TEXAS
GUN LAW
Armed And Educated

A Complete Guide To Gun Law In Texas

2015 Edition

By Attorneys Kirk Evans, Edwin Walker,
Michele Byington, and Darren Rice

Written by Kirk Evans, Edwin Walker, Michele Byington, and Darren Rice and published in the United States of America By Texas Law Shield, LLP
ISBN 978-0-578-15752-8

To order additional books by phone or for wholesale orders call (877) 448-6839.

TABLE OF CONTENTS

CHAPTER EIGHT 145

LAW OF CONCEALED CARRY: PART I
THE LICENSE QUALIFICATIONS, REQUIREMENTS,
APPEALS, AND REGULATIONS 145

CHAPTER NINE 158

LAW OF CONCEALED CARRY: PART II
WHAT, HOW, AND WHERE YOU CAN
LEGALLY CARRY WITH A CHL....................158

CHAPTER TEN 187

POSSESSING, CARRYING, AND TRANSPORTING
FIREARMS WITHOUT A CHL 187

PREFACE

As lawyers with years of representing law-abiding gun owners in cases all over the State of Texas, we have seen how well intended folks exercising their Second Amendment rights get mixed up in the legal system through just plain not understanding the law. For that reason, we set about creating a one volume resource that provides any gun owner with a base level of knowledge about laws that gun owners need to know.

The law can be complicated, overlapping, hard to understand, and in some cases, completely arbitrary to the point of confusion. Laws are often written by lawyers for lawyers or are the result of political compromises generating confusing laws that the courts are left to interpret. After years of legal work in the arena of firearms law, we found there did not exist a resource that explained gun law in a manner that was easy for everyone to understand, because understanding the law goes far beyond just reading statutes or regulations. If you do not know either the process by which the law is being administered or how the courts are interpreting the meaning of the law, then you don't understand the full legal story.

That is why we wrote *Texas Gun Law: Armed And Educated*. It is a one volume guide to the minimum law every gun owner needs to know to stay legal. Whenever appropriate, we tried to present useful analysis and real world applications. Our goal was to explain the "law" so gun owners who wanted to could inform and educate themselves. Thousands of attorney hours have gone into producing this resource, always with the goal in mind of education. Our collective legal experience has taught us well that anyone can become ensnared in the legal system. Many people firmly believe that "it" can't happen to them. Even people that have never been in trouble before find themselves in the world of law, lawyers, and law enforcement through ignorance of the law.

We are committed to helping protect Second Amendment rights for all legal gun owners. It is our passion and our mission. We want people to know the law, because only through eternal vigilance will we protect our cherished right to bear arms. If you own a gun, the laws concerning firearms and their use apply to you. Ignorance of the law is not a valid legal excuse. Therefore, if you want to stay legal, know the law!

CHAPTER ONE
BRIEF LEGAL HISTORY OF THE RIGHT TO BEAR ARMS AND THE LAWS REGULATING FIREARMS

I. Introduction and overview

To fully understand gun rights today in Texas or the United States, one should start first at the beginning: the formation document for our federal government, the United States Constitution. The Constitution was written without any enumerated guaranteed individual rights. The founding fathers thought it obvious and apparent that individuals had rights; therefore, there was no reason to elucidate them in a document that was supposed to control the government. James Madison also thought that by naming certain rights, it would imply that those were the only rights an individual possessed. After much discussion, and a complete change of opinion by Madison, the lack of enumerated rights was remedied in the first Congressional session and the state ratification process. When the dust settled, ten amendments were added to the Constitution; these ten amendments are the Bill of Rights. It is the Second Amendment that concerns firearms specifically, though throughout this book we will reference many others, including the Fourth and Fifth Amendment that both affect your rights to bear arms and the fundamental rights for us all.

II. Do I have a constitutional right as an individual to keep and bear arms?

Yes; the United States Supreme Court has decided that an individual has a constitutionally given right to keep and bear arms that flows from the Second Amendment, which states simply:

> *A well-regulated Militia, being necessary to the security of a free State, the right of the people to keep and bear Arms, shall not be infringed.*

From a plain reading, there are two important parts to this amendment: first, that a well-regulated militia is necessary to the security of a free state, and second, that there is a right of the people to keep and bear arms. For years, before the issue was decided, anti-gun activists have tried to argue that the Second Amendment only applied to "militias" and not to individuals. Luckily, this argument is not the law. Nevertheless, despite the Supreme Court rulings stating otherwise, this myth seems to persist. What do these parts of the Second Amendment mean? Are they the same, or are they different?

A. *What is a "Well-Regulated Militia?"*

As we discussed earlier, the first part of the Second Amendment references a "well-regulated militia." What is a well-regulated militia? The U.S. Supreme Court has held what this phrase does and does not mean. In 1939, in the case of *United States v. Miller*, 307 U.S. 174 (1939) (ironically, a ruling that upheld firearms regulation), the court defined a Militia as comprising "all males physically capable of acting in concert for the common defense." Based on how the amendment was drafted, the Court stated, it was clear that the Militia pre-dated Article I of the Constitution, because unlike armies and navies, it did not have to be created by Congress. What then is "well-regulated" per the court? It is exactly what it sounds like: the imposition of discipline and training. So, is this just the National Guard? No.

In the case of *D.C. v. Heller*, 554 U.S. 570 (2008), the Supreme Court stated that the well-regulated militia is not the state's military forces, but a separate entity altogether. The Supreme Court stated that the word "militia" referred to the body of the people, and they—the people—were required to keep a centralized government in check. The Supreme Court considered and rejected the position that the National Guard is the current militia under the Second Amendment.

B. *How has the phrase "right to keep and bear arms" been interpreted by the courts?*

One of the first cases to directly deal with the Second Amendment was *United States v. Miller*. In *Miller*, the Supreme Court found that the National Firearms Act ("NFA"), which imposed registration requirements on machine guns, short-barreled weapons, destructive devices, and other similarly unique firearms, did not violate the Second Amendment. The Court used the reasoning that possession of weapons regulated by the NFA did not reasonably relate to the preservation or efficiency of a well-regulated militia, therefore, the NFA was held constitutional.

Court fight where it all began: *United States v. Miller*

United States v. Miller (1939)

The facts:

Defendants, Miller and Layton, transported a double barrel 12-gauge shotgun with a barrel length of less than 18 inches from Oklahoma to Arkansas, and were being prosecuted under the National Firearms Act (which required certain types of firearms to be registered and a tax to be paid). Defendants challenged the NFA as an unconstitutional violation of the Second Amendment.

The legal holdings:

Upheld the National Firearms Act as Constitutional.

An interesting quirk of history in the Miller case (and not a shining moment for the legal system) is that Miller's attorney never appeared at the arguments before the U.S. Supreme Court because he was court-appointed and had not been paid. There was no written brief and no legal representation at oral arguments by the party arguing that the law was unconstitutional. The Court only heard the government's side. To make matters worse, Miller was shot to death before the decision was rendered.

C. *69 years later, the Supreme Court interprets the Second Amendment again: D.C. v. Heller*

It would be 69 years after *Miller* until the U.S. Supreme Court addressed the Second Amendment directly again, except this time the Court would hear both the government's and the defendant's arguments. Fortunately, freedom and Second Amendment rights prevailed in court that day. The Court held that individuals have a right to keep and bear arms.

District of Columbia v. Heller (2008)

The Facts

Heller had applied for a handgun ownership permit and was denied; without such a permit, D.C. required that all firearms (including rifles and shotguns) be kept unloaded and disassembled, or bound by a trigger lock, even in a person's own home.

The Legal Holdings

1. The Supreme Court found that the Second Amendment protects an individual right of firearms ownership for purposes of self-defense, not connected with any militia or military purposes; it further elaborated that individual self-defense is 'the central component" of the Second Amendment. Further, handguns are the primary defensive weapon of choice and are protected by the Second Amendment.
2. A well-regulated militia is not the state's military forces.
3. The Court also discussed what the phrase "bear arms" meant: "wear, bear, or carry... upon the person or in clothing or in a pocket, for the purpose... of being armed and ready for offensive or defensive action in a case of conflict with another person."
4. The D.C. regulation was held to be unconstitutional.
5. The Court concluded that like other rights, the right to bear arms is not completely absolute. Reasonable provisions and restrictions have been upheld.

Keep in mind *D.C. v. Heller* was a split 5-4 decision; only one justice away from a completely different outcome, where the Second Amendment (according to the dissent) had "outlived its usefulness and should be ignored."

D. *Can states ignore the Second Amendment? McDonald v. City of Chicago*

D.C. v. Heller was fantastic, but there was a slight quirk: the District of Columbia is under the exclusive jurisdiction of Congress and is not part of any state. Therefore, the case shed no light on the question of what states can do when it comes to regulating or banning firearms. How do state constitutions interact with the Second Amendment and can states ban guns outright? *McDonald v. City of Chicago* sought to answer these questions.

> ### *McDonald v. City of Chicago*, 561 U.S. 742 (2010)
>
> **The Facts**
>
> *McDonald v. City of Chicago* was decided in 2010; Chicago ordinance banned handgun possession (among other gun regulations). McDonald was a 76-year-old retired maintenance engineer who wanted a handgun for self-defense. Chicago required that all handguns had to be registered, but refused all handgun registration after a 1982 citywide handgun ban.
>
> **The Legal Holdings**
>
> The Supreme Court held that the Second Amendment is fully applicable to the States and that individual self-defense is "the central component" of the Second Amendment. Therefore, the Second Amendment prohibits states from enacting bans on handguns for self-protection in the home.

E. *Legal limitations of the right to keep and bear arms*

The U.S. Supreme Court has stated: "Of course the right [to keep and bear arms] was not unlimited, just as the First Amendment's right of free speech was not." Courts may have struggled over the years with what the Second Amendment means, but they have been resolute that there is an element of self-defense. The *Heller* Court stated that, "The Second Amendment does not protect the right to carry arms for any sort of confrontation," focusing their decision on self-defense. Further, the *Miller* Court stated that the weapons protected were those "in common use at the time" of the decision. This is supported by historical traditions of prohibiting the carry of "dangerous and unusual weapons" that are commonly used by criminals offensively, as opposed to by law-abiding citizens for defensive purposes.

The Second Amendment does not protect against prohibitions on firearm possession by felons and the mentally ill; *Heller* made this point in its decision, and many circuit court cases such as *U.S. v. Everist* follow the same reasoning. The Court of Appeals in *U.S. v. Everist* states that the Second Amendment is subject to, "limited narrowly tailored specific exceptions or restrictions for particular cases that are reasonable; it is clear that felons, infants and those of unsound mind may be prohibited from possessing firearms." *U.S. v. Everist*, 368 F.3d 517, 519 (5th Cir. 2004). Along this same train of thought, the *Heller* Court did not want to eliminate laws that imposed conditions and qualifications on the commercial sales of firearms.

It also does not mean that the Second Amendment includes the right to carry anywhere a person wants. The *Heller* Court stated that their opinion was not meant to allow the carrying of firearms in sensitive places such as schools and certain government buildings.

Practical Legal Tip:

Currently, the two most important court decisions fortifying our gun rights are *Heller* and *McDonald*. But those cases were very, very close to going the other way! Both were decided by a 5-4 majority, meaning that if only one other Supreme Court Justice had decided differently, our individual right to possess and carry firearms could have been severely limited. *-Edwin*

III. Major firearms statutes every gun owner needs to know

At the Federal level, there are plenty of laws and regulations that concern firearms, but this section will focus on some of the more major legislative actions that all gun owners need to know.

A. *Gun Control Act of 1968*

The Gun Control Act of 1968 ("GCA") was enacted by Congress to "provide for better control of the interstate traffic of firearms." This law is primarily focused on regulating interstate commerce in firearms by generally prohibiting interstate firearms transfers except among licensed manufacturers, dealers, and importers, however, interstate commerce has been held by the courts to include nearly everything. It also contains classes of individuals to whom firearms should not be sold. For the specifics of who can and can't purchase a firearm, please refer to Chapter 3. Among other things, the GCA created the Federal Firearms License ("FFL") system, imposed importation restrictions on military surplus rifles (adding a "sporting purpose test" and a "points system" for handguns), and marking requirements.

B. *The Brady Handgun Violence Prevention Act*

The Brady Handgun Violence Prevention Act, commonly referred to as the Brady Law, instituted federal background checks (the National Instant Criminal Background Check System or NICS) for firearm purchasers in the United States. It also prohibited certain persons from purchasing firearms; for more information on who can or can't purchase a firearm, see Chapter 3.

C. *The Firearm Owners' Protection Act*

The Firearm Owners' Protection Act ("FOPA") revised many provisions of the original Gun Control Act, including "reforms" on the inspection of FFLs. This same Act updated the list of individuals prohibited from purchasing firearms that was introduced by the GCA. The FOPA also banned the ownership by civilians of any machine gun that was not registered under the NFA as of May 19, 1986. FOPA created what is called a "safe passage" provision of the law, which allows for traveling across states with a firearm. Finally,

FOPA prohibited a registry for non-NFA items that directly linked firearms to their owners.

D.   *The Public Safety and Recreational Firearms Use Protection Act*
The Public Safety and Recreational Firearms Use Protection Act, commonly referred to as the *Federal Assault Weapons Ban*, was a subsection of the Violent Crime Control and Law Enforcement Act of 1994. It banned outright the manufacture and transfer of certain semi-automatic firearms and magazines. This ban grandfathered-in previously legally owned weapons, but no prohibited firearm could be acquired or manufactured after September 13, 1994. With great foresight, the drafters of this law included a so-called "sunset provision," that stated the ban would expire ten years later unless renewed. The ban expired in 2004, and all attempts to renew have been unsuccessful.

E.   *The National Firearms Act*
The National Firearms Act ("NFA") regulates and imposes a statutory excise tax on the manufacture and transfer of certain types of firearms and weapons: machine guns, short-barreled weapons, suppressors, explosive devices, and "any other weapons" (AOWs can range from everyday objects that are actually firearms, such as an umbrella that can fire a round, to other weapons the ATF decides to place in this category). The tax is $200 if you make or transfer an item (other than for the transfer of AOWs); the tax for transferring AOWs is $5. The NFA is also referred to as Title II of the federal firearms laws. For more information on how to navigate the NFA while remaining legal, please see Chapter 14.

IV. **Do Texans have a right to keep and bear arms in the Texas Constitution?**
Yes. The Texas Constitution acknowledges the right to keep and bear arms in Article I, Section 23. This provision of the Texas Constitution has never been amended. Article I, Section 23 reads:

Every citizen shall have the right to keep and bear arms in the lawful defense of himself or the State; but the Legislature shall have power, by law, to regulate the wearing of arms, with a view to prevent crime.

The more observant will notice that, as opposed to the Second Amendment of the United States Constitution, this description specifically allows for legislation. The courts in Texas have acknowledged that Section 23 allows the legislature to create laws to prohibit certain types of carrying weapons, and have upheld "unlawful carrying" laws and license requirements (*Collins v. State*, 501 S.W.2d 876 (Tex. Crim. App. 1973), *Roy v. State*, 552 S.W.2d 827 (Tex. Crim. App. 1977)).

A. *Can Texas prohibit local municipalities from making certain gun laws?*

Yes.   The Texas Legislature can and does prohibit local municipalities from making certain gun laws by the legal doctrine known as "preemption." A preemption statute is a mechanism by which the Texas legislature sets certain areas off limits to local governments, which helps ensure the uniformity of law across the state, in this case, firearms law.

B. *What local governments may not regulate*

The Texas preemption statute can be found in Texas Local Government Code § 229.001. It states what areas of law municipalities are not allowed to regulate. Local municipalities <u>cannot</u> regulate:

- Anything relating to the transfer, private ownership, keeping, transportation, licensing, or registration of firearms, ammunition or firearm supplies;
- The discharge of a firearm at a sport shooting range;
- The discharge of a shotgun, air rifle, pistol, BB gun, or bow and arrow on a tract of land of 10 acres or more and more than 150 feet from a residence or occupied building

located on another property in a manner not reasonably expected to cause a projectile to cross the boundary line;

- The discharge of a center or rim fire rifle or pistol of any caliber on a tract of land of 50 acres or more, more than 300 feet from a residence or occupied building located on another property in a manner not reasonably expected to cause a projectile to cross the boundary line.

C. *What local governments may regulate*

Local municipalities under state law are empowered to and <u>may</u> regulate the following:

- The discharge of firearms within the limits of the municipality other than at a sport shooting range (Texas Local Government Code Annotated Section 229.001(a)(2));
- The use of property or location of a business under its fire code, zoning ordinances, or land-use regulations (Texas Local Government Code Annotated Section 229.001(b)(3));
- The use of firearms in the case of an insurrection, riot, or natural disaster if it is found necessary to protect public health and safety (Texas Local Government Code Annotated Section 229.001(b)(4));
- The storage and transportation of explosives to protect public safety;
  - o The statute provides an exception, that local municipalities cannot regulate 25 pounds or less of black powder for each private residence, or 50 pounds or less for each retail dealer (Texas Local Government Code Annotated Section 229.001(b)(5));
- The carrying of a firearm by a person who <u>does not</u> have a Concealed Handgun License ("CHL") at a public park,

public meeting of a governmental body, non-firearms-related school, college, or professional athletic events;

- This does not apply to a firearm carried to or from an area designated for lawful hunting, fishing, or other sporting events where firearms are commonly used in the activity (Texas Local Government Code Annotated Section 229.001(b)(6)).

Preemption even applies to municipal housing authorities, their municipal housing codes, or mass transit authorities; for example, it would be unlawful for a public housing project to prohibit the possession of firearms within the public housing project, evicting anyone who violated such prohibition, as the preemption statute above prohibits such regulations. Tex. Att'y Gen. Op No. DM-71 (1991).

CHAPTER TWO
LEGAL DEFINITIONS AND CLASSIFICATIONS OF FIREARMS: WHAT IS LEGAL?

I. Introduction and overview

Before discussing the law of firearms and all its different facets, it is important first to understand what the law defines as a "firearm." Firearms laws are governed on both the federal and state levels; therefore, throughout this chapter we will explore the interactions federal and state law have on the purchase and possession of firearms.

A. _What is a firearm?_
Federal definition

Under the federal law, a firearm is defined as "any weapon (including a starter gun) which will or is designed to or may readily be converted to expel a projectile by the action of an explosive." 18 U.S.C. § 921(a)(3). The federal definition of a firearm also includes the frame or receiver of any such weapon, any firearm muffler or silencer, or any "destructive device." This is similar to the Texas definition, but not exactly the same.

Texas definition

In the State of Texas, for purposes of applying state and not federal law, a firearm is defined by the Texas Penal Code in Chapter 46. Section 46.01(3) defines a firearm as "any device designed, made, or adapted to expel a projectile through a barrel by using the energy generated by an explosion or burning substance or any device readily convertible to that use."

Why might it be important to know the different ways the term "firearm" is defined under federal and state law? It is because if a person finds themselves charged with a crime by federal authorities, the federal definition of a firearm will apply. Likewise, if the charge is under a violation of state law, then the Texas definition will apply. Thus, the primary difference in the definitions and their impact on a defendant charged with a crime involving a firearm lies with how a person may be in trouble with the law. As we will see in the next section, the definitions of what does and does not constitute a firearm, although similar in many aspects, contain an array of differences that make violating the law unwittingly easy.

B. *Definitions for handguns, rifles, and shotguns*

In addition to defining what constitutes a firearm, federal and Texas law further classify and define firearms into categories of handguns and long guns (rifles and shotguns). This section will provide an overview of how federal and state laws classify firearms as well as the physical requirements for a firearm to be legal.

1. What is a handgun?

Ultimately, whether looking at the federal or Texas definition, the term handgun is defined in the same manner: it simply refers to any firearm that is designed to be fired by using only one hand. While it is true that most individuals will use two hands when firing a handgun for safety and accuracy purposes, the emphasis in the legal definition of a handgun rests purely in its design to be held or fired with a single hand.

Federal definition

The United States Code of Federal Regulations defines a handgun as "(a) any firearm which has a short stock and is designed to be held and fired by the use of a single hand; and (b) any combination of parts from which a firearm described in paragraph (a) can be assembled." 27 CFR § 478.11.

Texas definition

Under Texas law, handguns are defined by the Penal Code in Chapter 46. A handgun "means any firearm that is designed, made, or adapted to be fired with one hand." Tex. Penal Code § 46.01(5).

2. What is a rifle?

Federal law defines a rifle as "a weapon designed or redesigned, made or remade, and intended to be fired from the shoulder, and designed or redesigned and made or remade to use the energy of the explosive in a fixed metallic cartridge to fire only a single projectile through a rifled bore for each single pull of the trigger." 27 CFR § 478.11. In addition, a legal rifle must have a barrel length of 16 inches or greater, and includes any weapon made from a rifle which is at least 26 inches overall in length. Texas law does not provide a definition for a rifle under the Penal Code, but it does classify illegal short-barreled firearms, including rifles in the same manner as the federal definition. *See* Tex. Penal Code § 46.01(10).

Minimum lengths

In order for a rifle to not be subject to the National Firearms Act or classified as a short-barreled firearm under Texas law, it must have a <u>barrel</u> of at least 16 inches in length. The ATF procedure for measuring barrel length is accomplished by measuring from the closed bolt (or breech-face) to the furthermost end of the barrel or permanently attached muzzle device. Below is an example of a rifle that does not meet the minimum barrel length requirement after measurement:

The barrel is measured by inserting a dowel rod into the barrel until the rod stops against the bolt or breech-face. The rod is then marked at the furthermost end of the barrel or permanently attached muzzle device, withdrawn from the barrel, and then measured. Any measurement of less than 16 inches will classify the rifle as being short-barreled under Texas and federal law and subject the firearm to the NFA. For short-barreled rifles and other non-compliant firearms, see Chapter 14, which discusses the NFA. *Note:* for overall length, rifles with collapsible/folding-stocks are measured from the "extreme ends," unless the stock is "easily detachable," in which case it is measured without the stock.

3. What is a shotgun?

The federal definition of a shotgun is "a weapon designed or redesigned, made or remade, and intended to be fired from the shoulder, and designed or redesigned and made or remade to use the energy of the explosive in a fixed shotgun shell to fire through a smooth bore either a number of ball shot or a single projectile for each single pull of the trigger." 27 CFR § 478.11. Like rifles, legal shotguns have requirements for minimum barrel and overall lengths. Shotgun barrels must be at least 18 inches long and must also comply with the same 26 inch overall length requirement. Under Texas law, shotguns are classified in the same manner as they are under federal law. *See* Tex. Penal Code § 46.01(10).

Minimum lengths
In order for a shotgun to not be subject to the National Firearms Act or classified as a short-barreled firearm under Texas law, it must have a <u>barrel</u> of at least 18 inches in length. The ATF procedure for measuring the barrel length of a shotgun is the same as it is for a rifle. Below is an example of a shotgun that does not meet the minimum barrel length requirement after measurement:

Any measurement of less than 18 inches will classify the shotgun as a short-barreled weapon and illegal under Texas and federal law unless the requirements of the NFA are satisfied. For short-barreled shotguns and other non-compliant firearms, see Chapter 14. *Note:* the collapsible/folding-stock rule that applies to rifles applies to shotguns as well.

C. *Antique firearms and replica firearms*
When is a firearm not legally a "firearm?" It is when the law defines it as not being one, such as with "antique" firearms.

1. Federal definition of "antique firearm"
1898 or prior
The federal definition of firearm under Title 18, Section 921 of the United States Code excludes "antique firearms." Even though an antique firearm still functions ballistically similar to a "modern" firearm, under federal law, antique firearms are regulated differently, if at all. An antique firearm under federal law includes any firearm with a matchlock, flintlock, or percussion cap, or similar type of ignition system manufactured in or before 1898 or any replica of a firearm just described so long as the replica "is not designed or redesigned for using rimfire or conventional centerfire fixed ammunition, or uses rimfire or centerfire ammunition that is no longer manufactured in the United States and is not readily available in ordinary channels of commerce." 18 U.S.C. §§ 921(16)(A) and (B). So, an "antique firearm" is not a "firearm" for purposes of federal regulation; it is an "antique firearm."

Muzzle loading
In addition, federal law does not consider "any muzzle loading rifle, muzzle loading shotgun, or muzzle loading pistol, which is designed to use black powder, or a black powder substitute, and which cannot use fixed ammunition" as a firearm. Be aware, however, that the term "antique firearm" does not include any weapon which incorporates a firearm frame or receiver, any firearm which is converted into a muzzle loading weapon, or any muzzle loading weapon which can be readily converted to fire fixed ammunition

by replacing the barrel, bolt, breechlock, or any combination of these parts. 18 U.S.C. § 921(a)(16)(C).

2. Texas definition of "antique firearm"

Pre-1899

The Texas definition of firearm excludes antique firearms by not including any firearm that is an antique firearm manufactured before 1899; or a replica of an antique firearm manufactured before 1899, but only if the replica does not use rim fire or center fire ammunition. *See* Tex. Penal Code § 46.01(3). This is similar to the federal definition, simply stated differently.

3. Differences in federal and Texas law

The area where the federal and Texas definitions of what is not a firearm differ the most surrounds the use of black powder firearms. Although the language looks dissimilar, the years of manufacture for firearms that are classified as "antiques" are both the same under federal and Texas law; antique firearms are ones that were manufactured before 1899. However, the federal law takes things one step further by providing a separate section exempting out muzzle loading firearms designed to use black powder or a black powder substitute so long as the firearm cannot be readily convertible to fire fixed ammunition. Texas law has no such exception for black powder firearms: only firearms that were produced prior to 1899, or which are replicas of weapons that were actually produced prior to 1899, are excluded.

This demonstrates one of the few examples where the federal law is less restrictive than the state law. By these definitions, a person who could not otherwise legally possess a firearm, under federal law, could legally possess a muzzle loading rifle or pistol designed to use black powder that is not a replica of any weapon that was actually previously manufactured before 1899, because federal law does not consider such a weapon to be a firearm due to its mere use of black powder. However, under Texas law, if a black powder gun is a modern black powder firearm and not a replica of an "old" pre-1899 firearm, it is considered a firearm under the

Texas Penal Code, and it is not an "antique firearm." The possession or use of such a black powder firearm would be subject to all other Texas laws governing the use of firearms. Texas only excludes from its definition of firearms weapons designed to use black powder if they were actual weapons manufactured prior to 1899 or replicas of actual weapons manufactured prior to 1899.

D. *What firearms are illegal?*
Under Texas Penal Code § 46.05, certain firearms are prohibited or illegal under Texas law. These firearms include:
- machine guns;
- short-barreled firearms;
- firearm silencers or suppressors;
- zip guns (which includes any device which was not originally a firearm, but is adapted to become and act like one).

This section of the Penal Code also makes illegal other weapons such as knuckles, chemical dispensing devices, and armor-piercing ammunition. However, a person may have a defense to prosecution under state law if he or she has complied with the requirements of the National Firearms Act (see Chapter 14 for more information on the NFA).

Under federal law, the same firearms that are prohibited weapons under state law are regulated by the National Firearms Act. These firearms include:
- short-barreled shotguns;
- short-barreled rifles;
- machine guns;
- firearm silencers or suppressors;
- weapons or devices capable of being concealed on the person from which a shot can be fired;
- pistols or revolvers having a smooth bore (as opposed to rifled bore) barrel designed to fire a fixed shotgun shell;
- pistols or revolvers with a vertical handgrip;
- destructive devices; and

- weapons classified as "Any Other Weapon," or AOWs.

See 26 U.S.C. § 5845. For more information on these weapons, see Chapter 14 discussing the National Firearms Act.

On the surface, the prohibited firearms list is similar between both federal and state law with the primary difference existing merely in classification only (federal law classifies most of these items as firearms whereas Texas classifies the items not as firearms but prohibited weapons). However, although these firearms and/or weapons are prohibited by statute, it does not mean a person absolutely cannot possess one. Many of these weapons may be legally possessed with proper documentation under the National Firearms Act. For more information on these prohibited weapons and the NFA, see Chapter 14.

E. *How big of a gun can a person possess?*
Federal law dictates that any firearm which has any barrel with a bore of more than one-half inch in diameter is a "destructive device" and is subject to the National Firearms Act. Possession of any such firearm without the proper paperwork associated with NFA firearms is illegal. Note, however, that some shotguns are regulated differently. For more information on destructive devices and the NFA, see Chapter 14.

II. **Ammunition and the law**
No discussion concerning firearms laws would be complete without examining laws concerning the ammunition that goes into a firearm. Just like firearms, the law regulates the possession, sale, and even composition of "legal" ammunition. This section addresses the essential aspects of the law concerning ammunition and what gun owners need to know, both under federal and Texas law.

A. *How does the law define ammunition?*
Under federal law, the term ammunition is defined under 18 U.S.C. § 921(a)(17)(A) and means "ammunition or cartridge cases,

primers, bullets, or propellent powder designed for use in any firearm." Thus, the federal definition of ammunition includes the finished product and all of the components in making a round of ammunition. However, the federal definition of ammunition does not include (1) any shotgun shot or pellet not designed for use as the single, complete projectile load for one shotgun hull or casing, nor (2) any unloaded, non-metallic shotgun hull or casing not having a primer. *See* 27 CFR § 478.11. In other words, individual ammunition components are legally defined as ammunition themselves, even if they are simply parts, except that shotgun ammunition components, if not completely assembled, are not ammunition.

Under Texas law, there is no statutory definition for mere "ammunition." Texas law only provides a definition for armor-piercing ammunition (which we will discuss later in this chapter) and a definition for the way firearms are discharged: a "projectile [that is expelled] through a barrel by using the energy generated by an explosion or burning substance." Tex. Penal Code § 46.01(3).

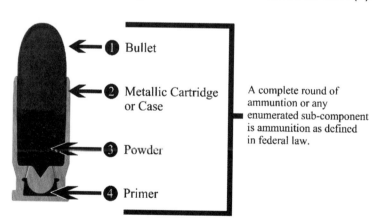

1. Bullet

2. Metallic Cartridge or Case

A complete round of ammuntion or any enumerated sub-component is ammunition as defined in federal law.

3. Powder

4. Primer

B. *Is there a difference in ammunition that is used in different types of firearms?*

Yes.   Ammunition can be divided into two classifications: ammunition for handguns and ammunition for long guns. Long gun ammunition can be further divided into ammunition for rifles and ammunition for shotguns.

Handgun ammunition means ammunition that is meant to be fired from a handgun, and it comes in many different calibers. Rifle ammunition is meant to be fired from a rifle and is similar to handgun ammunition in that it comes in many different calibers. Shotgun ammunition, on the other hand, comes in self-contained cartridges loaded with some form of shot or a shotgun slug which is designed to be fired from a shotgun.

Practical Legal Tip:

Even with firearms, having the right tool for the job is important. Practically speaking, you should choose the firearm and ammo that you feel most comfortable using. At the end of the day, why you started shooting is always more important than what you chose to shoot with. -Michele

C. *What ammunition is illegal?*

Armor-piercing handgun ammunition is the only ammunition which has explicit prohibitions under both federal and Texas law. The federal definition of armor-piercing ammunition is found in 18 U.S.C. § 921(a)(17)(B) and means "[1] a projectile or projectile core which may be used in a handgun and which is constructed entirely (excluding the presence of traces of other substances) from one or a combination of tungsten alloys, steel, iron, brass, bronze, beryllium copper, or depleted uranium; or [2] a full jacketed projectile larger than .22 caliber designed and intended for use in a handgun and whose jacket has a weight of more than 25 percent of the total weight of the projectile."

Federal law

Under federal law, while there is no blanket prohibition on the mere possession of armor-piercing ammunition, it is prohibited under four conditions:

1. *Prohibition one: it is illegal to make or import armor-piercing ammunition.* Under 18 U.S.C. § 922(a)(7) it is unlawful for any person to manufacture or import armor-piercing ammunition unless (1) the manufacture of such ammunition is for the use of the United States, any department or agency of the United States, any state, or any department, agency, or political subdivision of a state; (2) the manufacture of such ammunition is for the purpose of exportation; or (3) the manufacture or importation of such ammunition is for the purpose of testing or experimentation and has been authorized by the United States Attorney General.

2. *Prohibition two: it is illegal for manufacturers and importers to sell or deliver armor-piercing ammunition.* Federal law states that it is unlawful for any manufacturer or importer to sell or deliver armor-piercing ammunition unless such sale or delivery is (1) for the use of the United States, any department or agency of the United States, any state, or any department, agency, or political subdivision of a state; (2) for the purpose of exportation; or (3) for the purpose of testing or experimentation and has been authorized by the United States Attorney General. *See* 18 U.S.C. § 922(a)(8).

3. *Prohibition three: an FFL or other license-holder cannot sell or deliver armor-piercing ammunition without the proper documentation.* Under 18 U.S.C. § 922(b)(5), it is unlawful for any licensed importer, licensed manufacturer, licensed dealer, or licensed collector to sell or deliver armor-piercing ammunition to any person unless the licensee notes in his records, as required under 18 U.S.C. § 923, the name, age, and place of residence of such person if the person is an individual, or the identity and principal and local places of business of

such person if the person is a corporation or other business entity.

4. *Prohibition four: it is illegal to possess armor-piercing ammunition if a person is involved in a crime of violence or a drug-trafficking crime.* Pursuant to 18 U.S.C. § 924(c)(5), it is unlawful for "any person who, during and in relation to any crime of violence or drug trafficking crime (including a crime of violence or drug trafficking crime that provides for an enhanced punishment if committed by the use of a deadly or dangerous weapon or device) for which the person may be prosecuted in a court of the United States, use or carries armor piercing ammunition." Individuals who use or carry armor-piercing ammunition in the commission of a crime of violence or during a drug-trafficking crime are subject to heightened sentencing standards should they be found guilty.

As you can see, while possession of armor-piercing ammunition itself is not illegal, obtaining armor-piercing ammunition without violating one of the foregoing prohibitions is almost impossible.

Texas law
Texas Penal Code § 46.01(12) defines armor-piercing ammunition as "handgun ammunition that is designed primarily for the purpose of penetrating metal or body armor and to be used principally in pistols and revolvers." Texas Penal Code § 46.05(a)(6) makes the intentional or knowing possession, manufacture, transport, repair, or sale of armor-piercing ammunition a third-degree felony.

A couple of notable exceptions to this law are available, however. One is in the form of a defense to prosecution, and the other is an affirmative defense. First, under Texas Penal Code § 46.05(b), it is a defense to prosecution that a person's intentional or knowing possession, manufacture, transport, repair, or sale was "incidental to the performance of official duty by the armed forces or national guard, a governmental law enforcement agency, or a correctional facility." Persons employed in any of these agencies should not be prosecuted so long as their use of armor-piercing ammunition was a part of their official duties. Second, it is an affirmative defense that a person's intentional or knowing possession, manufacture, transport, repair, or sale of armor-piercing ammunition was incidental to dealing with armor-piercing ammunition solely for the purpose of making the ammunition available to the Armed Forces or National Guard, a governmental law enforcement agency, or a correctional facility. *See* Tex. Penal Code § 46.05(d)(2).

By definition, it should be noted that not all ammunition that *can* pierce armor is actually armor-piercing. Both the federal and Texas definitions contain specific requirements for a particular round of ammunition's composition in order to make it armor-piercing. Federal law requires that the ammunition be comprised of certain alloys while Texas law requires that the ammunition be designed primarily for the purpose of penetrating armor. For instance, 5.7 millimeter ammunition for an FN57 handgun or a PS90 rifle, while capable of piercing armor based on its size and velocity, is not ammunition that is armor-piercing as defined under the law because such ammunition, sold commercially, is primarily for sporting purposes according to the ATF.

PS90

D. *Does modifying traditional ammunition make it illegal?*
No, outside of armor-piercing ammunition, there is no handgun or long gun ammunition that is prohibited under the federal or Texas law. In fact, there are many examples of hollow-point rounds which are modified in a way to become more lethal such as the

R.I.P. ammunition, Black Talons, *etc.*, which star outward upon impact in order to do more internal damage. Such ammunition, though it looks different from traditional ammunition rounds, is perfectly legal.

Factory and Expanded Hollow Point Rounds

E. *Is it legal to use ammunition that works in both handguns and rifles?*

Yes, except for armor-piercing ammunition that is used principally in handguns. This is because the federal and Texas definitions of armor-piercing ammunition contemplate handguns only. Armor-piercing ammunition for a rifle is perfectly legal, though it may complicate matters at trial in trying to demonstrate to the jury any differentiation. Beyond armor-piercing ammunition, it is legal to use ammunition that is available in common calibers and that functions in both handguns and rifles.

With a solid understanding of what is and is not a firearm and ammunition, as well as what firearms and ammunition a person may legally possess without the necessity of obtaining additional documentation, we are now ready to move to the next chapter discussing the purchase and possession of firearms.

CHAPTER THREE
PURCHASING, TRANSFERRING, AND POSSESSING FIREARMS

I. Laws of purchasing and possessing: the basics

The laws of purchasing, selling, gifting, or otherwise transferring a firearm are distinct and different from the laws of possessing a firearm. It may be legal for someone to possess a firearm, and it still be illegal for them to "purchase" the firearm. Further, each of these sets of laws for "purchasing" or "possessing" has a federal and a state component both of which must be satisfied in order to start on the right side of the law.

On the federal level, the Bureau of Alcohol, Tobacco, Firearms and Explosives ("ATF") is charged with regulating firearms including sales, purchases, and transfers through Federal Firearms Licensees ("FFLs" or "dealers"), however, a multitude of federal agencies can be involved in any given firearms law investigation or police function most currently falling under a branch of the U.S. Department of Homeland Security. Texas has no direct state-level counterpart to the ATF.

A. *What is an FFL?*

FFL or Federal Firearms License is a license required by federal law for those persons or entities that are engaged in the business of buying and selling firearms. A federal firearms licensee is often called an "FFL" or "dealer." When an individual purchases, sells, or transfers a firearm through a dealer, the FFL and the individual must both comply with specific federal law requirements, paperwork, and procedures concerning the buying, selling, or transferring of those firearms. These requirements will be addressed throughout this chapter.

B. *Who must obtain an FFL?*

Federal law requires a federal firearms license if a person is engaged in <u>business</u> as a firearms dealer, manufacturer, or importer. For the purposes of our discussion in this chapter, a person is engaged in the business when the person "devotes time, attention, and labor to dealing in firearms as a regular course of trade or business with the principal objective of livelihood and profit through the repetitive purchase and resale of firearms, but such term shall not include a person who makes occasional sales, exchanges, or purchases of firearms for the enhancement of a personal collection or for a hobby, or who sells all or part of his personal collection of firearms." 18 U.S.C. § 921(a)(21)(C).

C. *What is a private sale?*
A private sale is just what it sounds like: a sale, purchase, or transfer of a firearm by parties that are not licensed dealers. A private sale is perfectly legal for both handguns and long guns in Texas, as long as all other legal requirements are met. We will discuss the ins-and-outs of private sales in greater detail in this chapter under Section IV.

D. *What is the legal age to purchase and possess a firearm?*
Federal law controls all FFL firearms transactions and requires that a person be 21 years of age or older before they may purchase a handgun or 18 for the purchase of a long gun. However, under Texas law, a handgun or long gun may be purchased in a private sale by a person who is age 18. Texas Penal Code § 46.06(a)(2) makes it a crime if a person "intentionally or knowingly sells, rents, leases, or gives or offers to sell, rent, lease, or give to any child younger than 18 years any firearm, club, or illegal knife." Note the exceptions to follow.

Required Age to Purchase Firearms	Federal Law: From Dealer	Texas Law: Private Sale
Handgun	21	18
Long gun	18	18

Under federal law, a person must be at least 18 years of age in order to possess a handgun or ammunition for a handgun. *See* 18 U.S.C. § 922(x)(2). Unlike the law on purchasing a long gun, there is no federal age requirement for the possession of a rifle or shotgun. There is no Texas law directly specifying that persons under a certain age are prohibited from possessing a firearm, however, Texas law does specify that persons under 17 must be supervised or that certain other conditions must be met in order for a juvenile to possess a firearm.

E. *Can I buy a firearm if I have a note from my parents?*

If a person finds themselves charged with selling a firearm to a minor, Texas law does provide an affirmative defense to prosecution under State law if the sale or transfer of the firearm was made "to a minor whose parent or the person having legal custody of the minor had given written permission for the sale or, if the transfer was other than a sale, the parent or person having legal custody had given effective consent." Tex. Penal Code § 46.06(c). This is the law whether the sale is for a handgun or a long gun. For the federal law regarding juveniles and handguns, see 18 U.S.C. § 922(x). Note, however, that this state-law exception does not apply to FFL transactions, and an individual must be 21 years old to purchase a handgun from an FFL.

F. *Criminal liability for allowing a minor access to firearms*

In Texas, under Texas Penal Code § 46.13, a person may be guilty of a crime if a child (younger than 17) gains access to a readily dischargeable firearm and the person with "criminal negligence: (1) failed to secure the firearm; or (2) left the firearm in a place to which the person knew or should have known the child would gain access."

If the child discharges the firearm and causes death or serious bodily injury to himself or another person, it is a class A misdemeanor. Otherwise, it is a class C misdemeanor.

The law defines "readily dischargeable firearm" as a "firearm that is loaded with ammunition, whether or not a round is in the chamber." The statute also defines "secure" as meaning to "take steps that a reasonable person would take to prevent the access to a readily dischargeable firearm by a child, including but not limited to placing a firearm in a locked container or temporarily rendering the firearm inoperable by a trigger lock or other means." Tex. Penal Code § 46.13(a)(3).

However, if a minor commits a crime to gain access to a firearm, the firearm's owner is not guilty of a crime. It is an affirmative defense to prosecution when a child gains access to a firearm "by entering property in violation of this code." Tex. Penal Code § 46.13(c)(3). This means that if a child illegally breaks into a person's home or vehicle and then takes possession of a weapon illegally, the gun owner has not committed a crime.

G. *When may children legally possess firearms?*
Texas law allows for the legal possession of firearms under specific exceptions included in the law. These exceptions or "affirmative defenses" include the following:

1. Exception for hunting or sporting purposes
The first affirmative defense to prosecution under section 46.13 is that the child's access to the firearm "was supervised by a person older than 18 years of age and was for hunting, sporting, or other lawful purposes." Tex. Penal Code § 46.13(c)(1). An adult is legally permitted to take a child hunting, or to the shooting range and permit the child to have access to a firearm, so long as that adult supervises the child.

2. Self-defense
Second, if the child's access to the firearm "consisted of lawful defense by the child of people or property." Tex. Penal Code § 46.13(c)(2). For obvious reasons, if a child uses a firearm in self-defense, or in defense of another person or property, there is a general public policy interest in not prosecuting those persons.

Example:
> One night, armed intruders break into Timmy's home and hold Timmy's parents at gunpoint

while burglarizing the home. Timmy, who is 14, covertly sees what is transpiring from the top of the stairs and knowing that his father keeps a loaded handgun in his nightstand, retrieves the weapon. Timmy then shoots the burglar threatening his parents.

Two questions arise in this scenario: first, is Timmy legally justified in shooting the armed burglar? As we will see later in Chapters 4, 5, and 7, yes, he is. Timmy is justified in defending a third person and property with deadly force under the circumstances. Second, is Timmy's father in trouble legally for leaving his firearm accessible to Timmy? No, he is not in trouble. Timmy's access to the firearm was the result of his necessity in defending his parents who were staring down the barrel of a burglar's gun! This accessibility to a firearm is contemplated under the Penal Code in the form of the affirmative defense—"lawful defense."

3. Exception for ranching or farming

There is an affirmative defense if the child has a firearm "during a time when the child was engaged in an agricultural enterprise." Tex. Penal Code § 46.13(c)(4). This affirmative defense covers situations where a child may need a firearm for protection or other necessary situations that arise while farming, ranching, or other activities associated with agriculture.

H. *Special duty of firearms dealers involving minors*

Texas law requires that a dealer of firearms post in a conspicuous place on the premises where the dealer conducts his business a sign that contains the following warning written in block letters, not less than one inch in height:

"IT IS UNLAWFUL TO STORE, TRANSPORT, OR
ABANDON AN UNSECURED FIREARM IN A
PLACE WHERE CHILDREN ARE LIKELY TO BE AND
CAN OBTAIN ACCESS TO THE FIREARM."

Tex. Penal Code § 46.13(g).

Federal law requires that FFLs who deliver handguns to non-licensees display at their licensed premises (including temporary business locations at gun shows) a sign that customers can readily see. These signs are provided by the ATF and contain the following language:

(1) The misuse of handguns is a leading contributor to juvenile violence and fatalities.
(2) Safely storing and securing firearms away from children will help prevent the unlawful possession of handguns by juveniles, stop accidents, and save lives.
(3) Federal law prohibits, except in certain limited circumstances, anyone under 18 years of age from knowingly possessing a handgun, or any person from transferring a handgun to a person under 18.
(4) A knowing violation of the prohibition against selling, delivering, or otherwise transferring a handgun to a person under the age of 18 is, under certain circumstances, punishable by up to 10 years in prison.

In addition to the displayed sign, federal law requires FFLs to provide non-licensee customers with a written notification containing the same four points as listed above as well as sections 922(x) and 924(a)(6) of Title 18, Chapter 44 of the United States Code. This written notification is available as a pamphlet published by the ATF entitled "Youth Handgun Safety Act Notice" and is sometimes referred to as ATF information 5300.2. Alternatively, this written notification may be delivered to customers on another type of written notification, such as a manufacturer's brochure accompanying the handgun or a sales receipt or invoice applied to the handgun package. Any written notification delivered to a customer other than the one provided by the ATF must include the language described here, and must be "legible, clear, and conspicuous, and the required language shall appear in type size no smaller than 10-point type." 27 CFR § 478.103(c).

II. Federal law disqualifications for purchasing and possessing firearms

Federal law lists categories of persons disqualified from legally purchasing and possessing a firearm. This list comprises disqualifications that come from several different pieces of federal legislation including the Gun Control Act of 1968, the Brady Handgun Violence Protection Act, and the Violence Against Women Act. If a person buys or attempts to buy a firearm from an FFL, they must not be disqualified under any of the laws. Before an FFL may sell or otherwise transfer a firearm, the purchaser must fill out an ATF Form 4473. This form has questions concerning each of the criteria that disqualify a person to purchase a firearm under federal law. These disqualifications include:

(1) if the person is not the actual purchaser of the firearm— also known as a "straw man purchaser;"

(2) if the person is under indictment or information in any court for a felony or any other crime for which the judge could imprison the person for more than one year;

(3) if the person has ever been convicted in any court for a felony or other crime for which the judge could imprison the person for more than one year;

(4) if the person is a fugitive from justice;

(5) if the person is an unlawful user of, or addicted to, marijuana, or any depressant, stimulant, narcotic drug, or controlled substance;

(6) if the person has ever been adjudicated as mentally defective or has been committed to a mental institution;

(7) if the person has been dishonorably discharged from the Armed Forces;

(8) if the person is subject to an active protective order restraining the person from harassing, stalking, or threatening the person's child, or an intimate partner or child of such partner;

(9) if the person has been convicted in any court for a misdemeanor crime of domestic violence;

(10) if the person has ever renounced their United States citizenship;

(11)   if the person is an alien illegally in the United States; and

(12)   if the person is admitted under a non-immigrant visa and does not qualify for an exception.

The purchaser must legally affirm that they are not subject to any of the criteria listed above before they may purchase a firearm. If a prospective purchaser answers any question on the form in a manner that indicates they are legally disqualified, it is illegal for the FFL to sell that person the firearm, and it is illegal for the purchaser to complete the transaction or possess the firearm.

A.   *Understanding who is disqualified*
   1.   Can I buy a firearm for another person?

No. This would be a "straw man" purchase. In order to legally purchase a firearm from a dealer, you must be the "actual purchaser or transferee." If you are not the actual purchaser or transferee, it is illegal for you to complete the transfer or sale under federal law. Purchases for third persons are often called "straw man" purchases and are illegal. If you are not the actual purchaser, beware!

In fact, the ATF has a campaign called "Don't Lie for the Other Guy" that is targeted at (as they term it on their website) detection and deterrence of "straw man" purchases. The ATF website lists numerous examples of prosecutions for "straw man" purchases and a United States Supreme Court case examined and upheld federal law on this matter. *Abramski v. United States*, 134 S.Ct. 2259 (2014).

So who is the "actual" buyer or transferee so as not to be a "straw man?" The ATF states that you are the actual "transferee/buyer if you are purchasing the firearm for yourself or otherwise acquiring the firearm for yourself (*e.g.*, redeeming the firearm from pawn/retrieving it from consignment, firearm raffle winner)." The ATF goes on to state "you are also the actual transferee/buyer if you are legitimately purchasing the firearm as a gift for a third party."

Example:

> *Mr. Smith asks Mr. Jones to purchase a firearm for Mr. Smith. Mr. Smith gives Mr. Jones the money for the firearm. Mr. Jones then buys the firearm with Mr. Smith's money and gives Mr. Smith the firearm.*

Mr. Jones is not the "actual buyer" (he is legally a "straw man") of the firearm and if Mr. Jones indicates that he is the "actual buyer" of the firearm on ATF Form 4473, he has committed a federal crime. The Supreme Court ruling in *Abramski*, however, did not make "gifts" of firearms illegal.

When completing ATF Form 4473: if a person checks "yes" to the box asking if the person is the "actual purchaser," then that person cannot have engaged in a separate transaction to sell or transfer the firearm privately. Please note: the Supreme Court's ruling held that a person cannot legally purchase a firearm on behalf of another even if the person receiving the firearm would not otherwise be prohibited from making the purchase themselves. So don't buy a firearm for another person no matter how good a friend, relative, or person they are—it is a crime!

FREQUENTLY ASKED QUESTION FROM ATF WEBSITE
Q: May I buy a firearm from an FFL as a "gift" for another person?   **A**: Yes.
Editor's note: Instead of the previous example where Mr. Smith paid Mr. Jones to purchase a firearm for him, if Mr. Jones decides to buy a firearm with his own money and then give the firearm to Mr. Smith as a present, then Mr. Jones is the actual buyer/transferee of the firearm. Since Mr. Jones is the actual buyer, there exists no sham or "straw man," and the purchase is legal.
Q: May a parent or guardian purchase a firearm as a gift for a juvenile?   **A**: Yes, however, possession of handguns by juveniles is generally unlawful under federal law. Juveniles may only receive and

possess handguns with the written permission of a parent or guardian for limited purposes, *e.g.*, employment, ranching, farming, target practice, or hunting.

See www.atf.gov.

2. **A person cannot purchase a firearm if they have been convicted or are under "indictment or information" for a felony or certain misdemeanors**

If a person has been convicted of a felony or other crime for which a judge may sentence, or could have sentenced the person to more than one year imprisonment, that person may not legally purchase a firearm (unless the crime was a state misdemeanor punishable by imprisonment of two years or less). *See* 18 U.S.C. § 921(a)(20)(B). Likewise, if a person is under "indictment" or "information" for a felony, or any other crime for which a judge may sentence the person to more than one year imprisonment, that person is disqualified from purchasing a firearm. An "indictment" or "information" is a formal accusation of a crime punishable by imprisonment for a term exceeding one year. It is important to point out that the actual sentence received is not the determining factor for disqualification, rather, it is the possible maximum sentence. A person may have only been sentenced to 30 days imprisonment, but if the crime for which they were charged allowed a maximum penalty of five years, then that person is disqualified. *See Schrader v. Holder*, 831 F.Supp.2d 304 (D.D.C. 2011, *aff'd*, 704 F.3d 980 (D.C. Cir. 2013)).

3. **What does it mean to be a "fugitive from justice" so as to be disqualified from purchasing a firearm?**

A "fugitive from justice" is a person who, after having committed a crime, flees from the jurisdiction of the court where the crime was committed. A fugitive from justice may also be a person who goes into hiding to avoid facing charges for the crime of which he or she is accused. Such individuals are not eligible to purchase or possess firearms.

4. <u>Unlawful users of or persons addicted to drugs are disqualified from purchasing firearms</u>

Federal law is very broad in that it disqualifies persons from the purchase of firearms if they are either users of or addicted to marijuana or any depressant, stimulant, narcotic drug, or any controlled substance. Under federal law, an "addict" is defined as a person that "habitually uses any narcotic so as to endanger the public morals, health, safety, or welfare, or who is so far addicted to the use of narcotic drugs as to have lost the power of self-control with reference to his addiction." 21 U.S.C. § 802(1). However, in using the terms "users of," no such frequency or dependence seems contemplated in the words, nor did Congress give further guidance. Illegal users and addicts are prohibited from purchasing firearms from any person under federal law, and are likewise prohibited from possessing firearms. *See* 18 U.S.C. §§ 922(d) and (g).

5. <u>A person can't legally buy or possess firearms if they are "mentally defective"</u>

What does "mentally defective" mean? A person is considered to have been adjudicated as "mentally defective" if there has been a "determination by a court, board, commission, or other lawful authority that a person, as a result of marked subnormal intelligence, or mental illness, incompetency, condition, or disease: is a danger to himself or others, or lacks the mental capacity to contract or manage his own affairs." The term "mentally defective" includes "a finding of insanity by a court in a criminal case, and those persons found incompetent to stand trial or found not guilty by reason of insanity or lack of mental responsibility." 27 CFR § 478.11.

"Mentally defective" also includes a person who has been committed to a mental institution by a court, board, commission, or other lawful authority, or a commitment to a mental institution involuntarily. The term includes commitment for mental defectiveness or mental illness, and also includes commitment for other reasons, such as drug use. However, it does not include a person in a mental institution for observation or a voluntary admission to a mental institution. Individuals who have been adjudicated as mentally defective are also prohibited from possessing firearms under federal law. *See* 18 U.S.C. § 922(g)(4).

6. A person subject to a restraining order may not purchase or possess a firearm

Under 18 U.S.C. § 922(g)(8), firearms may not be sold to or received by person subject to a court order that: (a) was issued after a hearing which the person received actual notice of and had an opportunity to participate in; (b) restrains the person from harassing, stalking, or threatening an intimate partner or child of such intimate partner or person, or engaging in other conduct that would place an intimate partner in reasonable fear of bodily injury to the partner or child; and (c) includes a finding that such person represents a credible threat to the physical safety of such intimate partner or child; or by its terms explicitly prohibits the use, attempted use, or threatened use of physical force against such intimate partner or child that a person would reasonably be expected to cause bodily injury. An "intimate partner" of a person is the spouse or former spouse of the person, the parent of a child of the person, or an individual who cohabitates with the person.

7. Domestic violence issues and disqualifications

A person who has ever been convicted of the crime of domestic violence may not purchase or possess firearms under federal law. These restrictions were passed in what is known as the *Violence Against Women Act* in 1994 and amended in 1996. This is an often misunderstood law, and, in fact, the ATF has numerous "Frequently Asked Questions" concerning this disqualification on its website: www.atf.gov. The ATF does a good job of explaining the scope of this subject in their FAQs. Due to the complexity of this issue, the ATF examples are included here:

FREQUENTLY ASKED QUESTION FROM ATF WEBSITE

Q: What is a "misdemeanor crime of domestic violence?"

A: A "misdemeanor crime of domestic violence" means an offense that:

1. is a misdemeanor under federal or State law;
2. has, as an element, the use or attempted use of physical force, or the threatened use of a deadly weapon; and
3. was committed by a current or former spouse, parent, or guardian of the victim, by a person with whom the victim shares a child in common, by a person who is cohabiting with or has cohabited with the victim as a spouse, parent, or guardian, or by a person similarly situated to a spouse, parent, or guardian of the victim.

However, a person is not considered to have been convicted of a misdemeanor crime of domestic violence unless:

1. the person was represented by counsel in the case, or knowingly and intelligently waived the right of counsel in the case; and
2. in the case of a prosecution for which a person was entitled to a jury trial in the jurisdiction in which the case was tried, either-
   1. the case was tried by a jury, or
   2. the person knowingly and intelligently waived the right to have the case tried by a jury, by guilty plea or otherwise.

In addition, a conviction would not be disabling if it has been expunged or set aside, or is an offense for which the person has been pardoned or has had civil rights restored (if the law of the jurisdiction in which the proceedings were held provides for the loss of civil rights upon conviction for such an offense) unless the pardon, expunction, or restoration of civil rights expressly provides that the person may not ship, transport, possess, or receive firearms, and the person is not otherwise prohibited by the law of the jurisdiction in which the proceedings were held from receiving or possessing firearms. 18 U.S.C. 921(a)(33), 27 CFR 478.11.

Editor's note: A significant number of people make the mistake of overlooking or forgetting about a court issue or family law judicial proceeding. However, if you meet the above criteria, you are federally disqualified from possessing a firearm. The fact that it may have happened a long time ago, or that you did not understand the ramifications, is legally irrelevant.

Q: What is the effective date of this disability?
A: The law was effective September 30, 1996. However, the prohibition applies to persons convicted of such misdemeanors at any time, even if the conviction occurred prior to the law's effective date.

Editor's note: For those wondering why this is not an unconstitutional *ex-post facto* law, multiple federal appeals courts have ruled against that argument and the Supreme Court has consistently declined to review any of those cases, effectively accepting the ruling of the courts of appeals and upholding the law.

Q: X was convicted of misdemeanor assault on October 10, 1996, for beating his wife. Assault has as an element the use of physical force, but is not specifically a domestic violence offense. May X lawfully possess firearms or ammunition?
A: No. X may not legally possess firearms or ammunition. 18 U.S.C. 922(g)(9), 27 CFR 478.32(a)(9).

Editor's note: In this situation because X's conviction for assault was against a person in the statute's protected class, the conviction would be, for purposes of firearms purchasing disqualification, a domestic violence conviction.

Q: X was convicted of a misdemeanor crime of domestic violence on September 20, 1996, 10 days before the effective date of the statute. He possesses a firearm on October 10, 2004. Does X lawfully possess the firearm?
A: No. If a person was convicted of a misdemeanor crime of domestic violence at any time, he or she may not lawfully possess firearms or ammunition on or after September 30, 1996. 18 U.S.C. 922(g)(9), 27 CFR 478.32(a)(9).

Q: In determining whether a conviction in a State court is a "conviction" of a misdemeanor crime of domestic violence, does Federal or State law apply?

A: State law applies. Therefore, if the State does not consider the person to be convicted, the person would not have the Federal disability. 18 U.S.C. 921(a)(33), 27 CFR 478.11.

Q: Is a person who received "probation before judgment" or some other type of deferred adjudication subject to the disability?

A: What is a conviction is determined by the law of the jurisdiction in which the proceedings were held. If the State law where the proceedings were held does not consider probation before judgment or deferred adjudication to be a conviction, the person would not be subject to the disability. 18 U.S.C. 921(a)(33), 27 CFR 478.11.

Q: What State and local offenses are "misdemeanors" for purposes of 18 U.S.C. 922(d)(9) and (g)(9)?

A: The definition of misdemeanor crime of domestic violence in the GCA (the Gun Control Act of 1968) includes any offense classified as a "misdemeanor" under Federal or State law. In States that do not classify offenses as misdemeanors, the definition includes any State or local offense punishable by imprisonment for a term of 1 year or less or punishable by a fine. For example, if State A has an offense classified as a "domestic violence misdemeanor" that is punishable by up to 5 years imprisonment, it would be a misdemeanor crime of domestic violence. If State B does not characterize offenses as misdemeanors, but has a domestic violence offense that is punishable by no more than 1 year imprisonment, this offense would be a misdemeanor crime of domestic violence. 18 U.S.C. 921(a)(33), 27 CFR 478.11.

Q: Are local criminal ordinances "misdemeanors under State law" for purposes of sections 922(d)(9) and (g)(9)?

A: Yes, assuming a violation of the ordinance meets the definition of "misdemeanor crime of domestic violence" in all other respects.

Q: *In order for an offense to qualify as a "misdemeanor crime of domestic violence," does it have to have as an element the relationship part of the definition (e.g., committed by a spouse, parent, or guardian)?*

A: No. The "as an element" language in the definition of "misdemeanor crime of domestic violence" only applies to the use of force provision of the statute and not the relationship provision. However, to be disabling, the offense must have been committed by one of the defined parties. 18 U.S.C. 921(a)(33), 27 CFR 478.11.

Editor's note: This basically means that if illegal force was used against another person, regardless of the language in the underlying statute, if the illegal force was used against a member of the protected class under the statute, federal law will deem this as satisfying the requirements and disqualify the individual from purchasing and possessing firearms.

Q: *What should an individual do if he or she has been convicted of a misdemeanor crime of domestic violence?*

A: Individuals subject to this disability should immediately dispose of their firearms and ammunition. ATF recommends that such persons transfer their firearms and ammunition to a third party who may lawfully receive and possess them, such as their attorney, a local police agency, or a Federal firearms dealer. The continued possession of firearms and ammunition by persons under this disability is a violation of law and may subject the possessor to criminal penalties. In addition, such firearms and ammunition are subject to seizure and forfeiture. 18 U.S.C. 922(g)(9) and 924(d)(1), 27 CFR 478.152.

Q: *Does the disability apply to law enforcement officers?*

A: Yes. The Gun Control Act was amended so that employees of government agencies convicted of misdemeanor crimes of domestic violence would not be exempt from disabilities with respect to their receipt or possession of firearms or ammunition. Thus, law enforcement officers and other government officials who have been convicted of a disqualifying misdemeanor may not lawfully possess or receive firearms or ammunition for any purpose, including performance of their official duties. The disability applies to firearms and ammunition issued by government agencies, purchased by government employees for use in performing their official duties, and personal firearms and ammunition possessed by such employees. 18 U.S.C. 922(g)(9) and 925(a)(1), 27 CFR 478.32(a)(9) and 478.141.

Q: Is an individual who has been pardoned, or whose conviction was expunged or set aside, or whose civil rights have been restored, considered convicted of a misdemeanor crime of domestic violence?

A: No, as long as the pardon, expungement, or restoration does not expressly provide that the person may not ship, transport, possess, or receive firearms.

See www.atf.gov.

Practical Legal Tip:

If you or a loved one are going through court proceedings involving family issues and a restraining or protective order is entered in your case, it can suspend your ability to purchase or possess firearms. Language in the court order prohibiting any acts of family violence whether or not family violence actually occurred, make it so the person whom the other impacts is legally barred from the purchase or possession of any firearm. Believe it or not, the Family Courts have the ability to suspend your Second Amendment rights. *-Michele*

8. **Illegal aliens or aliens admitted under a non-immigrant visa**

Persons who are illegally in the United States may not legally purchase, possess, or transport firearms. Generally, non-immigrant aliens are also prohibited from legally purchasing, possessing, or transporting firearms.

Exceptions for nonimmigrant aliens

However, a nonimmigrant alien who has been admitted under a non-immigrant visa is not prohibited from purchasing, receiving, or possessing a firearm if the person falls within one of the following exceptions:

1. if the person was admitted to the United States for lawful hunting or sporting purposes or is in possession of a hunting license or permit lawfully issued in the United States;
2. if the person is an official representative of a foreign government who is accredited to the United States Government or the Government's mission to an international organization having its headquarters in the United States;
3. if the person is an official representative of a foreign government who is *en route* to or from another county to which that alien is accredited;
4. if the person is an official of a foreign government or a distinguished foreign visitor who has been so designated by the Department of State;
5. if the person is a foreign law enforcement officer of a friendly foreign government entering the United States on official law enforcement business;
6. if the person has received a waiver from the prohibition from the Attorney General of the United States.

See 18 U.S.C. § 922(y).

III. Texas law disqualifications: who cannot buy a firearm under Texas law?

As mentioned earlier, Texas has restrictions on the sale, transfer, and possession of firearms that are separate and distinct from the federal restrictions. If a person runs afoul of the law, they could potentially face prosecution in both state and federal court.

A. *Texas law disqualifications for "purchasing" a firearm*

The disqualifications for purchasing firearms under Texas law are contained in section 46.06 of the Texas Penal Code and apply to all transactions in Texas. This section of the Penal Code makes it a crime—a class A misdemeanor or, under certain circumstances, state jail felony—for a person to:

(1) sell, rent, lease, loan, or give a handgun to a person that the seller knows intends to commit an unlawful act;

(2) intentionally sell, rent, lease, or give (or even offer to do so) a firearm to any child;

(3) intentionally, knowingly, or recklessly sell a firearm or ammunition to an intoxicated person;

(4) knowingly sell a firearm or ammunition to any person convicted of a felony before the lapsing of five years from release from confinement or supervision;

(5) sell, rent, lease, loan, or give a handgun to a person knowing that the person is subject to an active protective order.

If a person falls under any of the categories (see full explanations below) listed in the foregoing sections, Texas law makes it illegal for a person to "sell" the other person a firearm.

B. *Texas law disqualifications for "possessing" firearms*

Similar to the disqualifications for purchasing firearms under Texas law, Chapter 46 of the Penal Code also includes prohibitions on the possession of firearms. These prohibitions on possession are specifically found in section 46.04 of the Penal Code and include:

(1) persons convicted of a felony until after the fifth anniversary of the person's release from confinement,

supervision under community supervision, parole, or mandatory supervision—whichever date is later; and after the time expires, it cannot be possessed in any other place than the person's home;

(2) persons convicted of domestic or family violence punishable as a Class A misdemeanor before the fifth anniversary of the later of the date of the person's release from confinement, or the date of release from community supervision following the conviction of the misdemeanor;

(3) persons (other than law enforcement officers) who are subject to a domestic protective order and have received notice of the order and before the expiration of the order.

Note: even though a person may not be disqualified from possession of a firearm under state law, that person may nevertheless still be disqualified to possess a firearm under federal law.

Example:
> *Scott was convicted of a class A misdemeanor of family violence in 1992. He has a Smith & Wesson .357 Magnum in his nightstand for self-defense.*

Under Texas law, Scott may be in legal possession of his firearm because more than 5 years have lapsed following either his conviction or release from supervision. However, if push-comes-to-shove and the Feds ever care, Scott is in unlawful possession of a firearm under 18 U.S.C. § 922(g)(9) and 27 CFR § 478.32(a)(9), regardless of how legal he might be under state law.

C. *Understanding who is disqualified under Texas law*
   1. How does a seller "know" a person intends to commit an unlawful act?

Under Texas Penal Code § 46.06(a)(1), a person is prohibited from selling a firearm to another person when the seller *knows* that the buyer intends to commit some unlawful act. Let's take a look at a couple of examples to highlight the difficulties a seller can face.

The issue of knowledge as it relates to the law can be a mine-field to navigate. Under the law, whenever a statute prohibits a person from doing any certain thing because they "know" it is tantamount to *actual knowledge*. *See City of San Benito v. Cantu*, 831 S.W.2d 416, 421 (Tex.App.—Corpus Christi 1992); *Ethics Advisory Opinion No. 333* (Texas Ethics Commission, July 12, 1996). In fact, Texas Penal Code § 6.03(b) states that a "person acts knowingly, or with knowledge, with respect to the nature of his conduct or to circumstances surrounding his conduct when he is aware of the nature of his conduct or that the circumstances exist. A person acts knowingly, or with knowledge, with respect to a result of his conduct when he is aware that his conduct is reasonably certain to cause the result." That is, a person must actually know that the thing which is prohibited, as opposed to being "pretty sure," "probable," or even "likely." It is also a much higher standard than "should have had reason to know." A person's knowledge can only be established by the facts of each incident.

Example:

> *Tim arranges to sell a handgun to Bob. When Bob arrives at the pre-arranged meeting location to conduct the transaction, Bob inspects the handgun and, without humor, tells Tim, "This will be perfect to rob First State Bank down the street this afternoon. I've been looking for a gun just like this one! Now I don't have to wait any longer!"*

Can Tim legally sell his handgun to Bob? No. Bob has clearly communicated his plan to commit a serious crime with Tim's handgun.

Example:

> *Alex arranges to sell a hunting rifle to Jim, a man he met briefly at a gun show a couple of weeks prior. When Jim comes over to buy the rifle, he remarks while examining the firearm, "Boy, it'd sure be great to get on my neighbor's land sometime and shoot some deer."*

In this example, does Alex have actual knowledge that Jim is going to commit an unlawful act, like trespassing or hunting without a license? No, he only has an idea of what Jim would like to do sometime. He does not know if the hunting is with or without the land owner's permission, whether it would even be legal to shoot deer or if a neighbor or deer even exists at all. With only this information in hand, it would not be illegal for Alex to sell the rifle to Jim. Ultimately, what a seller did or did not know can only be established by looking at the totality of the circumstances and may ultimately be decided by a jury in court.

2. **What does Texas law define as a "child" for the purpose of selling a firearm?**

A "child" refers to any person who is under 18 years of age. *See age discussion under Section I(D) of this Chapter.*

3. **A person may not sell a firearm or ammunition to an "intoxicated person"**

A person may not <u>intentionally</u>, <u>knowingly</u>, or <u>recklessly</u> sell a firearm to an intoxicated person.

a. What is "intoxicated?"

Texas Penal Code § 46.06(b)(1) provides the most relevant definition for "intoxicated" with respect to the purchase of a firearm. Under that section of the Penal Code, intoxicated means "substantial impairment of mental or physical capacity resulting from introduction of any substance into the body." Note that under this definition, intoxication is not limited to alcohol, nor is a specific legal limit on the amount of whatever impairing-substance is found in the body. Under Texas law, no person who is intoxicated can be sold a firearm, and concealed handgun license holders are also prohibited from carrying a firearm concealed while intoxicated. Tex. Penal Code §§ 46.06(a)(3), 46.035(d). Again, when a person knew another may be intoxicated or knew whether a person was actually intoxicated may ultimately be decided by a jury.

b. Mental state

The law has three different "mental states" under which a person may be guilty of a crime for selling a firearm to an intoxicated person: intentionally, knowingly, or recklessly. Intentionally and knowingly are the higher standards and reckless the lesser.

When does a person recklessly sell a firearm to an intoxicated person? Texas Penal Code § 6.03(c) states that "a person acts recklessly, or is reckless, with respect to circumstances surrounding his conduct or the result of his conduct when he is aware of but consciously disregards a substantial and unjustifiable risk that the circumstances exist or the result will occur. The risk must be of such a nature and degree that its disregard constitutes a gross deviation from the standard of care that an ordinary person would exercise under all the circumstances as viewed from the actor's standpoint." Likewise, if a person's mental state that they are selling a firearm or ammunition to an intoxicated person rises above reckless to knowingly or intentionally, that is also illegal.

4. Illegal to sell to certain felons

If a person knows that another person was convicted of a felony, they may not legally sell that other person a firearm under Texas law unless the person has been out of imprisonment or released from community supervision for five years—whichever is later. Note, however, that a person may still be guilty of unlawfully transferring a firearm to a felon under federal law.

5. Differences in federal and Texas law concerning convicted felons possessing firearms

Under federal law, a person convicted of a felony is prohibited from possessing firearms. Texas law, however, relaxes such restrictions. Under Texas law, a convicted felon is permitted to possess firearms in the person's home after five years from the date of the person's release from confinement, supervision under community supervision, parole, or mandatory supervision— whichever date is later. *See* Tex. Penal Code § 46.04(a). A convicted felon is not, however, able to purchase firearms under Texas law.

6. Will my juvenile record prevent me from purchasing and possessing a firearm?

Generally, if any person, including a juvenile, has been convicted of a crime which carries a punishment of imprisonment for more than one year, then that person will not be permitted to purchase a firearm under either federal or Texas law unless their firearm rights are restored. *See* 18 U.S.C. § 922(g); and *United States v. Walters*, 359 F.3d 340 (4th Cir. 2004).

IV. Understanding "private sales" laws

A. *What are the legal restrictions on "private sales" of firearms?*

Private individuals may legally buy, sell, gift, or otherwise transfer firearms to another private individual in Texas. However, when doing so, careful attention needs to be paid to not violate the laws regulating these transactions. So what are the legal restrictions? First, the ATF website has an informative pamphlet entitled "Best Practices: Transfers of Firearms by Private Sellers" located on its website. This pamphlet should be a must-read before entering into a "private sales" transaction involving a firearm. So what are the rule in Texas regarding private sales?

1. Residency requirements

In order for the private sale of a firearm to be legal in Texas, both parties must reside in the same state. This means, for our purposes, that both the buyer and seller of the firearm must be

Texas residents. Similarly, under federal law, an unlicensed (non-dealer) may only "transfer" a firearm to another unlicensed person in the <u>same</u> state. This means that if a person is a resident of Texas, federal law prohibits the person from directly (not through a dealer) selling or transferring the firearm to a resident of another state. Federal law makes these transactions illegal from both the buyer/transferee and seller/transferor perspective. It is illegal for a private individual to transport into or receive within his own state a firearm which was purchased in another state from a private seller. *See* 18 U.S.C. § 922(a)(3). Likewise, it is illegal for a private seller to sell or deliver a firearm to an individual whom the private seller knows or has reason to believe is not a resident of the seller's state. *See* 18 U.S.C. § 922(a)(5).

Example:

> *Bob is visiting his best friend from high school, Jim. Ten years ago after high school was over, Bob moved to Nebraska from Texas. One night, Bob and Jim decide to go to the shooting range during Bob's trip, and Bob borrows one of Jim's handguns. After shooting at the range, impressed with both the feel and action of Jim's handgun, Bob asks Jim if he could buy it from him. Since they've been friends for so many years, Jim says yes, and even offers him a good price for the transaction. Before leaving to go home to Nebraska, Bob pays Jim and packs his new handgun.*

Has Bob committed a crime in selling the handgun to Jim? Has Jim committed a crime in purchasing the handgun from Bob? The answer to both questions is yes! Under federal law, Bob is not allowed to privately purchase a handgun in another state and transport it back to his home state. Likewise, Jim is not allowed to sell a firearm legally to a person he knows lives in another state. In this example, both Bob and Jim <u>know</u> that Jim is not a Texas resident—the place where Bob has sold his firearm. Bob has committed the crime of willful receipt of a firearm from out-of-state by an unlicensed person while Jim has committed the federal crime of willful sale of a firearm to an out-of-state resident. *See 18 U.S.C. § 924(a)(1)(D).* The penalties for these crimes include jail time up to 5 years and/or a fine of $250,000.00!

What if the situation is less obvious? Let's take a look at an example where "reasonable cause to believe" comes into play.

Example:

> *Frank, a Texas resident, recently posted his Glock 19 for sale on an internet message board in Texas. Frank receives an email from a person named Ted who would like to buy the handgun. Frank and Ted agree, via email, on a purchase price and arrange to meet at a place in Texas one week later to facilitate the transfer. When Ted pulls up in his 1978 Ford LTD Wagon, Frank notices the car's Tennessee license plates. Nevertheless, Frank shrugs and sells Ted the gun anyway without going through any of the formalities of a bill-of-sale, or asking for identification. Two weeks later, Frank finds himself at an FBI field office in Houston answering questions about a shooting that took place with his (former) Glock 19.*

Is Frank in trouble? It is highly likely. Although Frank is not the center of the shooting investigation, Frank is probably the center of an investigation for illegally selling the firearm to an out-of-state resident under federal law.

2. Private sales: don't knowingly sell to the "wrong" people

A private individual may sell a firearm to a private buyer in the same state so long as the seller does not know or have reasonable cause to believe that the person purchasing the firearm is prohibited from possessing or receiving a firearm under federal or state law. *See* 18 U.S.C. § 922(d). *Also, see discussion in the previous sections on "disqualifications."*

Example:

> *Gordon and Josh are friends and Josh tells Gordon that he has just attempted to buy a gun from a local FFL and that he was denied because he was disqualified for some reason under federal law (something about a conviction or restraining order or drug use or psychiatric problems—Josh was too mad to remember!). Gordon says, "no problem, I'll just sell you one of mine," and he does.*

Gordon has just committed a federal and state crime, because he knew (or at least had reasonable cause to believe) that Josh was prohibited from purchasing a firearm under the law. *See our earlier discussion concerning disqualifications.*

B. *How does the law determine a person's residence when buying or selling a firearm?*
   1. Individuals with one residence

For the purpose of firearms purchases, the person's state of residence is the state in which the person is present and where the individual has an intention of making a home. 27 CFR § 478.11.

   2. What if a person maintains a home in two states?

If a person maintains a home in two (or more) states and resides in those states for periods of the year, he or she may, during the period of time the person actually resides in a particular state, purchase a firearm in that state. However, simply owning property in another state does not qualify a person as a resident of that state so as to purchase a firearm in that state. To meet the residency requirements, a person must actually maintain a home in a state which includes an intention to make a particular state a residence. *See* 27 CFR § 478.11. This issue may ultimately be a fact question with evidence of residency being things like a driver's license, insurance records, recurring expenses in the state, as well as other things related to making a particular state a person's residence.

3. Members of the Armed Forces

A member of the Armed Forces on active duty is a resident of the state in which his or her permanent duty station is located. If a member of the Armed Forces maintains a home in one state and the member's permanent duty station is in a nearby state to which he or she commutes each day, then the member has two states of residence and may purchase a firearm in either the state where the duty station is located or the state where the home is maintained. *See* 18 U.S.C. § 921(b). *See also ATF FAQs on residency at www.atf.gov.*

4. Nonimmigrant aliens

Persons who are legally present in the United States are residents of the state in which they reside and where they intend to make a home. Such persons, provided they meet all other requirements and are not otherwise prohibited from purchasing a firearm are lawfully permitted to purchase a firearm.

C. *Suggestion on how to document a private firearms sale*

Protect yourself! This is practical advice that should not be ignored. If you engage in the private sale of a firearm, here are some practical tips:

- Ask for identification whether you are the buyer/transferee or seller/transferor to establish residency;
- Get and/or give a "bill of sale" for the transfer and keep a copy—identify the firearm including make, model, and serial number, as well as the date and place of transfer;
- Put the residency information on the "bill of sale" including names, addresses, and phone numbers;
- Do not sell or transfer a firearm or ammunition if you think the person may not be permitted or is prohibited from receiving the firearm.

Why do this? Not only will it help establish residency, but if you unfortunately happen to buy or sell a firearm that was previously used in a crime, or if you sell or transfer a gun that is later used in a crime, you want to be able to establish when you did and did not own or possess the firearm.

Further, as a matter of good course, if you are a seller or transferor in a private sale, you might ask whether there is any reason the buyer/transferee cannot own a firearm. Why? So that if there is an issue later, you can at a minimum say that you had no reason to know the buyer could not legally possess firearms. However, do not overlook behavior that may indicate the buyer is not telling you the truth, because law enforcement will not overlook facts that show you did know, or should have had reasonable cause to believe that the buyer/transferee could not own a firearm at the time of the transfer if a legal issue arises later. Protect yourself!

V. Buying, selling, and transferring through an FFL
A. *Basic procedures*
Persons purchasing firearms through dealers must comply with all legal requirements imposed by federal law. These include both paperwork, and appropriate background checks or screenings to ensure that the purchaser is not prohibited from the purchase or possession of a firearm under federal law.

When purchasing through a dealer, the first thing a prospective buyer will do is select a firearm. Once a selection has been made, the prospective purchaser is required to show proper identification and complete ATF Form 4473. This form requires the applicant, under penalty of law, to provide accurate identifying information, as well as answer certain questions in order to establish whether a person may legally purchase a firearm. The information provided on Form 4473 is then provided to the National Instant Criminal Background Check System (NICS) for processing and approval in order to proceed with the transfer (however, no NICS background may be required if the transferee is legally exempt for reasons such as possessing a state-issued firearms license like a Texas CHL). A FFL dealer can submit the check to NICS either by telephone or through the online website and only after the FFL completes all of these steps successfully is a purchaser/transferee allowed to take possession of the firearm.

B. *What is Form 4473?*

ATF Form 4473 is the ATF's form known as a Firearms Transaction Record which must be completed when a person purchases a firearm from an FFL. *See* 27 CFR § 478.124. Form 4473 requires the applicant to provide their name, address, birth date, state of residence, and other information including government issued photo identification. The form also contains information blanks to be filled-in including the NICS background check transaction number, the make, model, and serial number of the firearm to be purchased, and a series of questions that a person must answer. *See* 27 CFR § 478.124(c). This series of questions and the corresponding answers help determine a purchaser's eligibility under federal law to purchase a firearm. Once the form is completed, the prospective purchaser will sign the form and attest that the information provided thereon is truthful and accurate under penalty of federal law. This means that if you lie or make false statements on this form, the Feds can and will prosecute you for a crime!

Likewise, the dealer must also sign Form 4473 and retain it for at least 20 years. The ATF is permitted to inspect, as well as receive a copy of Form 4473 from the dealer both during audits and during the course of a criminal investigation. The 4473 records must be surrendered to the Bureau of Alcohol, Tobacco, Firearms and Explosives in the event the FFL dealer retires or ceases business.

C. *How are background checks administered when purchasing a firearm?*

1. NICS: National Instant Criminal Background Check System

Background checks by dealers when transferring firearms are completed through the National Instant Criminal Background Check System or NICS, if required, prior to the transfer of a firearm from an FFL dealer to a non-dealer. When the prospective purchaser/transferee's information is given to NICS, the system will check the applicant against at least three different databases containing various types of records. Applicants are checked against the records maintained by the Interstate Identification Index (III) which contains criminal history records, the National Crime Information Center (NCIC) which contains records including warrants and protective orders, as well as the NICS Index which contains records of individuals who are prohibited from purchasing or possessing firearms under either federal or state law. In addition, if the applicant is not a United States Citizen, the application is processed for an Immigration Alien Query (IAQ) through the Department of Homeland Security's Immigration and Customs Enforcement Division.

2. <u>Responses from NICS</u>

NICS responses to background checks come in three basic forms: proceed, delay, or deny. The "proceed" response allows for the transfer to be completed. The "delay" response means that the transfer may not legally proceed. If the dealer receives a response of "delay," NICS has three business days to research the applicant further. If the dealer has not received a notice that the transfer is denied after the three business days, then the transfer may proceed. "Deny" means the transfer does not take place; a transferee's options after a "deny" are discussed below.

3. <u>What transactions require background checks?</u>

A background check is required before each and every sale or other transfer of a firearm from an FFL to a non-licensee unless an exception is provided under the law. For every transaction that requires a background check, the purchaser/transferee must also complete ATF Form 4473. This includes:

- The sale or trade of a firearm;
- The return of a consigned firearm;
- The redemption of a pawned firearm;
- The loan or rental of a firearm for use off of an FFL's licensed premises;

- Any other non-exempt transfer of a firearm.

Practical Legal Tip:

Thinking about buying a gun on behalf of your buddy? Not a good idea! One of the purposes of ATF Form 4473 is to conduct a background check on individuals who want to purchase firearms in order to make sure they are legally allowed to do so. Acting as a "straw man" by purchasing it for your buddy circumvents this process and is a crime. -Kirk

4. <u>What transactions do not require a background check?</u>

A background check is not required under the following circumstances:

- The sale or transfer of a firearm where the transferee presents a valid state permit/license that allows the transferee to carry a firearm (for example, a CHL) from the state where the FFL is located <u>and</u> the state permit/license is recognized by the ATF as a qualifying alternative to the background check requirement;
- The transfer of a firearm from one FFL to another FFL;
- The return of a repaired firearm to the person from whom it was received;
- The sale of a firearm to a law enforcement agency or a law enforcement officer for official duties if the transaction meets the specific requirements of 27 CFR § 478.134 including providing a signed certification from a person in authority on agency letterhead stating that the officer will use the firearm in official duties and where a records check reveals the officer does not have any misdemeanor convictions for domestic violence;

- The transfer of a replacement firearm of the same kind and type to the person from whom a firearm was received;
- The transfer of a firearm that is subject to the National Firearms Act if the transfer was pre-approved by the ATF.

Note: a Texas Concealed Handgun License currently qualifies as an alternative to the NICS background check requirement as long as the license was issued within 5 years of the date of the transfer. A complete permit chart for all states is available on the ATF's website at www.atf.gov.

5. If a person buys multiple handguns, a dealer must report that person to the ATF

Under federal law, FFLs are required to report to the ATF any sale or transfer of two or more pistols, revolvers, or any combination of pistols and revolvers totaling two or more to an unlicensed (non-FFL) individual that takes place at one time or during any five consecutive business days. This report is made to the ATF on Form 3310.4 and is completed in triplicate with the original copy sent to the ATF, one sent to the designated State police or local law enforcement agency in the jurisdiction where the sale took place, and one retained by the dealer and held for no less than five years.

6. FFLs must report persons who purchase more than one rifle in southwest border states

In Texas, Arizona, New Mexico, and California, dealers are required to report the sale or other transfer of more than one semiautomatic rifle capable of accepting a detachable magazine and with a caliber greater than .22 (including .223 caliber/5.56 millimeter) to an unlicensed person at one time or during any five consecutive business days. *See* 18 U.S.C. § 923(g)(3)(A). This report is made via ATF Form 3310.12 and must be reported no later than the close of business on the day the multiple sale or other disposition took place. This requirement includes (but is not limited to) purchases of popular semiautomatic rifles such as AR-15s, AK-47s, Ruger Mini-14s, and Tavor bullpup rifles.

VI. What if I'm denied the right to purchase a firearm?

A. If I am denied the right to purchase, how do I appeal?

Persons who believe they have been erroneously denied or delayed a firearm transfer based on a match to a record returned by the NICS may request an appeal of their "deny" or "delay" decision. All appeal inquiries must be submitted to the NICS Section's Appeal Service Team (AST) in writing, either online or via mail on the FBI's website at www.fbi.gov. An appellant must provide their complete name, complete mailing address, and NICS Transaction Number. For persons appealing a delayed transaction, a fingerprint card is required and must be submitted with the appeal, although the fingerprint card is merely recommended on appeals for denied applications. This may seem counter-intuitive, but it is required per the FBI's website.

B. What if I keep getting erroneously delayed or denied when I am attempting to buy a firearm?

Apply for a PIN (personal identification number) that is designed to solve this issue. Some individuals may have a name which is common enough (or happens to be flagged for other reasons) that it causes undue delays or denials in the background check verification process through NICS. For that reason, NICS maintains the Voluntary Appeal File database (VAF) which allows any applicant to apply by submitting an appeal request and then obtain a UPIN or Unique Personal Identification Number. A person who has been cleared through the VAF and receives a UPIN will then be able to use their UPIN when completing Form 4473 in order to help avoid further erroneous denials or extended delays. A person can obtain a UPIN by following the procedures outlined on the FBI's website at www.fbi.gov.

VII. Additional considerations in firearms purchasing and possession laws

A. *How can I legally purchase a firearm from someone in another state?*

Any individual who wishes to purchase a firearm from a person that lives in another state than the purchaser must complete the transaction through an FFL. Sellers or transferors are legally authorized to facilitate a private transaction or transfer by shipping the firearm to the purchaser's FFL in the recipient/buyer's state, where the FFL will complete the transfer process. It is a federal crime to sell or transfer a firearm between persons who are residents of different states, or where a transfer takes place in a state other than the transferee/transferor's singular state of residence.

B. *Can I purchase firearms on the Internet?*

Yes. However, all legal requirements for a transfer must be followed. If the buyer and seller are both residents of Texas, then the two may lawfully conduct a private sale so long as all other legal issues are satisfied (see our earlier discussion on disqualifications to purchasing and possessing firearms in this chapter). However, if buyer and seller are not residents of the same state, the transaction can only be legally facilitated through the intervention of an FFL.

C. *Shipping firearms*

1. Can I ship my firearm through the postal service?

Long guns: yes. Handguns: no. However, under federal law, a non-licensed individual may not transfer (and this would include shipping to someone) a firearm to a non-licensed resident (non-FFL) of another state. However, a non-licensed individual may mail a long gun to a resident of his or her own state, and they may also mail a long gun to an FFL of another state. To that end, the USPS recommends that long guns be mailed via registered mail and that the packaging used to mail the long gun be ambiguous so as to not identify the contents. Handguns are not allowed to be mailed. *See* 18 U.S.C. §§ 1715, 922(a)(3), 922(a)(5), and 922(a)(2)(A). Rather, handguns must be shipped using a common or contract carrier (*e.g.*, UPS or FedEx).

2. Shipping handguns and other firearms through a common or contract carrier

Under federal law, a non-licensed individual may ship a firearm (including a handgun) by a common or contract carrier (*i.e.*, UPS or FedEx) to a resident of his or her own state, or to a licensed individual (FFL) in another state. However, it is illegal to ship any firearm to a non-FFL in another state. It is a requirement that the carrier be notified that the shipment contains a firearm, however, carriers are prohibited from requiring any identifying marks on the package which may be used to identify the contents as containing a firearm. *See* 18 U.S.C. §§ 922(a)(2)(A), 922(a)(3), 922(a)(5), 922(e), 27 CFR 478.31 and 478.30.

D. *Can I ship my firearm to myself for use in another state?*

Yes. In accordance with the law as described in the preceding section, a person may ship a firearm to himself or herself in care of another person in another state where he or she intends to hunt or engage in other lawful activity. The package should be addressed to the owner and persons other than the owner should not open the package and take possession of the firearm.

E. *If I am moving out of Texas, may I have movers move my firearms?*

Yes, a person who lawfully possesses firearms may transport or ship the firearms interstate when changing the person's state of residence so long as the person complies with the requirements for shipping and transporting firearms as outlined earlier. *See* 18 U.S.C. § 922(e) and 27 CFR § 478.31. However, certain NFA items such as destructive devices, machine guns, short-barreled shotguns or rifles, and so forth require approval from the ATF before they can be moved interstate. *See* 18 U.S.C. § 922(a)(4) and 27 CFR § 478.28. It is important that the person seeking to move the firearms also check state and local laws where the firearms will be relocated to ensure that the movement of the firearms into the new state does not violate any state law or local ordinance.

F. *May I loan my firearm to another person?*

There is no prohibition on loaning a firearm to another person, so long as the person receiving the firearm may lawfully possess one. However, under Texas law, Penal Code § 46.06(a)(2) states that it is unlawful for a person to intentionally or knowingly sell, rent, lease, give or offer to sell, rent lease, or give a firearm to any child younger than 18 years of age. The law does provide an affirmative defense for persons charged with a crime of unlawful transfer of weapons in the event that the loan of the firearm to a minor was done with the effective consent of the parent who is the person with legal custody of the child. Although this statute does not specifically use the word "loan," the term "give" is not defined and, thus, Texas firearms owners should be aware of this statute anytime the loan of a firearm to a minor takes place.

G. *What happens to my firearms when I die?*

Depending on the manner in which a person leaves his or her estate behind, firearms may be bequeathed in a customary manner like other personal property. However, firearms held in an estate are still subject to the laws of transfer and possession. This careful consideration needs to be given in estate planning with consideration for firearms law of both the jurisdiction in which the estate is located as well as consideration of who is to receive the firearms.

VIII. Ammunition: the law of purchasing and possession

A. *Who is legally prohibited from purchasing ammunition under federal law?*

Under federal law, there are six primary situations where a person is prohibited from buying, selling, or possessing ammunition (beyond armor-piercing ammunition which was discussed in Chapter 2).

1. Under 18 U.S.C. § 922(b)(1), it is unlawful for a person to sell long gun ammunition to a person under the age of 18;

2. Under 18 U.S.C. § 922(b)(1), it is unlawful for a person to sell handgun ammunition to a person under the age of 21;
3. Under 18 U.S.C. § 922(x)(2)(B), it is unlawful for a juvenile to possess handgun ammunition;
4. Under 18 U.S.C. § 922(d), it is unlawful to sell ammunition to a person who is prohibited from purchasing firearms;
5. Under 18 U.S.C. § 922(g), it is unlawful for a person who is disqualified from purchasing or possessing firearms to possess firearm ammunition if such ammunition has moved in interstate commerce (which is nearly all ammunition); and
6. Under 18 U.S.C. § 922(h), it is unlawful for a person who is employed by a person who is disqualified from purchasing or possessing ammunition to possess or transport ammunition for the disqualified individual.

For the statutes that involve juveniles, there are a couple of notable exceptions to the law: first, the law against selling handgun ammunition to a juvenile and possession of handgun ammunition by a juvenile does not apply to a temporary transfer of ammunition to a juvenile or to the possession or use of ammunition by a juvenile if the handgun and ammunition are possessed and used by the juvenile in the course of employment, in the course of ranching or farming-related activities at the residence of the juvenile (or on property used for ranching or farming at which the juvenile, with the permission of the property owner or lessee, is performing activities related to the operation of the farm or ranch), target practice, hunting, or a course of instruction in the safe and lawful use of a handgun. The law also does not apply to the temporary transfer to or use of ammunition by a juvenile if the juvenile has been provided with prior written consent by his or her parent or guardian who is not prohibited by federal, state, or local law from possessing firearms. *See* 18 U.S.C. § 922(x)(3).

Additionally, juveniles who (1) are members of the Armed Forces of the United States or the National Guard who possesses or is armed with a handgun in the line of duty, (2) receive ammunition by inheritance, or (3) possess ammunition in the course of self-defense or defense of others are permitted to possess ammunition.

B. *When is a person prohibited from purchasing or possessing ammunition under Texas law?*

The Texas Penal Code provides two occasions where the sale of ammunition is prohibited: (1) to intoxicated persons, and (2) to felons prior to the fifth anniversary of their release. However, there is no crime for the purchase or possession of ammunition by those or any other individuals, with the exception of armor-piercing handgun ammunition (see Chapter 2).

Under Texas Penal Code § 46.06(a)(3), it is a class A misdemeanor if a person "intentionally, knowingly, or recklessly sells a firearm or ammunition for a firearm to any person who is intoxicated." Likewise, under section 46.06(a)(4), is it a class A misdemeanor if a person "knowingly sells a firearm or ammunition for a firearm to any person who has been convicted of a felony before the fifth anniversary of the later of the following dates: (A) the person's release from confinement following conviction of the felony; or (B) the person's release from supervision under community supervision, parole, or mandatory supervision following conviction of the felony." The Texas statutes only criminalize the selling of ammunition to these individuals; they do not criminalize the possession or purchase of it.

C. *Can a person be disqualified from purchasing ammunition if they are disqualified from purchasing firearms?*

Yes, under federal law. Under 18 U.S.C. § 922(g) it is unlawful for a person who is disqualified from purchasing or possessing firearms if the ammunition has moved in interstate commerce. Since nearly all ammunition or ammunition components move through interstate commerce in one form or another, this disqualification includes essentially all ammunition. There is no disqualification under Texas law, however.

D. *Can a person purchase ammunition that is labeled "law enforcement use only"?*

Yes. Although some handgun ammunition is sold with a label "law enforcement use," such a label has no legal meaning and is only reflective of a company policy or, viewed less positively, as a marketing strategy.

CHAPTER FOUR
WHEN CAN I LEGALLY USE MY GUN: PART I
UNDERSTANDING THE LAW OF JUSTIFICATION
SOME BASIC LEGAL CONCEPTS

I.   Ignorance of the law is NO excuse!

Now we start to get into the meat of our discussion: when is it legal to use a gun as a weapon? The purpose of this chapter is to look at the essential, basic legal concepts of the law of when and under what circumstances a person is legally justified in using force or deadly force against other persons or animals. Know when you may legally shoot, because ignorance of the law holds no weight in a courtroom! That is why it is critical you know the law so that you are in the best possible situation to preserve your legal rights if you ever need them.

II.   Gun owners need to know Chapter 9 of the Texas Penal Code

In Texas, legal justifications appear in numerous places and areas of the law. Of particular importance to gun owners are the defenses found in Chapter 9 of the Texas Penal Code entitled "Justification Excluding Criminal Responsibility" which we cover in detail throughout this book. The full text of relevant provisions of that chapter of the Texas Penal Code are found in the Appendix.

III. To legally use force or deadly force, you must be "justified." What is legal justification?

A.   *Basic definition of justification: an acceptable excuse*

So, when is it legal to use force or deadly force against another person? When is it legal to even threaten to use force or deadly force against another? The answer is when there is a legal "justification," or defense. A legal justification is an acceptable reason or excuse under the law for taking an action that would otherwise be a crime.

Example:
> *Rick is in his suburban back yard with his faithful dog when out of nowhere, a coyote appears and is about to attack.   Rick draws his handgun and shoots the coyote.*

Rick has discharged his firearm in the city limits, which is ordinarily a crime.   Why will Rick likely be not guilty of the crime of "discharging a firearm within city limits?" Because he was <u>legally justified</u> in shooting the coyote! That is, the law will likely say the excuse for discharging the firearm in the city limits—protecting himself and his dog from coyotes—makes Rick's action of discharging a firearm in the city limits reasonable and, therefore, legally justified.

Practical Legal Tip:

A <u>defense to prosecution</u> is not the same as a <u>bar to prosecution</u>.   A "bar to prosecution" is where a person can't be prosecuted for engaging in certain conduct, whereas a "defense to prosecution" allows prosecution for the conduct, but offers defendants a justification that must be demonstrated with evidence in court. *-Kirk*

B. *Basic requirement: you must admit your action*

If a person wants the potential protection of legal justification in Texas, in order to raise the defense of justification in court, a person is required to admit all of the elements of the crime for which they are charged.   Then, the person must present "some evidence" of justification before a jury will be given an instruction that "a person is legally justified to use force if..." In plain English, a person will not be allowed to say "I didn't do it, but if I did do it,

I was justified!" You must admit the underlying elements of the charge.

Example:

> *Jane is walking home one night, when a man jumps out of the bushes and demands her purse. Jane pulls out her handgun and points it at the man, who then runs away. Unfortunately, Jane does not call the police, but the criminal immediately does, reporting a crazy woman threatening him with a gun. Jane ends up charged with aggravated assault, even though Jane was the victim.*

Because justification is a legal defense in Texas, if Jane's case goes all the way to trial, in order to offer a legal justification for committing "aggravated assault," she must admit in court that she did pull her handgun and point it at the would-be robber. Then, in order for the jury to consider a legal justification defense (*i.e.,* receive a jury instruction from the judge), she must offer some evidence of why she is legally justified under the law for having pulled her weapon (in this example, Jane believed she was being robbed). The result is that Jane is entitled to have the judge instruct the jury that they may find Jane not guilty because she was justified in her action. The jury will then decide whether they believe Jane and whether she is guilty or not guilty of the crime of aggravated assault.

Practical Legal Tip:

A jury instruction is a statement made by the judge to the jury informing them of the law applicable to the case in general, or some aspect of it. *-Edwin*

On the other hand, if Jane does not admit to the elements of the criminal offense she is charged with, she will not be allowed to offer a legal justification defense under Chapter 9 of the Texas Penal Code. Legal justification is, therefore, literally the law of "Yes, I did it, BUT...!"

IV. Categories of force for justification under Chapter 9

Anytime a person takes a physical action against another person, they have used force. Chapter 9 of the Texas Penal Code divides or categorizes uses of force into different levels. Whether or not a use of force was justified under the law often depends on how that force is categorized. These categories, which we will address throughout this book, are: 1) *force*, 2) *deadly force*, and 3) *the threat of force*.

A. *What if a person uses greater force than the law allows?*

The use of a legally appropriate level of force is important because if a person uses more force than is "reasonably believed to be immediately necessary" (see Section V), that person may not be legally justified in using that level of force. It is important to understand the differences in the levels of force and the circumstances under which the law allows the use of each.

For example, if a person uses deadly force, and the law allows only for the use of force, that person will not be legally justified. Likewise, if a person uses force when no force is legally allowed, that use of force will not be legally justified.

Example:

> *Harry Homeowner looks out his window and sees a person standing on his front lawn. Harry yells at the fellow to get off his land. The fellow on the lawn does not respond. Harry rushes out to confront the fellow and demands that he leave Harry's lawn.*

This fellow is now clearly a trespasser! What degree of force may Harry use to remove the trespasser? The law, as discussed later, will show that Harry is only allowed to use force in response to a mere trespasser. If Harry uses deadly force against the trespasser, he will not be legally justified and would be guilty of using unlawful force against the trespasser. Ultimately, using the correct degree of force is critical in determining whether a person has committed a crime or a legally justified action.

B.   *What is the legal definition of "force?"*
Surprisingly, "force" is not defined in the Texas Penal Code. However, "deadly force" *is* defined. Under Chapter 9 of the Penal Code, a prerequisite for being able to legally use deadly force is the requirement that a person must be able to use force in the same situation. Therefore, one may conclude that mere force must be something less than deadly force. Texas courts have further helped define force by holding that force occurs anytime a person engages in conduct that inflicts harm on another person or puts another person in fear of harm.

Example:
> Timmy is being harassed and insulted by a bully, when the bully suddenly clenches his first and takes a swing at Timmy, but misses. Timmy reacts to the swing by punching the bully in the face.

The bully's action was a use of force. Even though he missed Timmy, the bully placed Timmy in fear of harm. Timmy's action of striking the bully was likewise a use of force, and as will be discussed later, legally justified because Timmy engaged in conduct which caused harm or a fear of harm to the bully.

C. *What is deadly force?*

Definition of Deadly Force: Tex. Penal Code § 9.01(3)
"Deadly force" means force that is intended or known by the actor to cause, or in the manner of its use or intended use is capable of causing, death or serious bodily injury.

1. Deadly force does not have to cause death!

On the surface, the legal definition of deadly force seems simple. However, the meaning of what is and is not deadly force can be legally tricky. A particular action does not necessarily have to result in death to be legally defined as deadly force—it just needs to be *capable* of causing death or serious bodily injury. *Note:* serious bodily injury is defined as the substantial risk of death, permanent disfigurement, protracted loss, or impairment of the function of any bodily member or organ. *See* Tex. Penal Code § 1.07(a)(46).

Example:

> *Jim is being robbed and beaten by a group of individuals when he manages to draw his handgun and fire it at one of the most aggressive assailants. His shot misses his intended target but breaks the group up, causing the would-be robbers to flee.*

In our example, even though the bullet did not kill or even strike any of his assailants, Jim legally used deadly force because his conduct fit the legal definition of "capable of causing death or serious bodily injury." Thus, death is not a prerequisite for the existence of deadly force! Likewise, almost any object can be used as a weapon in a particular circumstance. Therefore, in this section of the law, the focus is on the object's intended use and not just on the object itself.

2. "Intended or known" as a component of deadly force

Deadly force, by its legal definition, occurs when a person takes an action that is *intended* or *known* by the actor to cause death or serious bodily injury. This knowledge or intention to cause serious bodily harm or death is called a person's mental state. A prosecutor must prove beyond a reasonable doubt that a person possessed a particular mental state applicable to a crime in order to meet the state's burden of proof and convict someone of a crime.

Often a person's intent is easily ascertainable by the circumstances. For example, if a person is the would-be victim of robbery, and the person resists by pulling his or her gun and firing at the robber, the law will likely find the victim used justifiable deadly force, because the victim of the crime resisted and used force that the victim intended to cause death or serious bodily injury.

However, the weapon used is not always dispositive evidence of someone's intent to use deadly force. Hammers, toasters, knives, baseball bats, and almost any other object can be "capable of causing" serious bodily injury or death under a particular circumstance. The case legally turns, then, on how the person is using the force.

D. *What are threats of force? "Stop or I will…"*

> ### Threat of Force by Production of a Weapon: Tex. Penal Code § 9.04
>
> The threat of force is justified when the use of force is justified by this chapter. For purposes of this section, a threat to cause death or serious bodily injury by the production of a weapon or otherwise, as long as the actor's purpose is limited to creating an apprehension that he will use deadly force if necessary, does not constitute the use of deadly force.

Texas law provides that if you are legally justified to use force in any particular situation, then you may also legally *threaten* to use force in the same situation. Likewise, if you are justified in using deadly force in a particular situation, you may legally threaten the use of deadly force in the same situation.

Section 9.04 of the Texas Penal Code states that if a person threatens deadly force by the production of a weapon, it is not a use of <u>deadly force</u> so long as the person's only purpose is to create an apprehension that they will use deadly force, if necessary.

Example:

> *Billy is walking to his car after work when three individuals with baseball bats confront him in the parking lot and surround him in an aggressive manner. Fearing that they are about to assault him with the bats, Billy draws his gun and clearly demands that the aggressors leave him alone, at which point they all flee from the scene.*

Has Billy legally used deadly force by showing his gun? Probably not under the plain language of section 9.04. Billy's threat was to create apprehension that he would use deadly force if necessary. Thus, the legal argument would say his production of a weapon was a use of force by Billy and not a use of deadly force.

By defining the action of the production of a weapon to create apprehension as <u>not</u> "the use of deadly force," the legislature (by its express language and the legislative history) wanted to make the action only a use of force. Therefore, a person could be legally justified to "produce" a weapon to create apprehension when use of force was legally justified—not just when the use of deadly force is justified! This is what the text of the law says. However, some courts have failed to interpret the law this way. Read on...

Section 9.04 is not the end of the story
Contrary to the plain language of section 9.04, some Texas courts
seem to indicate (and prosecutors and trial courts followed) that a
person may <u>only</u> legally produce a weapon as a threat in response
to <u>deadly force</u>. Although the plain language of section 9.04
appears to give a legal justification for a person to threaten force
by producing a weapon in response to an unlawful use of force <u>or</u>
deadly force, some Texas appellate court cases have significantly
muddied the water in interpreting the meaning of section 9.04.

These court decisions arguably take the position that one can only
threaten deadly force in response to situations under which you
can legally use deadly force, contrary to the plain language of
section 9.04. Until further clarification by Texas courts, the matter
seems less settled than the statute's language would suggest. For
those interested, the cases include *Smith v. State*, No. 04-95-
00337-CR, 1997 WL 94151 (Tex.App.—San Antonio 1997, *pet.
ref'd*)(mem. op. not designated for publication), *Flores v. State*, No.
01-10-00531-CR, 2013 WL 709100 (Tex.App.—Houston [1st Dist.]
Feb. 26, 2013, *pet. dism'd* (Aug. 21, 2013), *pet. ref'd* (Feb. 5,
2014))(mem. op. not designated for publication), *Reynolds v. State*,
371 S.W.3d 511 (Tex.App.—Houston [1st Dist.] 2012, *pet. ref'd*).
The two latter decisions were based on the unpublished (and,
therefore, non-binding, although often cited by prosecutors) ruling
from the San Antonio Court of Appeals, *Smith v. State* (cited
above), which stated that the only time you can point your gun is
in response to the use, threatened use, or appearance of deadly
force. *See Smith v. State*. Are you confused? We are too!

E. *Warning shots*
Warning shots get a lot of good folks in legal trouble! Warning
shots are commonly portrayed in movies and television as a good
idea—and people like to mimic what they see in movies and on TV!
Leaving completely aside all practical issues of whether under a
particular set of circumstances a warning shot is a good idea (and
experience has taught us that very rarely are they a good idea),
what does Texas law say about warning shots?

1. Are warning shots a use of deadly force?

First, the term "warning shot" does not appear in the Texas Penal Code. Without clear guidance from statutory law, courts are left to determine if the action of firing a warning shot is to be considered under either the use of force standard or the use of deadly force standard.

Although the firing of a warning shot is not *per se* legally forbidden, you should be aware that if you fire a warning shot, it is highly likely that your conduct will be judged under the legal standard that you have used deadly force and not just mere force. This means that a person may only be allowed the legal argument of justification if a warning shot is fired in situations in which deadly force is justified under the law, similar to how the courts evaluated the *Smith*, *Flores*, and *Reynolds* cases discussed earlier. There is little appellate court case law demonstrating how Texas courts have addressed the issue of warning shots. Every gun owner should be aware that one likely argument a prosecutor may put forth against a defendant at trial is that the simple discharge of a firearm is an action that is capable of causing death or serious bodily injury. Such an argument, if successful, will shift the analysis of warning shots into the use of deadly force arena of whether a person intended that action or not.

Why is it important whether the law classifies a warning shot as a use of force or a use of deadly force, even if no one is injured? Let's take a look at an example:

Example:

> *Harry Homeowner looks outside during broad daylight and sees a trespasser on his property. Not knowing what the trespasser is doing, Harry grabs his firearm to investigate. Harry confronts the trespasser and demands that he leave the property, but the trespasser ignores Harry. Being both scared and agitated, Harry fires a "warning*

shot" to get the trespasser's attention and compliance.

Does Harry's discharging his gun fit the definition of the use of deadly force? Likely, yes. Harry very likely may be guilty of a crime and not have a justification available as a defense, because he used a higher degree of force than the law allows.

2. Warning shots: "But, I never meant to hurt anyone!"

Going back to our example, assume Harry will say he fired the warning shot, but that he never aimed at or even meant to hit anyone. In fact, assume Harry will say he only shot into the dirt to get the trespasser to leave. How will the law view Harry's "warning shot?"

First, Harry Homeowner was confronted in this example with a mere trespasser and under Texas law as we will see later, a person may legally use force, **but not** deadly force to remove a trespasser. Therefore, if the "warning shot" that was fired by Harry is legally classified as deadly force under the law, Harry will not be legally justified, and instead, a jury may decide he is guilty of a crime such as aggravated assault. So, the classification is the difference between guilt and innocence in this example.

Now, let us change the example a bit to see how things may get even more complicated:

Example:

Harry Homeowner confronts the same trespasser (Tom) as before and fires a warning shot. This time, however, the shot startled Tom out of his zoned state of self-meditation and wandering in which he likes to contemplate the universe. Tom was so deep in his personal world, he didn't realize he had accidentally wandered onto Harry's property. In fact, Tom the trespasser was so deep in meditative strolling and enjoying the

Texas air that he didn't even hear Harry's verbal demands, but, the sound of Harry's 30.06 hunting rifle got Tom's full attention! As a result, Tom does exactly what his 25 years of police training have taught him—he draws and fires at Harry, believing that Harry's shot had meant to end his days of strolling and meditation!

Where do we start the legal analysis? First, Harry Homeowner is in what Texas legal circles often call a "big mess!" Harry has very likely used unlawful deadly force against a mere trespasser. After Harry's shot, does this turn our absent-minded wandering Tom into a victim who reasonably believes his life is threatened? Does this fact then allow Tom the trespasser some legal justification to return fire, *etc.*?

Continuing the issue, if our wandering Tom Trespasser then returns fire at Harry, is Harry then legally justified in using deadly force to defend himself? Or, because Tom is an accidental trespasser, is Tom required to retreat first before he takes any action? Keep in mind that Harry knows nothing about Tom's meditation or walks—he is just confronted with a trespasser who did not respond to verbal requests, but has now responded to Harry's "warning shot" with muzzle flashes from a pistol. Ultimately, you can see how messy this type of scenario can become, which all started with a well-intentioned "warning shot."

After the dust clears (assuming perfect knowledge), Harry likely used a higher degree of force than the law allows. But who decides if a "warning shot" is a "warning shot" and not a shot at someone that simply missed? Who decides if a response to a situation is reasonable? In the vast majority of cases in Texas, a jury ultimately decides. There are no bright lines on warning shots, so be advised that a warning shot can potentially be viewed as a use of deadly force, whether you subjectively intended it to or not, and, therefore, should never be used without careful consideration.

V. What does it mean to "reasonably believe force is immediately necessary?"

In Texas law, the legal standard for a justified use of force is generally expressed as a person must "<u>reasonably</u>" believe that the use of force is "<u>immediately necessary</u>" to protect against the unlawful use of force.

But what does "reasonable" mean? Further, when is something immediately necessary—and who decides whether it is or not? The answers to these questions are how the legal process decides guilt or justification. For all gun owners, these concepts are critical.

A. *How does the law determine "reasonable?"*

In determining what is reasonable, the law often uses a standard known as the "reasonable person" standard to evaluate a person's conduct. It uses a hypothetical "reasonable person." Who is a reasonable person, and how does he or she act? Ultimately, a reasonable person is whatever a jury says it is.

Practical Legal Tip:

Throughout this book, we refer to juries making the ultimate determination of fact. There are, however, some limited occasions where a judge makes the determinations. For example, if all parties waive their right to a jury, the Court may conduct what is called a "bench trial." *-Kirk*

The legal analysis behind the reasonable person goes like this: if a person used force or even deadly force, they must act like a reasonable person would have acted under the same or similar circumstances in order to be legally justified! However, if a person fails to act like a reasonable person, their conduct will fall below the acceptable legal standard and will <u>not</u> be justified. The reasonable person standard is the law's attempt to make the concept of reasonableness an objective and measurable test.

Under this standard, the law does not focus on whether you *subjectively* (or personally) believed force was reasonable, but whether a "reasonable person" would have considered it reasonable, an objective standard. If the legal system (and ultimately, again, this could be a jury) determines that a reasonable person would have believed that force was immediately necessary in response to another person unlawfully using force against you, then you will be found legally justified in using force.

Keep in mind, however, that judges, juries, and prosecutors are simply human beings, and people can have vastly different ideas of how a reasonable person should act under any given circumstances. This is particularly true if asked to decide whether force or deadly force was immediately necessary or not.

B. *What does "immediately necessary" mean under the law?*
When does someone have a reasonable belief that force is immediately necessary? In Texas, it ultimately may be a jury that is tasked with determining whether someone had a reasonable belief if an action was immediately necessary or not. With that said, courts have held that immediately necessary means that when a person took his action, he had to take that action right then, right there, and without delay, otherwise he may have suffered harm or injury. *See McGarity v. State* 5 S.W.3d 223 (Tex.App.—San Antonio, 1999, *no pet. h.*). Clearly, "immediately necessary" attempts to convey a sense of urgency for the use of force, but again, it usually falls back to the jury to decide if this standard was met in a particular case.

C. *Legal presumptions: stop legal second-guessing*
Under certain circumstances, a person's belief in the necessity of immediate force or deadly force will be presumed "reasonable" under Texas law. This legal presumption can be a very powerful

legal tool to stop legal second-guessing or "Monday morning quarterbacking" of the amount or time of the force used. A jury will be told that if a given set of circumstances exists (*e.g.*, a person is the victim of a sexual assault), the law will presume "reasonable" a person's belief in the immediate necessity of using force or deadly force, and that use of force or deadly force would, therefore, be legally justified.

Example:

> *Harry Homeowner is asleep in his house when he hears a noise in his kitchen. Harry enters his kitchen with his .45 drawn and confronts an armed burglar. Harry fires his weapon and the burglar will burgle no more!*

In this situation, was Harry's use of deadly force in firing his gun immediately necessary, or, more precisely, was Harry's belief that deadly force was immediately necessary reasonable? Did Harry, legally, have to take additional actions before firing in order to have acted reasonably? In Harry's current situation, the law will give Harry a powerful legal <u>presumption</u> that his belief that the use of deadly force was immediately necessary was "reasonable." In Harry's example, section 9.32 of the Penal Code will provide him with this presumption of "reasonableness" (as a victim of a home invasion in his occupied habitation). In Texas statutes, these legal presumptions read: "the actor's belief that deadly force was immediately necessary is presumed to be reasonable if... (fill in the appropriate circumstances: *e.g.*, prevent murder, sexual assault, *etc.*)." This presumption will prevent any second-guessing by prosecutors that deadly force was not immediately necessary. This has a practical effect of preventing arguments like a person should have used less force, no force, or retreated first. The legal presumption of reasonableness is a powerful tool for anyone facing a criminal charge and claiming legal justification.

Practical Legal Tip:

Note: a presumption is not an <u>absolute</u> ticket to victory. A prosecutor may attempt to overcome the presumption with other evidence that shows you did not act in self-defense. *-Edwin*

D. *No presumption of reasonableness: prosecutors are allowed to second-guess*

As we discussed above, under certain circumstances, the law will presume the reasonableness of a person's belief that force or deadly force is immediately necessary. However, if a person uses force or deadly force under circumstances that do not qualify for this presumption, the issue of whether a belief of the immediate necessity to use force or deadly force was or was not reasonable is left to the jury, and prosecutors are allowed to second-guess the reasonableness of the timing and/or degree of force used by a defendant.

Accordingly, when a defendant does not qualify for a legal presumption, a prosecutor has the opportunity to argue that a person's use of force or deadly force was not immediately necessary. This allows for arguments in court like "should have retreated," "should have used lesser force," and so forth. In many circumstances (such as situations involving defense of property), no legal presumption of reasonable belief is afforded for uses of force or deadly force at all! In those cases, a jury will decide the issue of the reasonableness of a person's belief and, ultimately, whether or not a person is guilty of a crime.

VI. The burden of proof in criminal cases

In criminal cases, the state attorneys or prosecutors have the burden of proof. This means that it is the State's responsibility to present enough evidence to prove the defendant committed a crime. This burden of proof that the prosecutor bears is a standard called "beyond a reasonable doubt." It is the highest level of proof used in the American justice system. The state's job at trial in attempting to prove the defendant's guilt includes eliminating any reasonable doubt that the defendant's conduct was justified.

We are now ready to look at under what circumstances Texas law allows a person to use deadly force to protect themselves and others in the next chapter.

Practical Legal Tip:

A word about juries. Juries are not "picked" in Texas. Rather, they are the first twelve people that are not "struck" from the pool of folks called a jury pool. Most of the time, in my opinion, juries get it "right," but after years of practice, some juries' decisions leave you scratching your head... That is why these legal presumptions can be critical. *-Edwin*

CHAPTER FIVE

WHEN CAN I LEGALLY USE MY GUN: PART II
SELF-DEFENSE AND DEFENSE OF OTHERS
UNDERSTANDING WHEN FORCE AND DEADLY
FORCE CAN BE LEGALLY USED
AGAINST ANOTHER PERSON

I. Introduction and overview

The question of "when can a person legally use deadly force against another person" is of critical importance if you are a legal Texas firearms owner. Although a firearm is nothing more than a tool, it is a tool that by its very nature has the ability to deliver deadly force. Thus, all responsible firearms owners should understand when they are justified in using force and deadly force under the law. Failure to understand the law gets lots of good folks in serious trouble!

The primary Texas statutes dealing with self-defense and defense of other people are contained in three Texas Penal Code Sections:
> 9.31: Self-Defense
> 9.32: Deadly Force In Defense of Person
> 9.33: Defense of Third Persons

The law of justified self-defense is split between justification for the use of <u>force</u> in section 9.31 and justification for the use of <u>deadly force</u> in section 9.32. Each of these sections also contain legal presumptions of reasonableness that are available under certain circumstances and are extremely powerful when deciding if a use of force or deadly force was legally justified. Likewise, the language of both sections contains Texas' versions of the "Castle Doctrine" and "Stand Your Ground" laws, even though those specific terms are not mentioned in the statutes. Section 9.33 combines force and deadly force in providing justification for "Defense of Third Persons."

In the previous chapter, several legal concepts, such as reasonableness, immediate necessity, and the categorization of force and deadly force were discussed. Those concepts have practical applications in this chapter. In this chapter, we will expand upon those topics to include when a person may be justified in using force or deadly force in self-defense, as well as those circumstances when the law specifically prohibits the use of force or deadly force.

II. Defending people with force or deadly force

A. *General self-defense justification: no presumption of reasonableness*

The primary self-defense statutes in Texas are sections 9.31 and 9.32 of the Texas Penal Code. Section 9.31(a) lays out the legal requirements for the justified use of force, but not deadly force, for self-defense. This section establishes that a person is legally justified in using force against another "when and to the degree the actor reasonably believes the force is immediately necessary to protect the actor against the other's use or attempted use of unlawful force."

Likewise, section 9.32(a) establishes the general standard for the justified use of deadly force. The first requirement is that force must be justified under section 9.31. A person must legally be able to use force before the law will ever allow deadly force to be justified. Thereafter, a person is legally justified in using deadly force for self-defense "when and to the degree the actor reasonably believes the deadly force is immediately necessary" to protect himself or herself against another's use or attempted use of unlawful deadly force. As discussed in the previous chapter, what a person believes is immediately necessary and whether that belief is reasonable is the difference between justification (not guilty) and conviction (guilty).

Who decides whether an actor's belief is or is not reasonable that force or deadly force is immediately necessary? Who decides if the degree of force used by someone was reasonable under a particular set of circumstances? The answer to both of these questions is the jury.

Therefore, if a person finds himself or herself facing a criminal charge and is claiming self-defense under the general self-defense provisions of sections 9.31 and 9.32, the jury will decide if that person's belief was or was not reasonable regarding the immediate necessity of the use of force or deadly force by that person. As can be imagined, this leaves a lot of room for juries to interpret what actions are reasonable or not. It also leaves the door open for legal second-guessing by prosecutors as to when and how much force was used, including arguments that there was no imminent threat and as such, the force or deadly force was not really "immediately necessary." If the prosecutor convinces a jury that a person used force or deadly force when or to a degree that was not "reasonably" believed to be immediately necessary, a person's use of force or deadly force will not be legally justified, and that person will be guilty of using unlawful force or deadly force. However, under certain circumstances, sections 9.31 and 9.32 allow persons a powerful additional protection in the form of a legal presumption of reasonableness in their belief that the use of force or deadly force was immediately necessary.

B. *Presumption of reasonableness under sections 9.31 and 9.32*
Sections 9.31 and 9.32 contain several circumstances when the law gives far more protection than is available under the general self-defense standard. Under these statutes, a person's belief that it was immediately necessary to use force or deadly force will be legally presumed reasonable. This legal presumption, if available to an accused, is a potentially powerful legal argument and limits prosecutors in court from second-guessing either when or the amount of force used by the accused in defending himself or herself (*e.g.*, should have used non-deadly force, dispute resolution methods, or should have retreated, and so forth). If a defendant meets the conditions enabling him or her to be afforded the protection of this presumption, the law will deem "reasonable" a belief that the force that was used was immediately necessary,

limiting any argument that the force used by the accused was unreasonable.

> ## Practical Legal Tip:
>
> In law school, they taught us that "reasonable minds can differ." Yet, reasonableness is a standard that we are held to whenever we face a legal issue. Thankfully, Texas provides us with presumptions of reasonableness so that even when reasonable minds do differ, you know where you stand with the law. -Michele

C. _Legal presumptions for victims of certain violent crimes_

If a person is a victim or would-be victim of unlawful force or deadly force, Texas law allows for the justified use of force or deadly force when and to the degree that the person reasonably believes that it is immediately necessary to protect himself or herself. However, if a person is forced to defend himself or herself against someone who is committing or is about to commit one of the 6 crimes listed in sections 9.31 and 9.32 and satisfies the other requirements of the statutes, the law will provide a legal presumption that a victim's belief in the immediate necessity of force or deadly force was "reasonable." These 6 crimes are: aggravated kidnapping, murder, sexual assault, aggravated sexual assault, robbery, and aggravated robbery.

1. Aggravated kidnapping

If a person is a victim or a would-be victim of an aggravated kidnapping, a felony of the first degree, then the law will presume reasonable his or her belief that the use of force (section 9.31), or deadly force (section 9.32) was immediately necessary to defend against an attacker, and therefore, force or deadly force will be legally justified.

What is aggravated kidnapping? Generally, aggravated kidnapping occurs anytime a person abducts another person and "uses or exhibits a deadly weapon during the commission of the offense." This is the definition found in Texas Penal Code § 20.04(b).

However, under Texas law, the crime of aggravated kidnapping can actually occur in several different circumstances. Texas Penal Code § 20.04(a) defines aggravated kidnapping as anytime a person: "intentionally or knowingly abducts another person with the intent to:

- hold him for ransom or reward;
- use him as a shield or hostage;
- facilitate the commission of a felony or the flight after the attempt or commission of a felony;
- inflict bodily injury on him or violate or abuse him sexually;
- terrorize him or a third person; or
- interfere with the performance of any governmental or political function."

Example 1:
> *Jane is out jogging one evening, when a white van pulls up next to her, and a masked man with a gun jumps out, trying to grab her and drag her into his van. Jane pulls out her pepper spray, sprays the man in the face, and runs away to call police.*

Example 2:
> *Jane is out jogging one evening, when a white van pulls up next to her, and a masked man with a gun jumps out, trying to grab her and drag her into his van. Jane pulls out her Glock 42 and fires two shots, killing her attacker.*

In the first example, was Jane legally justified in her use of force against the man? What about her use of deadly force in example two? The answer to both is yes. Jane's belief that the use of force (pepper spray) was immediately necessary will be presumed reasonable under section 9.31, because the man in the white van was attempting to commit aggravated kidnapping! Likewise, in the second example, under section 9.32, Jane's belief that deadly force was immediately necessary will also be presumed reasonable for the same reason, and also results in the conclusion that Jane's use of deadly force was justified.

In these hypotheticals, the masked man with the gun was trying to abduct Jane. Whatever his ultimate purpose for trying to grab her, if Jane reasonably believed she was about to be a victim of an aggravated kidnapping, she will be entitled to a legal presumption that her belief was "reasonable" in that the use of force or deadly force was immediately necessary to stop the aggravated kidnapping. Thus, with this presumption, prosecutors will be limited in their ability to second-guess whether Jane should have used less force than she did, or that she should have retreated first. The law will deem her belief in the immediate necessity of her use of force or deadly force "reasonable." These are clear examples, however. We will discuss later how the law is applied in more ambiguous cases.

2. Victims of attempted murder

It is basic self-preservation set forth in the law that if someone is trying to end your days, you may defend yourself with force or deadly force. Thus, it is no surprise that sections 9.31 and 9.32 of the Texas Penal Code combine to allow for the use of force or deadly force to prevent someone from murdering you. As with the other listed violent crimes, a person who defends himself or herself against murder is justified in using force or deadly force in self-defense against the attacker. The victim is also given a legal presumption of "reasonableness" to any belief that force or deadly force was immediately necessary to defend his or her life.

Murder

So, what is murder? Texas Penal Code § 19.02 defines murder as any time a person:

- "intentionally or knowingly causes the death of an individual;
- intends to cause serious bodily injury and commits an act clearly dangerous to human life that causes the death of an individual; or
- commits or attempts to commit a felony, other than manslaughter, and in the course of and in furtherance of the commission or attempt, or in immediate flight from the commission or attempt, he commits or attempts to commit an act clearly dangerous to human life that causes the death of an individual."

How should the law under sections 9.31 and 9.32 be applied after a self-defense shooting?

Example:

> One busy day at his job, David is working quietly at his desk when he hears an angry voice yell out, "I hate this company, and I'm going to kill every one of you!" About that time, David spots a machete in a deranged-looking stranger's hand. The stranger turns toward David with an evil look. David draws a gun from his desk drawer. As the man continues toward David with the machete raised, David fires two shots at the attacker, killing him.

In this situation, the law allows David to use force or deadly force when and to the degree he reasonably believes it is immediately necessary to defend himself. Here, David skipped mere force and immediately used deadly force. Was this reasonable? Should David have first used non-deadly force? Should he have used a method of dispute resolution? If he could have retreated out of a back door, was his use of deadly force really immediately necessary? If David does not qualify for the legal presumptions under sections 9.31 and 9.32, these are the types of questions and issues that will be presented to the jury to determine.

However, in this example, because David is about to be a victim of murder, the law will deem "reasonable" his belief that deadly force was immediately necessary! This is a powerful legal presumption and limits prosecutorial arguments regarding the reasonableness of when the force was used or the degree of force used, because it is legally deemed "reasonable." How do we know David acted in self-defense? In this example, the attacker makes it easy, because he cleared up any ambiguity of his intentions when he declared "I am going to kill every one of you" while wielding a machete. Thus, under Texas law, David, as a would-be victim of murder, is entitled to a legal presumption that he had a reasonable belief that it was immediately necessary to use force or deadly force against the attacker to prevent his own murder. Therefore, David is legally justified in using deadly force. See also the discussion on "Stand Your Ground" under Section E later in this chapter.

If, for some reason, David was ever charged with a crime for killing the would-be murderer, and David puts forth "some evidence" in trial that he was about to be the victim of murder, the jury would then get to decide whether David acted in self-defense under sections 9.31 and 9.32. For a discussion of the legal concept of "some evidence," see Section D. The jury will be told that if David reasonably believed he was about to be murdered, the law will presume "reasonable" that deadly force was immediately necessary. The prosecution would then have the burden of establishing beyond a reasonable doubt that David did not act in self-defense (*i.e.*, David did not know or have reason to believe he was about to be murdered). If the jury finds that the prosecution did not meet this burden of proof, it will decide his use of deadly force was legally justified.

But, how does the self-defense statute work when the example is not so clear?

Example:

> *Police respond to a two-car collision in a parking lot. When the police arrive, they discover that the collision has sparked a violent road-rage incident. At the scene, one man is dead on the ground with a tire iron beside him. The remaining driver—the shooter—Michael, a 45 year-old man with no previous criminal record, fired two shots and is now a suspect in a murder investigation. Michael claims that the other driver became irate after the collision, threatened him, and aggressively came toward him with the tire iron raised in his hand. However, the position of the physical evidence makes it so that determination of who was the true victim in this incident is unclear. In fact, one investigator thinks Michael is lying. There are no other witnesses.*

If Michael ultimately faces criminal charges for murder and claims self-defense at his trial, how does the determination of presumption and, ultimately, legal justification under sections 9.31 and 9.32 work in practice?

In order to receive the protection of a presumption of "reasonableness" for victims of crimes under sections 9.31 and 9.32, Michael has the initial burden of producing "some evidence" in court to support that he "knew or had reason to believe" that he was about to be the victim of murder (*e.g.*, the man screamed threats at him and was about to strike him with the tire iron, and Michael was in fear of his life, so he shot the man). If Michael puts forth "some evidence" that the dead man was about to murder him, the law requires the prosecution to then prove beyond a reasonable doubt that the accused (in this case, Michael) did not act in self-defense. *See Saxton v. State*, 804 S.W.2d 910 (Tex. Crim. App. 1991), and *Jenkins v. State*, 740 S.W.2d 435 (Tex. Crim. App.

1987). The prosecution will have an opportunity to put forth evidence that Michael was not about to be the victim of murder based on the physical evidence found at the scene as well as the investigating officer's testimony. This presumption of reasonableness puts Michael's legal defense in a much better legal position than it would be without it.

If the jury believes Michael acted in self-defense to an attempted murder or, more precisely, that the prosecution did not prove beyond a reasonable doubt that Michael did not act in self-defense, sections 9.31 and 9.32 act to give Michael a legal presumption of "reasonableness" to his belief that the use of force or deadly force was immediately necessary (see also the discussion of *no duty to retreat* later in this chapter). This is a very powerful legal tool in court. Having the presumptions of section 9.31 and 9.32 could just be the difference between a verdict of guilty or not guilty!

3.   Victims of sexual assault and aggravated sexual assault
Like murder, if a person is the victim of a sexual assault or an aggravated sexual assault, Texas law allows for the legally justified use of force (section 9.31) or deadly force (section 9.32) to stop the assault. These two self-defense statutes will also provide any victim of these crimes who resists with force or deadly force a powerful legal presumption of "reasonableness" to his or her belief in the immediate necessity of force or deadly force against the attacker. How does the law define sexual assault and aggravated sexual assault?

Sexual Assault
Section 22.011 of the Texas Penal Code defines sexual assault as a felony of the second degree, or under certain circumstances, a felony of the first degree. A person commits sexual assault in the State of Texas any time that person "intentionally or knowingly:
- causes the penetration of the anus or sexual organ of another person by any means, without that person's consent;

- causes the penetration of the mouth of another person by the sexual organ of the actor, without that person's consent; or
- causes the sexual organ of another person, without that person's consent, to contact or penetrate the mouth, anus, or sexual organ of another person, including the actor; or
- causes the penetration of the anus or sexual organ of a child by any means;
- causes the penetration of the mouth of a child by the sexual organ of the actor;
- causes the sexual organ of a child to contact or penetrate the mouth, anus, or sexual organ of another person, including the actor;
- causes the anus of a child to contact the mouth, anus, or sexual organ of another person, including the actor; or
- causes the mouth of a child to contact the anus or sexual organ of another person, including the actor."

Aggravated Sexual Assault
The crime of aggravated sexual assault under Texas law is found in section 22.021 and is a first degree felony. Aggravated sexual assault is defined as when a person commits an intentional or knowing action of sexual assault under section 22.011, **and** if "the person:

- causes serious bodily injury or attempts to cause the death of the victim or another person in the course of the same criminal episode;
- by acts or words places the victim in fear that any person will become the victim of [human trafficking] or that death, serious bodily injury, or kidnapping will be imminently inflicted on any person;
- by acts or words occurring in the presence of the victim threatens to cause any person to become the victim of an offense under [the human trafficking statute] or to cause

the death, serious bodily injury, or kidnapping of any person;

- uses or exhibits a deadly weapon in the course of the same criminal episode;
- acts in concert with another who engages in conduct described by [the sexual assault statute in section 22.011] directed toward the same victim and occurring during the course of the same criminal episode; or
- administers or provides flunitrazepam, otherwise known as rohypnol, gamma hydroxybutyrate, or ketamine to the victim of the offense with the intent of facilitating the commission of the offense;
- the victim is younger than 14 years of age; or
- the victim is an elderly individual or a disabled individual."

4. <u>Victims of robbery and aggravated robbery</u>

Like the other violent crimes listed in sections 9.31 and 9.32 of the Penal Code, if a person is a victim or would-be victim of a robbery or aggravated robbery, Texas law allows the victim to protect himself or herself against the robber with legally justified force or deadly force. Further, like the other crimes listed in these two sections, the presumptions of reasonableness of force or deadly force being immediately necessary without a duty to retreat are available if all statutory requirements are met. How does Texas law define robbery and aggravated robbery?

Robbery

Under section 29.02 of the Texas Penal Code, robbery, a second degree felony, occurs when a person, in the course of committing theft and with the intent to obtain or maintain control of the property, 1) intentionally, knowingly, or recklessly causes bodily injury to another; or 2) intentionally or knowingly threatens or places another in fear of imminent bodily injury or death. For a robbery to occur, a robber does not actually have to acquire the property.

Aggravated Robbery

Aggravated robbery is a first degree felony and is defined in Texas Penal Code § 29.03 as when, during the commission of robbery, the robber: 1) causes serious bodily injury to another; 2) uses or exhibits a deadly weapon; or 3) causes bodily injury to another person or threatens or places another person in fear of imminent bodily injury or death, if that person is 65 years of age or older, or a disabled person.

Example:

> *Tina is on her way home from work. She stops by a local convenience store for some bread and milk. As she enters the store, a masked man suddenly approaches her with a knife, grabs her by the arm, and demands her money. Tina, scared and shaken, remembers her training, opens her purse and pulls a .357 revolver and fires, killing the masked robber.*

In this example, because an aggravated robbery was happening, sections 9.31 and 9.32 allow for the justified, legal use of force or deadly force when and to the degree Tina reasonably believes it is immediately necessary to stop the aggravated robbery. In addition, the law will provide Tina with a powerful legal presumption of "reasonableness" to her belief in the immediate necessity of deadly force to stop the aggravated robbery, and she has no legal duty to retreat. Thus, her use of deadly force is legally justified.

What if the example is less clear?

Example:

> *Hank, a sixty-six year old disabled man, works downtown. He has to park four blocks from his company's office buildings and has to walk*

through some rough parts of town in order to get to his car. A man suddenly appears in front of him and says, "Hey man—give me some money!" Hank, feeling very frightened and intimidated, walks on with the now more loud and aggressive panhandler demanding, "Hey! Man! I said give me some money!" Hank now becomes extremely concerned for his safety. About that time, Hank makes a wrong turn into an alley where he is cornered. He again hears, "HEY! MAN! I SAID GIVE ME SOME MONEY!" When Hank turns around, he sees the same man, now very aggressive, with something in his hand.

Is the panhandler just being annoying, or is Hank about to be the victim of robbery or aggravated robbery? This is the ultimate issue Hank may face if Hank decides to use force or even deadly force against the alleged aggressor. How will the law evaluate a use of deadly force under sections 9.31 and 9.32?

This is an example with a lot of gray area. The man never verbally threatened Hank, nor did he ever physically touch him. All the man said was "give me some money;" he didn't even demand *all* of Hank's money—just some. Do robbers ever demand just some money? If Hank is in genuine fear of an aggravated robbery, does he have a duty to retreat? What about the fact that Hank was cornered in an alley? If Hank takes out his legally concealed carry pistol and fires it to defend himself, what happens? Was Hank really about to be robbed, or is he a paranoid trigger-happy fellow as the prosecutor may try to portray him? Beyond that, who decides what the facts really were? This goes to show that there are lots of questions and gray area.

If Hank finds himself charged with unlawfully using force or deadly force against his alleged attacker, he can assert a legal justification based on self-defense under sections 9.31 and 9.32 of the Penal Code. Again, the law will allow Hank to use force or deadly force for self-defense when and to the degree he reasonably believes it is immediately necessary to stop unlawful force against him. In this example, before a jury will be allowed to decide if Hank acted in self-defense, Hank must present "some evidence" at trial that he reasonably believed he was about to be robbed (see our discussion of what constitutes "some evidence" in the next section).

Hank may attempt to satisfy the "some evidence" requirement by testifying that he was in fear for his safety and had seen the panhandler acting violently on the same street many times in the past. Hank may also say the man raised a weapon in his hand and was moving aggressively toward him, and that the assailant out-weighed Hank by 75 pounds and was about a foot taller. Hank will absolutely testify he felt he was being robbed. If Hank puts forth "some evidence" in court that he was the victim of an attempted aggravated robbery, the jury will get to decide if Hank is credible and if his belief was reasonable, and the law then requires the prosecution to prove beyond a reasonable doubt that Hank did not act in self-defense. *See Saxton v. State*, 804 S.W.2d 910 (Tex. Crim. App. 1991). However, if Hank fails to put forth "some evidence" that he acted in self-defense, he will not be entitled to a self-defense jury instruction concerning sections 9.31 and 9.32, and the jury will not get to decide the issue.

D. *What is "some evidence?"*
So, how much evidence does a person have to offer in a trial to constitute "some evidence" in order to be entitled to a jury charge regarding self-defense? Multiple Texas appeals courts have stated that "if [any] evidence raises the issue of self-defense, the defendant is entitled to have it submitted to the jury, whether that evidence is weak or strong, unimpeached or contradicted, and regardless of what the trial court may or may not think about the credibility of the defense." *Guilbeau v. State*, 193 S.W.3d 156, 159

(Tex.App.—Houston [1st Dist.] 2006). This means that in court, a defendant can literally offer anything as evidence that raises the issue of self-defense, and he is entitled to receive a jury instruction regarding self-defense under sections 9.31 and 9.32. The only requirement is that the evidence offered must be related to the incident of self-defense at issue.

The "some evidence" requirement may be satisfied where the evidence offered is as simple as the defendant's own testimony, which "alone may be sufficient to raise the defensive theory requiring a charge." *Guilbeau v. State*, 193 S.W.3d at 159, *See also Hayes v. State,* 728 S.W.2d 804 (Tex. Crim. App. 1987). In other words, a defendant testifying in court at his own trial that he was attacked first and feared for his life as a result of the attack, would have submitted sufficient evidence to be entitled to a jury instruction on self-defense. It is important to note that "in determining whether the testimony of a defendant raises an issue of self-defense, the truth or credibility of the defendant's testimony is not at issue." *Guilbeau,* 193 S.W.2d at 159. Rather, determining the truth or credibility of the defendant's testimony is the role the jury undertakes in its deliberations.

Practical Legal Tip:

My experience in over 20 years as a trial lawyer is that many people serving on juries tend to ignore the rule of "innocent until proven guilty." Even though every person has a Constitutional right to not testify against themselves, by not doing so, it can cloud a juror's mind so as to make the notion of innocent until proven guilty viewed with skepticism. *-Edwin*

Of course, relying on a defendant's testimony to be the sole source of evidence in order to obtain a jury instruction on self-defense can be fraught with peril as well. All defendants have the right to *not* testify at their trial—which can be a sound trial tactic in that it prevents the State from examining the defendant under oath and on the witness stand. Once a defendant takes the witness stand, however, that defendant will be subject to examination by not only his attorney, but also by the State, examination which may ultimately contain evidence which sways a jury away from seriously considering acquittal on self-defense grounds.

E. *The "Castle Doctrine" and "Stand Your Ground" laws*
   1. The "Castle Doctrine"

The term "Castle Doctrine" does not appear in Texas statutory law, however, the legal concept comes from the philosophy that every person is a King or Queen of his or her "castle." As such, no king or queen is required to retreat before using force or deadly force against an intruder in their castle. In Texas, the "Castle Doctrine" type laws are implemented under sections 9.31 and 9.32 of the Penal Code and take the form of powerful presumptions of reasonableness similar to those provided for the six violent crimes in these two sections. Texas "Castle Doctrine" laws extend to a person's occupied habitation, vehicle, or place of business or employment.

As we discussed earlier, the general rule is that a person is legally justified in using force or deadly force:

> When and to the degree a person reasonably believes the force or deadly force is immediately necessary to protect against the unlawful use of force or deadly force.

If you are a victim of unlawful force or deadly force when you are in your occupied habitation, vehicle, or place of business or employment, the law will provide you protection beyond the general rule. In these "Castle Doctrine" circumstances, the law will presume "reasonable" a person's belief that force or deadly force was immediately necessary to defend against unlawful force. This presumption applies to you when:

(a) A person has unlawfully and with force <u>entered</u>, or was <u>attempting to enter</u> your: occupied habitation, vehicle, or place of business or employment.

(b) A person has unlawfully and with force <u>removed</u>, or is <u>attempting to remove</u> you from your: occupied habitation, vehicle, place of business or employment.

As can be seen, section (a) covers conditions when someone is entering or attempting to enter your "castle" and section (b) covers situations when you are being unlawfully removed from your "castle." Like the presumptions available for victims of violent crimes, a "Castle Doctrine" presumption of "reasonableness" is a powerful legal tool for any person who is accused of a crime and claiming justification. The presumption will be further enhanced by having no duty to retreat (see *No Duty to Retreat* later in this chapter) and will prevent prosecutors in court from second-guessing when or the amount of force that was used. These presumptions are available only for occupied habitations, vehicles, or places of business or employment.

2. <u>What is a habitation under the "Castle Doctrine?"</u>

Texas law, in defining "Castle Doctrine" rights, does not use the term home, house, or property; it uses the term "habitation." The presumptions under sections 9.31 and 9.32 are specific, limited, and do not cover an entire piece of real property—just a habitation. The term "habitation" is defined by Texas Penal Code § 30.01 as:

> *a structure or vehicle adapted for the overnight accommodation of persons; and includes each separately secured or occupied portion of the structure or vehicle; and each structure*

appurtenant to or connected with the structure
or vehicle.

This means that structures which are detached from the building where you sleep at night are not considered to be your habitation. For example, Texas law does not consider your detached garage, shed, and/or barn part of your habitation. Therefore, any justified use of force or deadly force would not qualify for presumptions of reasonableness under this particular part of the law. However, if your garage, or front or back porch is connected to the structure containing your sleeping quarters (as exists in many suburban communities), it is considered part of your habitation as defined by the Texas Penal Code.

3. What is a vehicle under the "Castle Doctrine?"

Texas "Castle Doctrine" legal presumptions and protections are applicable to occupied vehicles. If a person is attempting to "car-jack" you, which is to unlawfully and with force enter your vehicle while you are in it, or unlawfully and with force remove you from your vehicle, you will fall under the "Castle Doctrine." What does Texas define as a vehicle? Under Texas Penal Code § 30.01, a vehicle is defined as:

any device, in, on, or by which any person or
property is or may be propelled, moved, or drawn
in the normal course of commerce or
transportation.

This is a very broad definition and appears to include anything that carries people or property from one place to another, including cars, trucks, boats, airplanes, golf carts, and so forth.

4. In Texas, "Stand Your Ground" means no duty to retreat!

"Stand Your Ground" is a common term for laws that provide that a person has no legal duty to retreat before using force or deadly force against a person that is a threat. The words "stand your ground" are not used in the Texas Penal Code but do appear in Texas case law. Prior to the amendments passed by the Texas legislature in 2007, Texas Penal Code § 9.32 imposed a requirement that deadly force could only be used when "a reasonable person in the actor's situation would not have retreated." The 2007 amendments to the self-defense statutes added provisions that allow a person under certain listed circumstances to "stand their ground" while defending himself or herself, and eliminated any legal duty to retreat. However, for circumstances that are not covered by the provisions of sections 9.31 and 9.32, "the failure to retreat may be considered in determining whether a defendant reasonably believed that his conduct was immediately necessary..." *Morales v. State*, 357 S.W.3d 1, 5 (Tex. Crim. App. 2011). Thus, the existence of no duty to retreat is also a powerful legal tool for any defendant.

The provisions establishing no duty to retreat are located in the self-defense statutes of sections 9.31(e) and (f), and section 9.32(c) and (d). These provisions will act to limit a prosecutor from arguing in court that a person's use of force or deadly force was not really "immediately necessary" because the person could have or should have first retreated.

Practical Legal Tip:

Numerous jurisdictions like Texas have "no duty to retreat" laws that do not require fleeing before the legal use of deadly force. However, several states impose a duty on a person to retreat if reasonably available as a prerequisite to using deadly force. So when traveling, make sure you know the law of the state you are visiting. *-Michele*

In order to receive the "No Duty to Retreat" protection under these statutes, first, a person must satisfy all the conditions in the Penal Code:

    (1) he or she has a legal right to be at the location where force or deadly force is used,

    (2) he or she did not provoke the person against whom force or deadly force was used, and

    (3) he or she is not engaged in criminal activity at the time force or deadly force was used.

All three of these conditions must be satisfied in order for the "No Duty to Retreat" provisions to apply. Further, if a person does not qualify for "No Duty to Retreat" provisions, it does not mean that the person's use of force or deadly force was not legally justified. It simply means that a jury will evaluate whether the person's belief was "reasonable" that the use of force or deadly force was immediately necessary. If a person cannot satisfy all three requirements, the prosecutor will be free to argue that because the accused could have but did not retreat, the accused's belief that the use of force or deadly force was immediately necessary was not reasonable.

Example:

> One day, looking for a shortcut through the neighborhood, Tom hops a fence (a trespass) and is walking across open property to reach the street on the other side of the property. Tom is confronted by the property owner and tries to explain that he meant no harm and was just taking a shortcut. However, the property owner becomes irate and cocks his gun, aims it at Tom, and says "I'm going to kill you!"

Under this example, Tom is a trespasser, and since this is considered being "engaged in criminal activity" under the statute, Tom is disqualified for any legal presumptions under sections 9.31 and 9.32 (see discussion later in this chapter regarding not being engaged in criminal activity). As such, any presumption of reasonableness to a belief in the immediate necessity of force or deadly force will not be given to Tom, even though the property owner made his intention to kill Tom very clear. Further, because he is a trespasser and has no legal right to be at his "location," Tom will not be entitled to the "No Duty to Retreat" protections of the law. This has the result as has been held by the highest Texas criminal court that "the failure to retreat may be considered in determining whether a defendant reasonably believed his conduct was immediately necessary to defend himself or a third person" *Morales*, 357 S.W.3d at 5. Thus, a prosecutor could argue that before the use of force or deadly force by Tom was immediately necessary, Tom should have retreated. It does not mean Tom may not be ultimately legally justified in defending himself, it just makes it more difficult to convince a jury of his justification.

Now let us take the example one step further:

> *Tom is scared out of his mind as he looks down the barrel of the property owner's shotgun. The two are about 20 feet apart. Tom, hearing the property owner's threat to kill him, draws his own firearm and fires two shots, killing the property owner.*

In this example, because Tom is not eligible for the presumptions under section 9.32, a prosecutor would be allowed to question and second-guess when and the degree of deadly force that was used. The prosecutor may argue that Tom did not really need to use deadly force immediately because a "reasonable" person would have retreated under the circumstances. Tom does not lose his legal right to self-defense under this example, just the presumptions of reasonableness, and the protection that the "No Duty to Retreat" provisions offer.

F. *A person who provokes an attack is not entitled to a presumption of reasonableness*

Sections 9.31 and 9.32 of the Texas Penal Code contain a requirement that in order for a person to take advantage of legal presumptions of reasonableness, the person must not have provoked the attack that led to the use of force or deadly force in the first place. See also section H discussing "Provocation" later in this chapter.

G. *Is a person legally entitled to a presumption of reasonableness if they were involved in criminal activity?*

Sections 9.31(a)(3) and 9.32(b)(3) of the Texas Penal Code also contain a requirement that you cannot be engaged in a crime (other than a Class C Misdemeanor regulating traffic) at the time force or deadly force is used in order to obtain a presumption of reasonable belief in the immediate necessity of the use of force or deadly force. Interestingly, the "Stand Your Ground" or no duty to retreat language in both 9.31(e) and 9.32(c) use the even broader words "not engaged in criminal activity" and does not exempt out Class C misdemeanors regulating traffic. The classic example is a drug deal gone bad: the drug dealer may not lose his legal right to self-defense, but the law will not allow the dealer a legal presumption of reasonableness. The general idea is that individuals involved in criminal activity simply do not receive the power of presumed legal justification in protecting themselves when they were doing things they were not legally entitled to be doing in the first place!

H. *When is the use of force or deadly force explicitly **not** legally justified under Texas Penal Code §§ 9.31 and 9.32?*

Texas Penal Code § 9.31(b) outlines five specific situations where a person is not justified in using force. Of course, since being justified in the use of force is an absolute prerequisite to the use of deadly force, any time a person is not justified to use force under section 9.31 that person is also automatically disqualified from being justified to use deadly force under section 9.32. Without being justified, a person cannot claim self-defense.

1. Force never legally justified for verbal provocation alone

No Justification for Words Alone: Tex. Penal Code § 9.31(b)(1)
The use of force against another is not justified in response to verbal provocation alone.

If you think back to your childhood, you probably remember the saying: "sticks and stones will break my bones, but words will never hurt me!" Believe it or not, the law agrees wholeheartedly with this concept. Under Texas law, a person is not justified in using force when words are the *only* provocation to a situation.

Example:

> *Samantha is walking to her car in the grocery store parking lot when a woman starts screaming at her: "you're a terrible driver, and you park like an idiot!" Samantha runs over to the woman and punches the woman in the face.*

In this instance, Samantha is not legally justified in her use of force because the only thing happening was the other woman screaming at her—a mere verbal provocation.

2. Force not legally justified to resist arrest or search

Resisting Arrest or Search Not Justified: Tex. Penal Code § 9.31(b)(2)
The use of force against another is not justified to resist an arrest or search that the actor knows is being made by a peace officer, or by a person acting in a peace officer's presence and at his direction, even if the arrest or search is unlawful.

Example:

> *Justin has been pulled over for speeding and is removed from his vehicle by a uniformed police officer. While sitting on the curb, the officer begins to search Justin's vehicle without his consent and without probable cause. Feeling violated, Justin gets up and pulls the officer out of his car and throws the officer to the ground.*

Even though the officer's behavior is unusual for a mere speeding violation, and even though it appears Justin is being subjected to an illegal search and seizure, his legally justifiable recourse is to pursue the matter through the court system—not to use force against the officer!

Unfortunately, there really are instances where police officers exceed their authority and use more force than they are allowed under the law. Sometimes there are many factors leading to that excessive use of force, but officers have to follow the law, too! For that reason, the legislature crafted a very limited and specific exception to this rule in section 9.31(c).

> ### Justification for Use of Force Against Peace Officer: Tex. Penal Code § 9.31(c)
>
> The use of force to resist an arrest or search is justified if, before the actor offers any resistance, the peace officer (or person acting at his direction) uses or attempts to use greater force than necessary to make the arrest or search; and when and to the degree the actor reasonably believes the force is immediately necessary to protect himself against the peace officer's (or other person's) use or attempted use of greater force than necessary.

This exception in the self-defense statute is crafted to protect a person in those rare scenarios where an officer is using greater force than necessary to make an arrest or search. Having said that, pay very close attention to how narrow and specific this statute is in its application—a person must meet some very specific requirements before he or she is afforded any legal protection:

1. A person must <u>not be resisting</u> when the officer uses <u>greater force than necessary</u>; and
2. That person must <u>reasonably believe</u> that resistance is <u>immediately necessary</u> to protect himself or herself from the officer's use of greater force than necessary to make the arrest or search.

The point of this section is to give fair warning: any time a person uses force against a law enforcement officer, he or she should be aware that the cards are stacked against him or her from the beginning! Ultimately, the lack of available evidence may make it so exceptionally difficult to claim this statute's protections legitimately that it loses its value except in rare instances.

Practical Legal Tip:

The right to remain silent is a fundamental Constitutional right which is why it is so disturbing that in 2010, the US Supreme Court held that you have to say the magic words of "I invoke my right to remain silent and to counsel" in order to trigger it. Seemingly, by the Court's standard, if you don't say the magic words, police could interrogate you until the end of time. *-Edwin*

3. Consent to force

> **No Justification When You Consent to Force:**
> **Texas Penal Code § 9.31(b)(3)**
>
> The use of force against another is not justified if the actor consented to the exact force used or attempted by the other.

Example:

> *Andy and Dwight are having an argument about whose favorite football team will win the championship. In the heat of the argument, Andy calls Dwight a derogatory name and Dwight asks if Andy wants to take it outside. Andy agrees, and they both begin fighting in the parking lot. Shortly after they begin fighting, the police show up and arrest them for disorderly conduct and assault.*

This statute serves the purpose of preventing individuals who arrange to fight each other from avoiding criminal responsibility for their actions by claiming self-defense. The statute here is clear: if a person agrees to the force used against him or her by another person, that person cannot later claim that he or she fought back in self-defense! *See Padilla v. State*, 03-07-00513-CR (Tex.App.—Austin 2008). This statute also applies to individuals who agree to participate in unlicensed "fight clubs." That now explains why "the first rule of fight club is you do not talk about fight club!"

4. Provocation/abandoning an encounter

What does it mean to provoke an attack so as to lose your right to self-defense presumptions? At the time of writing, there are no appellate cases directly interpreting this issue under sections 9.31 and 9.32. However, Texas' highest criminal court, the Court of Criminal Appeals, generally defined what it means to provoke an attack. The Court held that a person who provokes an attack loses the legal right of self-defense (so certainly any legal presumption would be lost as well) when three requirements are met:

1) A person must do some act or use some words which provoke the attack;
2) The act or words from a person must be reasonably calculated to provoke the attack;
3) A person's action or the words used must have been used for the purpose and with the intent that the defendant would have a pretext for inflicting harm on the other. *See Smith v. State*, 965 S.W.2d 509, 513 (Tex. Crim. App. 1998).

What the *Smith* Court is saying is that a person cannot effectively "bait" another person into a violent confrontation and then hide behind the law by claiming that their (the provocateur's) conduct should be presumed reasonable because the other fellow took the first swing! While the Court is considering protection in a different context, courts in the future will likely use this opinion with changes in statutory law to decide when a person has "provoked" another person under sections 9.31 and 9.32. The legal doctrine of provocation is best summed up in a 1914 case, *Sorrell v. State*:

> *A man may not take advantage of his own wrong to gain favorable interpretation of the law. He seeks the law in vain who offends against it. ... One cannot willingly and knowingly bring upon himself the very necessity which he sets up for his own defense.*

Sorrell v. State, 74 Tex. Cr. R. 505, 520, 169 S.W. 299 (Tex. Crim. App. 1914).

Under section 9.31(b)(4), if a person has provoked an attack, self-defense is not available as a defense to a resulting criminal charge.

**No Justification for Provoking Another Person:
Tex. Penal Code § 9.31(b)(4)**

The use of force against another is not justified if the actor provoked the other's use or attempted use of unlawful force.

What if a person who started a fight soon realizes they bit off more than they can chew? Under the law, that person can abandon or clearly communicate his or her desire to abandon the encounter. If, after a person abandons or attempts to abandon the encounter, the person who was provoked pursues and uses unlawful force against the provocateur, the provocateur may then be legally justified to fight back.

**Abandonment of Provocation May Allow Justification:
Tex. Penal Code § 9.31(b)(4)(A) and (B)**

The use of force against another is not justified if the actor provoked the other's use or attempted use of unlawful force, unless the actor abandons the encounter, or clearly communicates to the other his intent to do so reasonably believing he cannot safely abandon the encounter, and the other nevertheless continues or attempts to use unlawful force against the actor.

Example:

> *Dave is at a bar when he notices another man checking-out his girlfriend. Dave tells the other man, "take a hike or you'll regret it" and slightly shoves the admirer. The other man responds by punching Dave in the face. Dave, who didn't really want a confrontation, holds both his hands up in surrender and says, "I don't want any more trouble!" However, the other man pulls out a knife and lunges at Dave.*

In this scenario, Dave is legally justified to fight back: he attempted to abandon the incident and made his intention known to the other person. When the other man continued to attack, Dave is now legally justified to defend himself, even though he made the initial provocation.

5. Settling differences

> **No Justification for Settling Differences:**
> **Tex. Penal Code § 9.31(b)(5)**
>
> The use of force against another is not justified if the actor sought an explanation or discussion with the other person concerning the actor's differences with the other person while the actor was carrying a weapon in violation of Section 46.02; or possessing or transporting a weapon in violation of Section 46.05.

The purpose of the statute is to discourage people from seeking a confrontation to settle a dispute when in possession of a weapon illegally. Situations invoking things like road-rage, cheating spouses, and "where is my money?" are confrontations that are completely different situations than the one like when you are facing an armed burglar in your home at night. Therefore, if you violate the statute, you lose your legal justification for self-defense.

III. Do I have a legal responsibility to defend another person?

Under Texas law, the average person has no duty to come to the defense of another, so long as that actor was not the cause of the situation or occurrence. This is true even if a crime is in progress (but note: this lack of a legal duty does not include police officers and other professionals that may have affirmative legal duties to assist). If you see a third person that is the victim of what you believe to be the unlawful use of force or deadly force, you have no legal duty to aid that person—it is your decision. This is equally true if you are legally carrying a gun pursuant to a CHL. But what if you decide to help the third person?

A. *When does Texas law allow for the justifiable use of force or deadly force to protect someone else?*

Justified Use of Deadly Force to Protect Another Person: Tex. Penal Code § 9.33
A person is justified in using force or deadly force against another to protect a third person if (1) under the circumstances as the actor reasonably believes them to be, the actor would be justified under Section 9.31 or 9.32 in using force or deadly force to protect himself against the unlawful force or unlawful deadly force he reasonably believes to be threatening the third person he seeks to protect; and (2) the actor reasonably believes that the intervention is immediately necessary to protect the third person.

In the last sections, we addressed the law of legal justification for the use of force or deadly force for self-defense. We now turn to when the law allows the justified use of force or deadly force to protect another person or persons.

In general, if you place yourself in the "shoes" of the third person, and the law would allow the third person to use force or deadly force to protect themselves, then you are legally justified to use the same level of force to protect a third person. Texas Penal Code § 9.33 allows a person to protect a third person from the unlawful use of force or deadly force by another in the same circumstances in which a person could justifiably use force under section 9.31 or deadly force under section 9.32 to protect themselves, so long as the person reasonably believes that the intervention is "immediately necessary." By referencing back to the self-defense statutes in sections 9.31 and 9.32, the law makes the legal analysis for defending third persons the same as for self-defense.

Therefore, the same legal justifications and presumptions of "reasonableness" for self-defense are also available for the defense of third persons. If a person decides to aid a third person, the law of justifiable use of force will allow a person to defend a third person to the extent they may defend themselves. As long as the person defending another reasonably believes that the third person would be justified in using force or deadly force to protect him or herself, the person defending may step in and use force or deadly force on that person's behalf. *See Hughes v. State*, 719 S.W.2d 560, 564 (Tex. Crim. App. 1986). However, please note that the law still imposes a requirement that a person's belief in the immediate necessity of the use of force or deadly force be reasonable. If a person decides to defend a third person, prudence dictates that the person defending must be sure they know what is truly happening in a situation before using force or deadly force. If a belief in the immediate necessity of the use of force or deadly force turns out to be unreasonable, the use of force or deadly force will not be legally justified no matter how well intentioned a person may be.

B. *What if the situation is not as I thought it appeared to be?*
A third person and a "Good Samaritan" may not potentially see things as they really are. When a person elects to use force or deadly force to defend a third person, it can all go terribly wrong.

Example:
> *Peter, a licensed concealed handgun owner, decides to get some lunch, so he pulls into a local burger joint to eat. He parks and exits his vehicle whereupon he witnesses a man walking out of the restaurant and across the parking lot. Suddenly, another man comes running up and points a gun in the first man's face. Peter, not wanting to become a victim of a robbery, drops to one knee while drawing his handgun. Still seeing the gun pointed at the first man, Peter decides to protect the would-be victim of robbery and fires his gun striking the robber.*

If there was in fact an armed robbery taking place, Peter's use of deadly force is likely legally justified, because if we put Peter in the shoes of the third person (the first man in the example), Peter would be legally justified in using deadly force to stop the aggravated robbery. Thus, the law will deem Peter's belief that the use of deadly force was immediately necessary as reasonable. But what if there was no armed robbery?

In fact, what would happen if in the instant after Peter fires his gun, the man Peter sought to protect immediately turns to help the wounded suspected robber yelling "murderer!" at Peter while screaming in fear and grief, "why did you shoot my friend?" It turns out that there was not robbery, just a couple of fellows were pranking each other, and the gun Peter saw was a toy. How does the law deal with this scenario?

In such a situation, Peter's perspective and knowledge of the situation are very different from the person he sought to defend. The man clearly knew there was no robbery in progress since he recognized his friend, and that it was a prank. In this situation, if Peter's belief that an aggravated robbery was in progress was reasonable, then Peter will be legally justified. However, if a jury finds that his belief was unreasonable, Peter will not be legally justified and likely guilty of aggravated assault.

C. *Do I have a duty to report a crime?*
Under Texas Penal Code § 38.171, it is a class A misdemeanor for a person who "observes the commission of a felony under circumstances in which a reasonable person would believe that an offense had been committed in which serious bodily injury or death may have resulted" and the person fails to report the crime where he or she reasonably believes the crime has not been reported and where doing so would not have placed the person "in danger of suffering serious bodily injury or death."

IV. The use of force in preventing suicide
Texas law provides that a person may be justified in using force to prevent another from committing suicide or inflicting serious bodily injury on himself. If a person has a reasonable belief that it

is immediately necessary to use force in order to prevent another from committing suicide or inflicting serious bodily injury on himself, then the use of force is justified. Of course, the use of deadly force is not justified in that scenario: the purpose of this statute is to preserve life, not end it!

Justified Use of Force to Protect Life or Health: Tex. Penal Code § 9.34
(a) A person is justified in using force, but not deadly force, against another when and to the degree he reasonably believes the force is immediately necessary to prevent the other from committing suicide or inflicting serious bodily injury to himself. (b) A person is justified in using both force and deadly force against another when and to the degree he reasonably believes the force or deadly force is immediately necessary to preserve the other's life in an emergency.

Section (b) of this statute refers to the rare instances where it may be necessary to use what would be considered deadly force to perform some type of emergency procedure in order to save a life such as an amputation or tracheotomy. Although the language seems somewhat misleading, it is not suggesting that a person be justified in killing another in order to save their life!

CHAPTER SIX

WHEN CAN I LEGALLY USE MY GUN: PART III
UNDERSTANDING WHEN DEADLY FORCE
CAN BE USED AGAINST ANIMALS

I.   Can I legally use deadly force against animals?

When it comes to the law of use of force and deadly force to defend yourself, others, or property from animal attacks, Texas law is a hodgepodge of different laws that are not contained in one section of statutes.

A.   *No general defense against animals statute*

Texas has no general self-defense or defense of others statute that deals with all animals. There exist statutes that justify conduct against certain specific "dangerous wild animals" and ones for protection of domestic animals, crops, and livestock, but no justification for protecting people against animal attacks. For example, if a dog is attacking you, and you have to shoot the dog, there exists no provision of the Texas Penal Code that specifically justifies the use of deadly force. In this situation, persons will be forced to rely on a general defense called "justification by necessity." The typical laws you would expect to find such as self-defense against an animal attacking a human being don't exist under Texas law at all! What this means is that one may not find specific legal justification for using force or deadly force against an animal that is attacking if the animal is not a certain type of animal. Under this condition, a person may be forced to argue the general law of necessity. This chapter will examine the laws that do exist relating to the use of deadly force against an animal and how your right to self-preservation can best be accomplished.

B.   *The doctrine of necessity*

Because there is no specific Texas law that allows a person to use deadly force against an animal in self-defense, often the best claim for legal justification a person can make in a court is one of justification by necessity. Texas law does recognize a very broad justification to potential criminal liability called "necessity," which is defined in Texas Penal Code § 9.22.

Definition of Justification by Necessity: Tex. Penal Code § 9.22
Conduct is justified if: 1. the actor reasonably believes the conduct is immediately necessary to avoid imminent harm; 2. the desirability and urgency of avoiding the harm clearly outweigh, according to ordinary standards of reasonableness, the harm sought to be prevented by the law proscribing the conduct; and 3. a legislative purpose to exclude the justification claimed for the conduct does not otherwise plainly appear.

As this law applies to animal attacks, a person may be legally justified in using force or deadly force (such as firing their gun) against an attacking animal if that person has a *reasonable belief* that force or deadly force is *immediately necessary* to avoid *imminent harm*. However, the imminent harm a person is trying to avoid (by otherwise breaking the law) must be evaluated by a desirability and urgency test under the statute using a reasonable person standard. Further, there exist no legal presumptions of reasonableness such as ones that exist when there are human-on-human attacks. So, how does this all work in practice?

Example:

> *Jim is walking in his neighborhood when out of nowhere three large pit bulls spot him and immediately begin running toward him barking with sharp fangs showing. Jim barely has time to draw and fire his .40 caliber Glock at the lead dog just before it lunged at him. Having dispatched one dog, the other two dogs flee.*

If, for some reason, Jim finds himself charged with any form of crime for his shooting of the dog (this could be anything from cruelty to animals to discharge of a firearm in city limits, *etc.*), Jim will not be able to rely on a specific statute for self-defense because none exists. Rather, Jim will have to rely on the general legal doctrine of necessity as described above.

Practical Legal Tip:

Beware! Using deadly force against a dog or cat that is only digging into your flowerbed or getting into your garbage may not be justified even under the doctrine of necessity. -*Edwin*

This means that a jury would ultimately decide whether Jim's conduct met the requirements of section 9.22. First, did Jim "reasonably" believe his conduct (in this case, drawing and firing his gun) was immediately necessary to avoid imminent harm (being bit, mauled, *etc.*)? So, as was covered in Chapter Four, any time a reasonable person standard is used, it will be an issue for the jury. Further, without legal presumptions available under either of the Texas versions of "Castle Doctrine" or "Stand Your Ground" type laws, a prosecutor will fully be able to argue that Jim should have retreated, that he used too much force, or that that the threat really was not reasonable.

Second, if a defendant satisfies the first part, he or she must still pass a desirability and urgency test according to the standards of reasonableness. In the case of Jim, he would argue that the desirability of a human (in this case, himself) not being bit by a dog when walking in his neighborhood outweighs the law against either discharging a firearm in the city limits, or a charge of cruelty to animals, *etc.* However, a prosecutor would be free to question all aspects of his conduct and second-guess him in court. In this case, it will be for the jury to decide if Jim, or any person in a similar situation, acted reasonably.

C. _Lions and tigers in Texas: "dangerous wild animals"_
Frankly, it's amazing that there's a law specifically protecting you from prosecution in the event you need to kill a caracal—which is a wild cat found primarily in Africa, Asia, and India—but not one which would protect you from an attacking dog in your neighborhood. Nevertheless, Texas Penal Code § 42.092(d)(1) makes that the case.

> **Defense for Cruelty to Animals-Dangerous Wild Animal: Tex. Penal Code § 42.092(d)(1)**
>
> It is a defense to prosecution under this section that the actor had a reasonable fear of bodily injury to the actor or to another person by a dangerous wild animal as defined by Section 822.101, Health and Safety Code.

The _dangerous wild animals_ referenced in this section only include: a lion, tiger, ocelot, cougar, leopard, cheetah, jaguar, bobcat, lynx, serval, caracal, hyena, bear, coyote, jackal, baboon, chimpanzee, orangutan, gorilla, or any hybrid of one of the animals listed here. If the animal is not on the list, it is not covered.

This list is very important because these are the only animals for which a specific justification of self-defense of a person is statutorily authorized. Further, the legislature has addressed the issue of using a firearm as self-defense against these specific animals, in that it is a defense to the crime of disorderly conduct by discharging a firearm in a public place or across a public road if that person who discharged the firearm had a reasonable fear of bodily injury to the person or to another by a dangerous wild animal as defined in section 822.101 of the Health and Safety Code.

You may be asking yourself, "why cougars, bears, and gorillas?" The answer lies in the purpose of Chapter 822 of the Health and Safety Code, which governs the owning of wild animals for entertainment, exhibition or profit. This list is comprised of animals which are not traditionally domesticated animals but are in some cases allowed to be kept in captivity. So, if you are out and about and are confronted by one of the animals listed in section 822.101 which has escaped from confinement, and you have a reasonable fear of bodily injury, you may shoot without fear of prosecution for disorderly conduct or cruelty to animals. This list is conspicuously short and does not cover every non-native wild animal which may be held in a zoo, circus, or safari park. Many animals not included on the list can kill or maim at will such as the hippopotamus, elephant or ferocious cape buffalo. What if our favorite peanut-eating pachyderm charges in a rage? You are left with the defense of necessity as the elephant is not a "dangerous wild animal."

D. *Protecting livestock and crops*

> ### Defense for Cruelty to Animals-Protecting Livestock: Tex. Penal Code § 42.092(e)(1)
>
> It is a defense to prosecution under Subsection (b)(2) [killing, administering poison, or causing serious bodily injury to an animal] or (6) [causing bodily injury to an animal] that the animal was discovered on the person's property in the act of or after injuring or killing the person's livestock animals or damaging the person's crops and that the person killed or injured the animal at the time of this discovery.

With regard to cruelty to a non-livestock animal, Texas Penal Code § 42.092(e)(1) provides a specific statutory defense for killing or injuring an animal if a person discovers the animal on his property and it is in the act of, or has just killed or injured that person's livestock or crops. Subsections (b)(2) and (b)(6) of section 42.092 deal with the moments when you are forced to "intentionally, knowingly, or recklessly" kill, poison, or cause serious bodily injury to another person's animal. If you catch such an animal killing or destroying your livestock or crops, you will be justified in using force or deadly force against it.

E. *Dogs and coyotes attacking livestock or domestic animals*

> ### Authorization to Kill Attacking Dogs/Coyotes: Tex. Health and Safety Code § 822.013
>
> A dog or coyote that is attacking, is about to attack, or has recently attacked livestock, domestic animals, or fowls may be killed by any person witnessing the attack; or the attacked animal's owner or a person acting on behalf of the owner if the owner or person has knowledge of the attack.

Texas Health & Safety Code § 822.013, specifically allows a person to kill a dog or coyote that is attacking livestock, domestic animals or fowls. This statute came into application when Texas Governor Rick Perry was out jogging and a coyote attacked his dog in 2010. Governor Perry dispatched the coyote with his .380 Ruger. The Governor was fully within the scope of section 822.013.

It is notable that this section is specifically limited to dog and coyote attacks on animals, not people. This statute does not address the issue of defending people against animal attacks; you must look elsewhere for your legal justification there. If Governor Perry had not had his dog with him that day and the coyote had instead attacked him, he would have had to employ the general legal defense of necessity. The Texas Court of Criminal Appeals has approved this authorization statute as a defense to the crime of animal cruelty in the case of *Chase v. State*, 448 S.W.3d 6 (Tex. Crim. App. 2014).

F. *Fur-bearing animals*

> ### Defense for Illegal Collection of Fur-Bearing Animal: Tex. Parks and Wildlife Code § 71.004
>
> This chapter does not prohibit a landowner or his agent from taking a fur-bearing animal causing depredation on that person's land.

It's not uncommon to be troubled by fur-bearing pests on your property, such as wild beavers, otters, minks, ring-tailed cats, badgers, skunks, raccoons, muskrats, opossums, foxes, or nutria. Many of these animals destroy property, crops, and so forth in their attempt to build their own habitats. It's for that reason that this section of the Parks and Wildlife code exists: to provide you with some recourse in the event you and your property are troubled by one of these animals. Unlike the Health and Safety Code section for dogs and coyotes, this appears to be a defense, much like other sections, rather than an affirmative authorization to use deadly force against one. Chapter 71 of the Parks and Wildlife Code also defines a "taking" of a fur-bearing animal to include killing that animal.

G. *Federal law defenses*

The federal law, in a comprehensive fashion, has actually had the foresight to specifically provide that a person may kill an animal protected by federal law in self-defense, such as the regulations concerning the Mexican gray wolf in 50 CFR § 17.84(k)(3)(xii), or the grizzly bear in 50 CFR § 17.40(b)(i)(B). Unlike the Texas statutes, this makes the Federal law clear and comprehendible. Therefore, if you are carrying a firearm in a National Park (see Chapters 9 and 10), and you find yourself face to face with a grizzly bear, you will have a legal defense for protecting yourself.

CHAPTER SEVEN
WHEN CAN I LEGALLY USE MY GUN: PART IV
UNDERSTANDING WHEN DEADLY FORCE
CAN BE USED TO PROTECT PROPERTY

I.   Overview and location of the law to protect property

Texas law allows a person to protect, with force, their property from another's unlawful interference or trespass on their property or the property of another. Further, Texas law, under certain circumstances, will also allow a person to use legally justified deadly force to protect property. The statutes in the Penal Code dealing with legally justified force or deadly force to defend property are as follows:

> 9.41: Protection of One's Own Property
> 9.42: Deadly Force to Protect Property
> 9.43: Protection of a Third Person's Property

Protection of property will be analyzed under the same "reasonable person" standard discussed in Chapters 4 and 5 and will have the same requirements for a person reasonably believing that the force or deadly force used was "immediately necessary." In addition to the above sections, Texas Penal Code § 9.44 addresses the law of devices to protect property.

II.   When is someone legally justified to use "force" but not "deadly force" to protect their own property?

A.   *Prevent or terminate interference with property*

The law answers this question based upon the statutory law of the justified use of force to protect property contained in section 9.41 of the Penal Code. This section divides the justified use of force (but not deadly force) into two categories: the first category, under subsection 9.41(a) is when a person is justified in using force to prevent or terminate another person's unlawful trespass or interference with their property, *e.g.*, stealing property, vandalizing property, *etc.*

If you catch someone in the act

In plain terms, if someone is unlawfully taking your personal property, you are justified in using force to stop them. Of course, just like instances of self-defense, you must also meet the standard of *reasonable belief in the immediate necessity of the use of force.*

> **Justified Use of Force to Protect Your Property:**
> **Tex. Penal Code § 9.41(a)**
>
> A person in lawful possession of land or tangible, movable property is justified in using force against another when and to the degree the actor reasonably believes the force is immediately necessary to prevent or terminate the other's trespass on the land or unlawful interference with the property.

B.   *Recovery of property*

The second category, under section 9.41(b), is the justified use of force in <u>recovering</u> property that has been unlawfully taken from the person or to reenter land.

> **Justified Use of Force to Recover Your Property:**
> **Tex. Penal Code § 9.41(b)**
>
> A person unlawfully dispossessed of land or tangible, movable property by another is justified in using force against the other when and to the degree the actor reasonably believes the force is immediately necessary to reenter the land or recover the property if the actor uses the force immediately or in fresh pursuit after the dispossession and (1) the actor reasonably believes the other had no claim of right when he dispossessed the actor; or (2) the other accomplished the dispossession by using force, threat, or fraud against the actor.

Fresh pursuit after property is taken

In the event a person's property has already been stolen, a person is only legally justified to use force to recover it *immediately after it was stolen* or in *"fresh pursuit."* A person is not allowed to use force that is not immediate, or in "fresh pursuit," to go and recover the property days, weeks, or months later and also be justified if he or she beats up the thief in the process of recovery. What does it mean to recover property "immediately after" or in "fresh pursuit?"

While it appears that the appellate courts in Texas have been reluctant to provide a bright-line definition of what it means to be in "fresh pursuit," they have provided some guidance on what is not considered to be "fresh pursuit." For instance, one court stated that the use of force was not immediately after or in fresh pursuit after the dispossession of the defendant's property when the defendant walked down to his van, retrieved a shotgun, returned upstairs, and then shot the complainant who had refused to return the defendant's revolver. *See Salley v. State*, No. 14-97-0656-CR, 2000 WL 552193 (Tex.App.—Houston [14th Dist.] 2000, pet. ref'd). In another case, a court held that a defendant who used force in an attempt to recover a wrecker approximately one hour after it was taken did not act immediately or in fresh pursuit. *See Hall v. State, No. 01-88-00511-CR,* 1989 WL 21835 (Tex.App.—Houston [1st Dist.] 1989, no pet.). Finally, a recent case in Houston cited the Black's Law Dictionary by stating that fresh pursuit is sometimes referred to as "hot pursuit." *See Ordonez v. State*, No. 14-10-00132-CR, 2010 WL 5395808 (Tex.App.—Houston [14th Dist.] 2010, no pet.)(citing Black's Law Dictionary, 667 (6th ed. 1990)). Ultimately, it appears that courts view "fresh pursuit" to mean "immediate without delay," as even taking a few minutes to arm oneself is sufficient to lose legal justification in using force to recover property.

In addition to attempting recovery immediately after or in fresh pursuit after dispossession of property, a person must have a *reasonable belief* that the other person wasn't entitled to take it in the first place. In other words, if an ordinary, reasonable person would take the item back believing the thief had no right to it, then a person may be justified in doing the same thing. Keep in mind, though, this section only justifies the use of force. If the thief used force, a threat, or fraud to take it from you, you might also be justified.

C. *No legal presumption of reasonableness when defending property*

Texas law provides no legal presumptions of reasonableness for uses of force to protect property, whether it is preventing or terminating a trespass or interference or the recovery of property. Thus, the jury will be the ultimate arbiter of the reasonableness of conduct.

The analysis so far leads us to the question: if force may legally be used to prevent or terminate trespass or interference with property, what constitutes a trespass or interference with property?

D. *What is trespassing?*

The commonly understood meaning of trespass is "an unlawful interference with one's person, property, or rights." This definition has been expanded to refer typically to "any unauthorized intrusion or invasion of private premises or land of another." *Black's Law Dictionary, 6th ed.* This commonly understood definition of trespass is different and more expansive than the offense of criminal trespass found in section 30.05 of the Texas Penal Code. The Penal Code defines a criminal trespass as whenever:

> a person ... enters or remains on or in property of another, including residential land, agricultural land, a recreational vehicle park, a building, or an aircraft or other vehicle, without effective consent and the person:
> (1) had notice that the entry was forbidden; or
> (2) received notice to depart but failed to do so.

In other words, unlike the common definition of trespass where a person becomes a trespasser whether they realized it or not (unwittingly walking across the King's hunting grounds, for instance), under the Texas Penal Code prior to committing a criminal offense a person must have knowledge that they are in a place they do not belong or are not welcome. In addition, the crime of criminal trespass is strictly limited to when a person is found <u>in or on</u> a piece of property without permission—the offense does not cover situations involving personal property.

E.   *Trespass, for legal justification, is not just "Criminal Trespass"*
How, then, is "trespasser" defined in section 9.41 for purposes of defending property? Because the plain language of section 9.41(a) refers only to terminating "the other's trespass" and does not reference a "criminal trespass," it is clear that the statute intends to follow a broader definition of trespass than just the offense of criminal trespass found in section 30.05. In other words, a person may be potentially legally justified in using force against a person found trespassing on their land—even if that person has not committed the crime of criminal trespass, but only so long as the use of force is accompanied with a reasonable belief that it is immediately necessary to terminate the trespass. However, in the event an unwitting trespasser has no intention of remaining on or damaging the property, at least one Texas court has held that the use of force is not immediately necessary. *See Hudson v. State*, 145 S.W.3d 323 (Tex.App.—Fort Worth 2004, pet. ref'd). However, without a specific definition of what "trespass" means as found in section 9.41, in the vast majority of cases, a jury will be the ultimate arbiter of whether or not a person had a reasonable belief that it was immediately necessary to terminate another person's trespass on the land.

F.   *What is unlawful interference with property?*
You have a legal right to prevent or terminate "interference with property," but what does this mean? It can be a theft, destruction, vandalism, or anything else that diminishes a person's right to their property. Whether particular conduct rises to "interference with property" is an issue that a jury decides.

G. *Is there a statutory minimum value of property before force may be legally used to protect it?*

No. There exists no statutory minimum value for property before force may be used to protect it. Sections 9.41 and 9.42 do not specify that property a person seeks to protect must be of a certain, minimum dollar value in order for a person to protect it. Having said that, what the Texas Penal Code does specify, is that a person must have a reasonable belief that the use of force or deadly force is immediately necessary to protect that property before a person would be justified in using force or deadly force.

Realistically, even though a person may be in the process of taking tangible, movable property (as specified in section 9.41), some property may be of so little value that the use of force or deadly force to protect or recover it would not be deemed reasonable by a reasonable person (people on a jury).

Example:

> One day at work, Fred walks into Ricky's office and takes a half-eaten bag of chips off of Ricky's desk and walks away. Ricky, upset at having his favorite chips pilfered from his desk, jumps up, chases Fred down, shoves him to the ground, and starts beating on Fred to recover his chips. On his way to chase Fred, Ricky also passes the office kitchen where identical bags of chips are available for community consumption.

Was Ricky's use of force against Fred legally justified? Maybe, but very likely maybe not. It may be a very hard sell to a jury that a person was beat up over a potato chip. However, some members of a jury may value a potato chip much differently. What if a thief is stealing irreplaceable family photos? There's no monetary value to be placed there—only personal sentiment. Again, the law is silent on the subject of any monetary value of property to be defended.

The point to be made here is that some items simply may not have enough value (financial, sentimental, or otherwise) to provide a person with a *reasonable* belief that the use of force or deadly force is necessary to protect or recover the item. In this example, not only do the chips have little monetary value, but there are others readily available for replacement from the kitchen. It would be hard to imagine a jury finding a person to be justified in even using force, let alone deadly force, for such a petty larceny! To that end, in a case of deadly force in 1893, the Court of Criminal Appeals held that the taking of a nickel (which is worth about $1.32 today), did not justify the owner of the nickel in killing the thief who was fleeing with the money. *Bowman v. State*, 21 S.W. 48 (Tex. Crim. App. 1893, no pet. h.). Remember, your conduct will always be evaluated under a reasonable person standard and that there are no legal presumptions available for defending property under sections 9.41 and 9.42.

Practical Legal Tip:

There are plenty of clever signs and bumper stickers out there advocating the use of a firearm. "Keep honking, I'm reloading," and even "Trespassers Will Be Shot" are seen often on the bumpers of Texas cars and the fence posts of Texas homeowners. But these signs, despite the chuckle they may elicit from a passerby, are not a good idea. Even  if meant only to prompt a laugh, if you are forced to use your forearm to defend yourself and end up in court, you can bet that the prosecutor will bring these signs up to the jury for consideration. Remember, a prosecutor will use every avenue to paint you in the worst light possible. Keep the laughs to yourself and take the signs down! -*Michele*

III. When is someone legally justified in using "deadly force" to protect or recover their own property?

When a person may legally use deadly force (force that is intended to cause serious bodily injury or death) to defend his or her property is addressed in section 9.42 of the Texas Penal Code.

Justified Use of Deadly Force to Protect Your Property: Tex. Penal Code § 9.42

A person is justified in using deadly force against another to protect land or tangible, movable property: (1) if he would be justified in using force against the other under Section 9.41; and (2) when and to the degree he reasonably believes the deadly force is immediately necessary:

1. To prevent the other's imminent commission of arson, burglary, robbery, aggravated robbery, theft during nighttime, or criminal mischief during the nighttime; or
2. To prevent the other who is fleeing immediately after committing burglary, robbery, aggravated robbery, or theft during the nighttime from escaping with the property; and

(3) He reasonably believes that:

1. The land or property cannot be protected or recovered by any other means; or
2. The use of force other than deadly force to protect or recover the land or property would expose the actor or another to a substantial risk of death or serious bodily injury.

A. *Three requirements for legal justification under section 9.42*

Legal justification for deadly force to protect property under section 9.42 is not accompanied with any legal presumptions of reasonableness; the jury will be the ultimate arbiter in deciding whether a person acted reasonably in a given incident. Because section 9.42 requires three separate elements of reasonable belief, this means a jury will have their work cut-out for them in determining whether a person is justified or not.

1. Step one: justified under section 9.41 to use force?
First, the jury will be responsible for determining whether the person (now a defendant) involved in the use of deadly force was justified in using mere force under section 9.41. Because justification under section 9.41 requires a reasonable belief in the immediate necessity of the use of force, the jury's first task is to establish whether the use of force would have even been justified. That is, was there an interference with property or a trespass in the first place? If not, a person will not be legally justified in using deadly force; the analysis stops and no legal justification exists under section 9.42.

2. Step two: prevent crimes or stop those fleeing with property
Second, the jury must decide whether a defendant had a reasonable belief that deadly force was immediately necessary to prevent the imminent commission of arson, burglary, robbery, aggravated robbery, theft during the nighttime, or criminal mischief during the nighttime, or if deadly force was used to prevent a person who was fleeing immediately after the commission of burglary, robbery, aggravated robbery, or theft during the nighttime from escaping with property. The jury must decide whether the person (now the defendant) had a reasonable belief that deadly force was immediately necessary to prevent the other from escaping with property.

Practical Legal Tip:

Notice the difference between sections 9.42(a) and (b) is that a person is not provided with a justification to use force or deadly force against a person who has completed arson or criminal mischief and shows no intent on committing another one! -*Kirk*

3. Step three: no other means of recovery available

The third step to legal justification under section 9.42 is that the person who used deadly force to protect property must have reasonably believed that the property could not have been protected or recovered by other means *or* using something less than deadly force would expose the person to a substantial risk of death or serious bodily injury to themselves. If the jury finds that a person acted reasonably under all three of these steps, only then will the person be legally justified in using deadly force. Again, there are no legal presumptions available for justified uses of force or deadly force to protect property.

Example:

> After a long day at work, Gordon finally pulls into his driveway just in time to see two masked men running out of his front door with his favorite television and his grandfather's expensive watch on one of the man's wrists. Gordon gets out of his car and demands that the men stop where they are, but they ignore him and run away. Gordon pulls his Glock 17 and fires at the fleeing men, killing one and injuring the other.

Was Gordon justified under section 9.42 to use deadly force? To answer this question, start the three-step analysis under section 9.42. First, is Gordon justified under section 9.41 to use force? Gordon has to show a jury that he had a reasonable belief that it was immediately necessary to use force to stop the interference with his property or a trespass. It seems pretty clear that with his TV and watch being stolen, there is both interference with property and a trespass. So if Gordon reasonably believes (as decided by a jury) that force is necessary to stop the threat, he may use force under section 9.41. Gordon likely passes step one.

Next, under section 9.42, the jury will decide if Gordon had a reasonable belief that his use of deadly force was immediately necessary to prevent "burglary," "theft during nighttime," or to prevent the person he shot from fleeing immediately after the person committed a burglary or theft during the nighttime from escaping with his TV and watch. This second requirement seems fairly straight-forward, and Gordon likely passes step two, as well.

Finally, a jury must find Gordon's belief reasonable that his TV and watch could not have been protected or recovered by other means, or that using less than deadly force would have endangered him under the language of section 9.42. In this case, the jury is again the ultimate arbiter and persons may reasonably disagree. Because there are no legal presumptions of reasonableness available to Gordon in protecting property, we do not know how the jury will decide this case, but the facts definitely seem to be in Gordon's favor.

IV. Can I protect another person's property?

> ### Justified Use of Deadly Force to Protect Another's Property: Tex. Penal Code § 9.43
>
> A person is justified in using force or deadly force against another to protect land or tangible, movable property of a third person if, under the circumstances as he reasonably believes them to be, the actor would be justified under Section 9.41 or 9.42 in using force or deadly force to protect his own land or property and:
> 1. The actor reasonably believes the unlawful interference constitutes attempted or consummated theft of or criminal mischief to the tangible, movable property; or
> 2. The actor reasonably believes that:
>   a. the third person has requested his protection of the land or property;
>   b. he has a legal duty to protect the third person's land or property; or
>   c. the third person whose land or property he uses force or deadly force to protect is the actor's spouse, parent, or child, resides with the actor, or is under the actor's care.

Section 9.43 of the Texas Penal Code establishes a two-prong test in determining if force or deadly force may be legally used to defend another person's property. First, before force or deadly force may be used to protect another's property, a person must have been justified under sections 9.41 or 9.42, respectively, as if the land or property were his or her own. The inverse is also true: you can't legally protect another person's property if you wouldn't be justified in protecting your own.

If a person satisfies the first prong of the test, they must also satisfy the second. The second prong of section 9.43 may be satisfied in one of the following ways: 1) the person using the force must reasonably believe that the interference with property they are preventing or stopping is a "theft" or criminal mischief to tangible, movable property; 2) the owner of the property has requested the property's protection; 3) the person seeking to protect the property has a legal duty to protect the property, *e.g.*, police or security officer, *etc.*; or 4) if the property belongs to a spouse, parent, child, or another person who is residing with the person seeking to protect the property. If a person satisfies one of these requirements, then both prongs of the test are met and the person may be justified.

Let's return to our earlier example with Gordon and see how things would play out if another person's property was involved.

Example:

> *After a long day at work, Gordon pulls into his own driveway one night and witnesses two men climbing out of his neighbor's window which appears to be broken and with what looks to be his neighbor's television. Gordon exits his vehicle gun drawn and demands the two men stop. When the men ignore his command, Gordon shoots and wounds both men.*

Is Gordon legally justified in using deadly force under this scenario? Very likely. We evaluate legal justification by determining first, would Gordon have been justified in using deadly force if the property he was protecting was his own. The answer seems clear that he would have been (*e.g.*, burglary or theft during the nighttime, *etc.*). The second requirement of section 9.43 must also be satisfied for there to be legal justification. In this scenario, even if Gordon's neighbor had not specially asked Gordon to protect his property (although such a request would have satisfied the second prong of the test), because Gordon's belief was likely reasonable that the persons he shot were attempting or consummating a theft to tangible, movable property, he likely will be legally justified.

V. How are the crimes associated with defending property defined under Texas law?

In the previous sections, we discussed circumstances where if certain crimes are being or have been committed, a person may have a legal justification in using force or deadly force to defend their property. How does Texas law define those crimes?

1. *Arson:* When a person starts a fire, regardless of whether the fire continues after ignition, or causes an explosion with the intent to destroy or damage any vegetation, fence, or structure on open-space land, or any building, habitation, or vehicle under certain circumstances. *See* Tex. Penal Code § 28.02.

2. *Burglary:* Anytime a person, without the consent of the owner, enters a habitation or building (or any portion of a building) not then open to the public, or remains concealed in a habitation or building with the intent to commit a felony, theft, or assault, or enters a habitation or building and actually commits or attempts to commit a felony, theft, or assault. *See* Tex. Penal Code § 30.02.

3. *Burglary of a Motor Vehicle:* When a person breaks into or enters a vehicle or any part of a vehicle without the effective

consent of the owner and with the intent to commit any felony or theft. *See* Tex. Penal Code § 30.04.

4. *Burglary of a Coin Operated Machine:* When a person breaks or enters into any coin-operated machine, coin collection machine, or other coin-operated or coin collection receptacle, contrivance, apparatus, or equipment used for the purpose of providing lawful amusement, sales of goods, services, or other valuable things, or telecommunications with the intent to obtain property or services without the effective consent of the owner. *See* Tex. Penal Code § 30.03.

A note about "burglary"
Texas Penal Code § 9.42 uses the word "burglary" in the most general sense of the word. The statute gives no qualifiers or limitations on what type of "burglary" a person would be justified in using deadly force to thwart. This is important because there are four types of burglary that are criminalized in Chapter 30 of the Texas Penal Code. It is generally accepted that deadly force is justified to prevent a burglary of a habitation and burglary of a building that is not a habitation, since these are both felonies, they are contained in a penal code section simply titled "Burglary," and they are crimes of a more personal nature where the perpetrator intends on committing other felonies or theft. However, there is an unresolved potential legal issue of whether the crimes of "burglary of a motor vehicle" as defined in Texas Penal Code § 30.03 or "burglary of a coin-operated machine" as defined in Texas Penal Code § 30.04 are included in the scope of the term "burglary" under Texas Penal Code § 9.42. There exist legal arguments both for the inclusion and exclusion of these two crimes, however, until a court of appeals addresses the issue, they remain mere arguments.

5. *Robbery:* When, in the process of committing theft, a person intentionally, knowingly, or recklessly causes bodily injury to another or intentionally or knowingly threatens or places another person in fear of imminent bodily injury or death while

intending to obtain or maintain control of the stolen property. *See* Tex. Penal Code § 29.02.

6. *Theft:* When a person unlawfully appropriates property with the intent to deprive the owner of the property. *See* Tex. Penal Code § 31.03.

7. *Criminal Mischief:* When a person, without the effective consent of the owner: intentionally or knowingly damages or destroys the tangible property of another, tampers with the tangible property of another and causes pecuniary loss or substantial inconvenience to the owner or a third person, or makes markings, including inscriptions, slogans, drawings, or paintings, on the tangible property of another. *See* Tex. Penal Code § 28.03.

8. *Nighttime:* The period of time beginning thirty minutes after sunset and ending thirty minutes before sunrise. *See* Tex. Transp. Code § 541.401.

VI. How can I assist law enforcement?
A. *Acting under a police officer's direction*
Almost without fail, as attorneys we are regularly asked about whether you can make a citizen's arrest, and how you can best assist law enforcement in dicey situations. Since every legal situation is unique, here we'll just provide a brief summary of the general law, as well as reference some of the statutes governing the use of citizen's arrests and how to assist authorities.

First, Texas Penal Code § 9.51(a) states that you may detain an individual who is committing a crime if you are authorized and directed by a police officer to do so, *and if you are in that officer's presence.* This would appear to eliminate the very idea of a "citizen's arrest" in the traditional sense and looks much more like a field-commission to deputy! In addition, be aware that this section of the Texas Penal Code only authorizes you to use force, you are not authorized to use deadly force. Finally, any person assisting law enforcement must identify themselves as a person acting at an officer's direction, unless such identification is either impossible or already known to the person being arrested.

Section 9.51(a) operates as the statute under which law enforcement is able to use force against a suspect. In order to enable officers to use all available resources at their disposal (such as an ordinary citizen), the statute is expanded to include individuals acting at an officer's direction.

B. *Not acting under a police officer's direction*
More in the area of authorizing a "citizen's arrest" is the language found in section 9.51(b), the text of which is found in the box below, and which removes the obstacle of being in an officer's presence.

> **Justified Use of Force Assisting Law Enforcement:**
> **Tex. Penal Code § 9.51(b)**
>
> A person other than a peace officer (or one acting at his direction) is justified in using force against another when and to the degree the actor reasonably believes the force is immediately necessary to make or assist in making a lawful arrest, or to prevent or assist in preventing escape after lawful arrest if, before using force, the actor manifests his purpose to and the reason for the arrest or reasonably believes his purpose and the reason are already known by or cannot reasonably be made known to the person to be arrested.

This statute allows an ordinary person to use force when making or assisting in making an arrest, since it does not require the person to be in a peace officer's presence! Once again, you must meet the same "reasonable belief" and "immediate necessity" standards we've outlined throughout this chapter before you may use force. Where possible, you also need to identify yourself and the reason you're making the arrest, unless you believe such is already known or can't be made known. Take notice, however, this statute does not authorize the use of deadly force.

In addition, the Texas Code of Criminal Procedure authorizes the warrantless citizen's arrest of an individual in the event the offense is "committed in his presence or within his view, if the offense is one classed as a felony or as an offense against the public peace." Tex. Code Crim. P. art. 14.01(a). This statute also closely follows the authorization granted by the Texas Court of Criminal Appeals in *Miles v. State* authorizing the warrantless arrest of a person committing a "misdemeanor within the citizen's presence or view or if the evidence shows that the person's conduct poses a threat of continuing violence or harm to himself or the public." *Miles v. State*, 241 S.W.3d 28, 42 (Tex. Crim. App. 2007).

C. *When can a person use deadly force in assisting law enforcement?*

In order to be legally justified in using deadly force to help law enforcement, a person must comply with the requirements of section 9.51(d):

Justified Use of Deadly Force Assisting Law Enforcement: Tex. Penal Code § 9.51(d)
A person other than a peace officer acting in a peace officer's presence and at his direction is justified in using deadly force against another when and to the degree the person reasonably believes the deadly force is immediately necessary to make or assist in making a lawful arrest, or to prevent escape after lawful arrest if, the use of force would have been justified under Subsection (b) and: 1. the actor reasonably believes the felony or offense against the public peace for which the arrest is authorized included the use or attempted use of deadly force; or 2. The actor reasonably believes there is a substantial risk that the person to be arrested will cause death or serious bodily injury to another if the arrest is delayed.

Like nearly every law authorizing the use of deadly force, this statute also only justifies using deadly force if you would first be justified in using mere force. However, deadly force may only legally be used to assist the police if a police officer is present and directing you to do so.

In other words, there is not a circumstance under section 9.51 where you, as an ordinary citizen, are legally justified in using deadly force to execute an "arrest" if no police officer is present and has so directed. That doesn't mean you won't have any justification under other sections of the law, such as self-defense, just not under section 9.51.

Practical Legal Tip:

If you use your firearm for defensive purposes, the first number you should call is 911. But keep your call brief: you only need to tell the operator that you have been the victim of a crime, where you are located, and some identifying information. After that, hang up! You are not required to remain on the line and doing so could cause you problems later. Remember, all 911 calls are recorded and operators are trained to gather as much information as possible. No matter how justified you are in your use of a firearm, something you say on a 911 call may become a real headache later at trial.
-Edwin

D. *Detaining potential thieves: "retailer's privilege"*

The Texas Civil Practice and Remedies Code grants a person authority to detain a person in order to investigate potential theft:

Authorization to Detain Potential Thief: Tex. Civil Practice and Remedies Code § 124.001
A person who reasonably believes that another has stolen or is attempting to steal property is privileged to detain that person in a reasonable manner and for a reasonable time to investigate ownership of the property.

The most common application of this particular statute is in the retail-store setting. Thus, it is often called "retailer's" or "shop-keeper's privilege" or right. Common scenarios include when a loss prevention official for the store will take a person into some type of custody while they investigate whether an item was stolen from their business.

VII. What crimes can I be charged with when my use of deadly force is not justified?

We've reached the end of our discussion on when you may be justified to use a weapon in defense of your person or property. Now it's time to give a brief summary of where you'll find yourself in legal trouble if you don't meet the elements of justification as we've described throughout this book. The following tables list some of the crimes involving the use of deadly force or a firearm and where relevant provisions may be found in Texas law:

Crimes Involving Deadly Force or a Firearm:
1. Murder: see Texas Penal Code § 19.02
2. Manslaughter: see Texas Penal Code § 19.04
3. Aggravated Assault: see Texas Penal Code § 22.01
a. Includes pointing a gun at another
b. Shooting at another without provable intent to kill
c. Firing warning shots
d. Road Rage

Crimes Against the Public Involving a Firearm:

1. Display of Firearms:
   a. It is <u>disorderly conduct</u> to display a firearm or other deadly weapon in a public place in a manner calculated to alarm. *See* Tex. Penal Code § 42.01(a)(8);
   b. It is <u>deadly conduct</u> to recklessly engage in conduct with a firearm that places another person in imminent danger of serious bodily injury. *See* Tex. Penal Code § 22.05(a);
   c. It is the <u>unlawful carrying of a handgun by a license holder</u> if a license holder carries a handgun and intentionally displays the handgun in plain view of another person in a public place. *See* Tex. Penal Code § 46.035(a);
   d. It is <u>aggravated assault</u> if a person uses or exhibits a deadly weapon while making a threat. *See* Tex. Penal Code § 22.02(a)(2).
2. Discharge of Firearms:
   a. It is <u>disorderly conduct</u> to intentionally or knowingly discharge a firearm in a public place (other than a public road or shooting range). *See* Tex. Penal Code § 42.01(a)(7);
   b. It is <u>disorderly conduct</u> to intentionally or knowingly discharge a firearm across a public road. *See* Tex. Penal Code § 42.09(a)(9);
   c. It is prohibited to <u>recklessly discharge a firearm in a city of more than 100,000 persons</u>. *See* Tex. Penal Code § 42.12(a);
   d. It is <u>deadly conduct</u> to knowingly discharge a firearm at or in the direction of one or more people, or if you discharge a firearm at or in the direction of a habitation, building, or vehicle and you do so with reckless disregard as to whether that habitation, building, or vehicle is occupied. *See* Tex. Penal Code § 22.05(b);
   e. It may also be a crime under a specific city ordinance (check your local statutes).

What Do I Do Immediately After I Use My Firearm?

1. Make sure that the threat is contained or neutralized;
2. Return your firearm to safekeeping;
3. Call 911 and tell them you (or another person) has been the victim of a crime. Give the operator your location and description. Avoid giving any unnecessary information, and avoid telling them you shot someone. It may be wise to suggest an ambulance is needed. Then hang up with 911.
4. Call the Texas Law Shield Emergency Hotline and follow the instructions your program attorney gives you;
5. Wait for police and do not touch any evidence;
6. If directed by your attorney, provide police only simple details of the crime against you;
7. Be careful of police questions and always be ready to invoke your right to silence and your right to counsel at any time.

CHAPTER EIGHT

LAW OF CONCEALED CARRY: PART I
THE LICENSE QUALIFICATIONS, REQUIREMENTS, APPEALS, AND REGULATIONS

In 1995, the Texas Legislature passed a law allowing for the issuance of Concealed Handgun Licenses (CHLs). In Texas, qualified individuals may obtain a CHL, which allows the carrying of a concealed handgun on their person for any lawful purpose. To obtain a CHL, a person must meet certain requirements and submit an application to the Texas Department of Public Safety. This chapter deals exclusively with the licensed carrying of a handgun in Texas. A CHL only allows for the lawful carry of handguns; the license does not cover long guns or any other type of weapon.

I. The evolution of the Texas concealed carry law

Despite its reputation as being a "gun-friendly state," various concealed carry laws were proposed but ultimately defeated in every Texas legislative session from 1983 to 1991. In 1993, the legislature passed a law calling for a statewide referendum on CHLs, but Governor Ann Richards vetoed the bill. It wasn't until 1995 that the Legislature finally passed a "shall-issue" concealed carry law which Governor George W. Bush signed into law. The law went into effect on September 1, 1995, and the Texas Department of Public Safety was able to train 2,000 instructors in time to meet the more than 200,000 initial applicants that followed. There are currently more than 700,000 Concealed Handgun License holders in the State of Texas.

Texas Government Code Chapter 411, Subchapter H, entitled "License to Carry a Concealed Handgun," contains the law on how concealed handgun licenses are administered in Texas. Throughout this chapter, we will discuss the requirements, the application process, as well as the rights given to CHL holders for carrying a handgun in the State of Texas. At the time of publishing, open carry of handguns in public is not permitted under Texas law unless the person holds the appropriate police or security credentials. A CHL does not allow a person to open carry a handgun in public.

II. Qualifications for and steps to get a CHL
A. *Persons who are legally qualified to obtain a CHL*
In this section, we will discuss the requirements to apply for a Texas CHL, as well as potential disqualifications. In addition to the requirements listed below, applicants must also complete state mandated education with a CHL instructor certified by the Texas Department of Public Safety and demonstrate proficiency with a handgun of .32 caliber or greater.

Section 411.172 of the Texas Government Code states that to be eligible for a CHL in Texas, a person must:

1. be a legal resident of the state for the six-months prior to an application for a CHL;
2. be at least 21 years of age, or age 18 if the person is an active or honorably discharged member of the armed forces;
3. not have been convicted of a felony;
4. not have been charged with a class A or B misdemeanor or convicted of one within the five years preceding an application;
5. not be charged with the crime of Disorderly Conduct as outlined in section 42.01 of the Texas Penal Code, or be convicted of Disorderly Conduct within the five years preceding an application;
6. not be a fugitive from justice for any felony, class A misdemeanor, class B misdemeanor, or any equivalent offense;
7. not be a chemically dependent person;
8. not be incapable of exercising sound judgment with respect to the proper use and storage of a handgun;
9. be fully qualified under federal and state law to purchase a handgun;

10. not have been finally determined by a court to be delinquent in making child support payments;

11. not have been finally determined by a court to be delinquent in the payment of state taxes;

12. not be currently restricted under a court protective order or subject to a restraining order affecting the spousal relationship, other than a restraining order solely affecting property interests;

13. not have been adjudicated as a juvenile delinquent for a felony-level offense within the 10 years preceding an application;

14. not make any material misrepresentation, and a person must not fail to disclose any material fact in the application.

Practical Legal Tip:

Texas Government Code § 411.173 allows non-residents, who are otherwise qualified, to obtain a Texas Concealed Handgun License. *-Kirk*

B. *What does it mean to be a "chemically dependent person" so as to be disqualified from receiving a CHL?*

A person is legally disqualified from receiving a CHL if that person is "chemically dependent." Texas Government Code § 411.172(c) states that a person is a chemically dependent person if he or she has been convicted at least twice within the ten year period prior to an application for a CHL of any Class B misdemeanor or greater offense involving alcohol **or** controlled substances, or if he or she is found by a court to be a chemically dependent person in any other proceeding. In addition, section 411.171 specifically defines chemically dependent person to include a "person who frequently or repeatedly becomes intoxicated by excessive indulgence in alcohol or uses controlled substances or dangerous drugs so as to acquire a fixed habit and an involuntary tendency to become intoxicated or use substances as often as the opportunity is presented." Individuals that possess any of the characteristics listed in this section will not legally qualify for a CHL under Texas law.

C. _What does it mean to be "incapable of exercising sound judgment" so as to be disqualified from receiving a CHL?_

Texas Government Code § 411.172(d) states the different ways in which a person may be deemed incapable of exercising sound judgment. First, it may mean that a person "has been diagnosed by a licensed physician as suffering from a psychiatric disorder or condition that causes or is likely to cause substantial impairment in judgment, mood, perception, impulse control, or intellectual ability." The statute goes on to state that if the condition is in remission but is reasonably likely to redevelop at a future time, or if the person "requires continuous medical care" to avoid redeveloping the condition, the person is incapable of exercising sound judgment and may be disqualified from obtaining a CHL.

Second, it may mean that a person "has been diagnosed by a licensed physician, determined by a review board or similar authority, or declared by a court to be incompetent to manage his or her own affairs."

Finally, it may mean that a person "has entered a plea of not guilty by reason of insanity" in any criminal proceeding. If any of these three scenarios applies to an applicant, then that person will be deemed incapable of exercising sound judgment and will not meet one of the basic requirements to qualify for a concealed handgun license in Texas. Tex. Gov't Code § 411.172(d).

Persons that are currently receiving psychiatric treatment may be disqualified from holding a Texas CHL while undergoing treatment. The State of Texas considers the following to constitute evidence that a person has a psychiatric disorder or condition described in Texas Government Code § 411.172(d)(1):

1. Involuntary psychiatric hospitalization;
2. Psychiatric hospitalization;
3. Inpatient or residential substance abuse treatment in the preceding five-year period;
4. Diagnosis in the preceding five year period by a licensed physician that the person is dependent on alcohol, a controlled substance, or a similar substance; or
5. Diagnosis at any time by a licensed physician that the person suffers or has suffered from a psychiatric disorder or condition consisting of or relating to:
   a. Schizophrenia or delusional disorder;
   b. Bipolar disorder;
   c. Chronic dementia, whether caused by illness, brain defect, or brain injury;
   d. Dissociative identity disorder;
   e. Intermittent explosive disorder; or
   f. Antisocial personality disorder.

Tex. Gov't Code § 411.172(e).

Although most individuals that fall into one of the above categories may be prohibited from holding a CHL, if an applicant can provide a certificate from a licensed physician practicing psychiatry stating that the person's disorder or condition is in remission and is not likely to develop at a future time, then the applicant may still qualify for a CHL because the applicant will not be judged to be incapable of exercising sound judgment.

D. *If you don't disclose, you can expect your application to be delayed or denied!*

The qualifying factor that probably delays the majority of applications revolves around when a person fails to make a full disclosure of material facts. To qualify for a Texas CHL, a person must not make any material misrepresentation or <u>fail to disclose any material fact</u> in his or her CHL application. *See* Tex. Gov't Code § 411.172(a)(14). Most often, this is due to a person failing to disclose a criminal conviction of one nature or another.

Many applicants forget about things that may have happened many years ago, but which require disclosure in the application. The best practice is: when in doubt, disclose! Otherwise, a person may face unwanted delays or even a denial of their application. *Note:* be very careful in the wording of your disclosures. We have seen many applicants encounter difficulties in not using precise descriptions of their legal history, medical condition, *etc.* Be careful with your words!

E.   *What if I received "deferred adjudication?" Can I get a CHL?*
If a person received "deferred adjudication" as a result of a criminal charge, that person may still be eligible for a CHL under specific conditions. Section 411.1711 of the Texas Government Code states that orders of deferred adjudication against a person for certain crimes—including felonies—will not prevent a person from possessing a CHL.

If a person has been charged with a crime which resulted in an order of deferred adjudication more than 10 years prior to his or her application for a CHL **and** the crime for which the person received deferred adjudication was for any crime except the following felony offenses, then the person may be eligible to apply for a CHL. Persons who received deferred adjudication for any of the following felony offenses are permanently barred from holding a CHL:

(A) Title 5 of the Texas Penal Code, which includes violent crimes against people;
(B) Chapter 29 of the Texas Penal Code: robbery;
(C) Section 25.07 or 25.072 of the Texas Penal Code, which involves violating a court-issued protective order; or
(D) Section 30.02(c)(2) or (d): burglary of a habitation.

What this means is that persons who have received deferred adjudication for criminal offenses not listed above may be eligible to apply for and possess a Texas CHL after 10 years from the date of their deferred adjudication order.

F. *What is "deferred adjudication?"*

Under Article 42.12, Section 5 of the Texas Code of Criminal Procedure, "when in the judge's opinion the best interest of society and the defendant will be served, the judge may, after receiving a plea of guilty or plea of *nolo contendere*, hearing the evidence, and finding that it substantiates the defendant's guilt, defer further proceedings without entering an adjudication of guilt, and place the defendant on community supervision." Deferred adjudication is, therefore, the legal act of either accepting culpability for a crime or refusing to contest the culpability of a crime, without being actually convicted of the crime. Deferred adjudication is effectively a form of probation: a defendant is released back into society under the condition that the defendant will stay out of legal trouble for a period of time imposed by a judge. At the conclusion of the probationary period, the judge will dismiss the charges against the defendant and the defendant will not be convicted.

G. *Suspension and revocation of a CHL*
    1. <u>What is the difference between suspension and revocation?</u>

To begin, it is important to know that there *is* a difference between a suspension and a revocation of a person's CHL. A suspension is only temporary, and a person's license may be reinstated without the necessity of submitting a new application for a CHL. This means that a person will not have to go through the rigors of the application process nor the classroom requirements again in order to regain their CHL. On the other hand, a revocation means that the Texas DPS has decided that a person's CHL shall be terminated and in order for the person to ultimately regain the CHL, they must reapply from step one by attending a CHL class and submitting the application with the applicable fees.

2. Under what circumstances can the Texas DPS revoke a CHL?

Texas Government Code § 411.186 governs CHL revocation and states that a person's CHL may be revoked for any of the following reasons:

a. If the person was not entitled to a CHL at the time it was issued. If a CHL is revoked because a person was not entitled to be issued a CHL, the person may apply as a new applicant two years after the date of revocation so long as the reason for revocation no longer applies when the new application is made. If the reason for revocation exists on the two year anniversary, the person may apply for a new CHL two years after the cause no longer exists.

b. Misrepresentations and failure to disclose. If the person made a material misrepresentation or failed to disclose a material fact on their original application or on their renewal application, DPS may revoke the CHL. If a CHL is revoked for this reason, the person may apply as a new applicant two years after the date of revocation so long as the reason for revocation no longer applies when the new application is made. If the reason for revocation does apply on the two year anniversary, the person may apply for a new CHL two years after the cause no longer exists.

c. No longer meets the requirements. If, after receiving their CHL, the person no longer meets one of the eligibility requirements for possessing a CHL the license many be revoked. This is unless the person has been charged with a class A or B misdemeanor, a crime of disorderly conduct, or a felony by information or indictment. In such cases, the CHL is only suspended pending the outcome of the charges. If a CHL is revoked for this reason, the person may apply as a new applicant two years after the date of revocation so long as the reason for revocation no longer applies when the new application is made. If the reason for revocation does apply on the two year anniversary, the person may apply for a new CHL two years after the cause no longer exists.

d. Convicted of "Unlawful Carrying of Handgun by a License Holder." If a person is convicted under Texas Penal Code § 46.035 for unlawfully carrying by a license holder and that person's CHL is revoked, the person may apply as a new applicant two years after the date of revocation so long as the reason for revocation no longer applies when the new application is made. If the reason for revocation does apply on the two year anniversary, the person may apply for a new CHL two years after the cause no longer exists.

e. Three strikes. If the Texas DPS determines that the person's license has already been suspended twice before, the license is revoked on the third occurrence of suspendable conduct. If a CHL is revoked for this reason, the person may apply as a new applicant two years after the date of revocation so long as the reason for revocation no longer applies when the new application is made. If the reason for revocation does apply on the two year anniversary, the person may apply for a new CHL two years after the cause no longer exists.

f. Failure to pay fee. If the person submits an application fee that is dishonored or reversed, DPS may revoke the CHL.

The requirement of Texas Government Code § 411.186(c) that a person whose CHL was revoked be free of the ineligibility for 2 years leads to the apparent result that a person whose CHL is revoked for class A or B misdemeanor or crime of disorderly conduct would have to wait for 2 additional years after the 5 year ineligibility period. A CHL holder whose license was revoked because they were placed on deferred adjudication for a felony that is exempt from permanent disqualification has to wait 2 additional years after the 10-year ineligibility period.

3. Under what circumstances can the Texas DPS suspend a CHL?

Texas Government Code § 411.187 governs suspensions of Texas CHLs and states that a person's CHL may be suspended for any of the following reasons:

a. Charged with a crime: if the person is charged with a class A or B misdemeanor, a crime of disorderly conduct, or a felony by information or indictment. In such cases, the CHL is suspended for as long as the charges are pending and depending on the outcome of the case, when the matter is resolved the person's CHL will either be reinstated in the event of dismissal or acquittal, or revoked upon the person's conviction.

b. Failure to update information: if the person fails to notify DPS of a change of name, address, or special status as a CHL instructor, a judge, a spouse of a judge, or a prosecutor. A suspension under these circumstances lasts for 30 days.

c. Family violence protective order: if the person commits an act of family violence and the CHL holder is the subject of an active protective order under the Texas Family Code. Those person's CHLs are suspended for as long as the protective order is active.

d. Emergency protective order: if the person was arrested for an offense of family violence or stalking, and the CHL holder is the subject of a magistrate's emergency protection order issued under the Code of Criminal Procedure. That person's CHL is suspended for as long as the order for emergency protection is active.

4. What happens if my CHL expires while it is suspended?

If you are unfortunate enough to have your Texas CHL expire during your period of suspension, you must apply for a Texas CHL as a new applicant once your suspension period ends.

5. Procedure for revocation or suspension of a CHL

Concealed Handgun Licenses are not automatically suspended or revoked even if one of the elements of revocation or suspension as discussed above apply—the revocation or suspension requires law enforcement action before it actually occurs. Texas law allows a law enforcement officer to seize the physical CHL card of a person who the officer suspects will be subject to revocation or suspension. Once dispossessed of their physical CHL card, a person effectively no longer possesses a CHL due to the requirement that you must be in possession of your CHL card while carrying a concealed handgun. However, regardless of whether the officer does seize the physical CHL card, the officer will complete an affidavit stating the reasons why revocation or suspension is recommended and forward the affidavit to DPS. DPS will then make a decision on whether to revoke or suspend the license. If DPS decides to proceed with the revocation or suspension, then DPS will send the CHL holder a letter stating the reason for revocation or suspension and require the CHL holder to surrender their license to DPS within ten days of receipt of the letter unless the person requests a hearing and the request is received by DPS within 30 days of receipt of the letter.

In addition, there are two scenarios where a person's CHL can be suspended before the DPS takes action. If a person is the subject of an emergency protection order pursuant to the Code of Criminal Procedure, a magistrate shall suspend the CHL of the person who is the subject of the order, pursuant to Texas Code of Criminal Procedure article 17.292(l). Once DPS becomes aware of the matter, DPS will also follow its procedures as outlined in Texas Government Code § 411.187 as stated above. Likewise, for individuals that are subject to a protective order issued under the Texas Family Code, the court that issues a protective order shall suspend the CHL of the person who was found to have committed family violence, pursuant to Texas Family Code § 85.022(d). DPS will then also follow its procedures for revocation or suspension as outlined in Texas Government Code § 411.187.

6. If my CHL is denied, revoked, or suspended, can I appeal?
Any CHL denial, revocation, or suspension may be appealed within 30 days of receiving official notice in the form of the notice letter discussed above from Texas DPS that the CHL has been denied, revoked, or suspended. A person must request a hearing in writing and the written request for a hearing must be received by DPS within 30 days of the date the letter was received by the CHL holder.

Written appeal requests should be sent to:

Texas Department of Public Safety
ATTN: RLS-Legal Staff MSC-0246
P.O. Box 4087
Austin, Texas 78773

If no hearing is requested, then the denial, revocation, or suspension will be final and unappealable after the 30th day from receipt of notice from DPS that the license was denied, revoked, or suspended, pursuant to Texas Government Code § 411.180(g).

III. The CHL application and process
A. *The CHL application*
A Texas CHL application packet containing all required information is necessary to obtain a license. The packet must be completed and submitted to the Texas Department of Public Safety. The packet can be downloaded and printed out by visiting the Texas DPS website. For individuals who elect to complete the application online, the CHL application can also be started by following the links on the Texas DPS website. Either method of submission is acceptable as applicants can begin the application process online, or they can print the application forms and mail it back to the DPS. The application requires personally identifying information including a valid driver license or identification card, current demographic, address, and contact information, residential and employment information for the last five years, a valid email address, as well as personal background information including

information regarding any psychiatric, drug, alcohol, or criminal history from the applicant as described in section 411.174 of the Texas Government Code.

The process of completing the application requires a person to answer every question on the application—whether completed online or by hand. In addition, after the application has been submitted electronically, or DPS is in receipt of a paper application, applicants are required to submit fingerprints to DPS as part of a background check. CHL applicants must submit fingerprints electronically, unless the applicant resides in a county having a population of less than 46,000 and the applicant does not reside within a 25-mile radius of a facility with the capability to process digital or electronic fingerprints. Instructions on how to properly submit fingerprints to the DPS and the applicable fees for doing so are available on the DPS website.

B. *CHL class and shooting test*

In order to obtain a Texas CHL, applicants must complete a state-mandated education course taught by a Texas DPS certified CHL instructor. These classes generally consist of a classroom portion of four to six hours of instruction, followed by a shooting test in which the applicant must demonstrate proficiency with their handgun. Applicants for a CHL must take the class and pass both a written and shooting test in order to be qualified for a CHL. Texas Gov't Code §§ 411.174(a)(7) and 411.188. Without successfully passing both of these sections, a person's application will be denied. If a person fails either exam, the test results are required by law to be submitted to the Texas Department of Public Safety, where they will be kept on record.

In order to obtain a passing score, applicants must complete the course with a minimum score of 70%. Once an applicant successfully completes both the written and shooting proficiency examinations, the CHL instructor may certify that he or she has established proficiency, and the applicant will be ready to submit his or her application to the DPS for approval and licensing.

CHAPTER NINE
LAW OF CONCEALED CARRY: PART II
WHAT, HOW, AND WHERE YOU CAN
LEGALLY CARRY WITH A CHL

I. Concealed handguns must be concealed!

First, it is obvious that a handgun must be concealed when carrying pursuant to a Concealed Handgun License.

A. *Intentional display of a handgun is a crime*

It is only a crime when a handgun becomes unconcealed if it is the "intentional display of a handgun" in public. Therefore, our discussion will focus on what is legal under this standard.

> **Intentional Displays of Handgun Prohibited**
> **Tex. Penal Code § 46.035(a)**
>
> A license holder commits an offense if the license holder carries a handgun on or about the license holder's person under the authority of Subchapter H, Chapter 411, Government Code, and intentionally displays the handgun in plain view of another person in a public place.

This is an area that rightfully concerns a lot of CHL holders and is a very misunderstood area of the law. The legislature passed a law that states that a CHL holder commits a crime if the CHL holder "intentionally displays the handgun in plain view of another in a public place." An unintentional, accidental, or inadvertent display is not a crime under Texas Penal Code § 46.035(a). Likewise, any intentional display must take place in a public place—if you are on your own property, you are not in a public place.

Must have "intentionally" displayed to be a crime
The statute's use of the word "intentional" refers to a person's culpable mental state. In other words, a person must have

"intended" to display the handgun. Intentionally is defined in Texas Penal Code § 6.03(a): "[a] person acts intentionally, or with intent, with respect to the nature of his conduct or to a result of his conduct when it is his conscious objective or desire to engage in the conduct or cause the result." "Intentionally" is the highest degree of culpable mental state in the Texas Penal Code, meaning that it will be more difficult for a prosecutor to prove that you were intentional in your conduct than it would be to prove the lower-degree mental states of "knowingly" (being aware of the nature of your conduct or that a certain result will happen as a result of your actions) or "recklessly" (being aware of but consciously disregarding a substantial and unjustifiable risk that the circumstances exist, or the result will occur). In fact, the Texas legislature actually took into consideration that a CHL holder's handgun might become accidentally revealed and chose to not criminalize this conduct.

Obvious examples of intentionally displaying your concealed handgun would be pulling your shirt up to reveal a portion or all of your handgun to another person, while consciously desiring that they would see it, or simply pulling your handgun out of its holster and waving it in the air in front of somebody in order to frighten them. If you consciously desire that another person see your handgun or a portion of it, and you cause the other person to see it, then you have intentionally displayed your handgun. It is not enough that you were aware that it was *possible* for your handgun to become exposed, and it later does. You must have the *conscious objective or desire* to display or expose your handgun in a public place.

B. _Unintentional displays of a handgun are not a crime_
What do you do if a gust of wind picks up your shirt and shows off your 1911 handgun? What about when your pants accidentally split revealing your Spiderman underwear and your Sig Sauer? How about the time your purse comes accidentally open, flashing your Glock? The good news is that none of these incidents are crimes under Texas law.

If a CHL holder's concealed handgun becomes unconcealed inadvertently, such as by "flashing" or "printing," the CHL holder is not breaking the law. Texas law provides that a person must intentionally display his or her handgun in a public place to another person in order to be guilty of any unlawful carrying of a weapon by a CHL holder under section 46.035(a) of the Texas Penal Code.

C. *What is "printing" and is it a crime?*
What is printing? First, printing is not a legal term and printing is not a crime. Further, the word printing does not appear in the Texas Penal Code. Printing is a common street term. It generally refers to when the outline or characteristics of a handgun become visible under the clothing of a person. Imagine a person in a skin-tight spandex outfit who is carrying a full-size Glock 9mm pistol under the outfit. The outline of the gun would be clearly visible, however, since the gun is concealed by a layer of spandex, the gun is still concealed. It may be boorish behavior, bad taste, or even unwise, but under the plain meaning of the statute, it is not a crime.

II. **Where can a CHL holder legally carry a concealed handgun?**
A person in possession of a CHL may legally carry their handgun concealed any place where it is not illegal for them to possess a concealed handgun under either state or federal law. The places prohibited under Texas law are located in section 46.035 of the Texas Penal Code. In addition, because a CHL is issued by the State of Texas and not the federal government, a CHL holder may not legally carry their concealed handgun on federal property unless specifically authorized by federal law.

A. *Prohibited places for CHL holders*
    1. Understanding the legal term "premises"
Before we get started on the analysis of the particular places prohibited by statute for CHL holders, it is useful to become familiar with the term "premises." In the Texas Penal Code, the carrying of a firearm is often prohibited on the "premises" of the place listed in the statute. What does the law define as a

premises? Texas Penal Code § 46.035(f)(3) defines "premises" as "a building or a portion of a building. The term does not include any public or private driveway, street, sidewalk or walkway, parking lot, parking garage, or other parking area." Throughout this section, wherever the term "premises" is used, this is the definition that will apply, unless otherwise noted.

2. Any place where 30.06 notice is given

   a. *Oral, written, or sign notice to exclude CHL holders*

If someone wants to exclude CHL holders from legally carrying on his or her property, he or she must give effective legal notice that CHL holders are prohibited from carrying pursuant to Texas Penal Code § 30.06. Chapter 30 of the Texas Penal Code deals with areas in which a person is guilty of criminal trespass. Relevant to the discussion of CHL holders is section 30.06, the crime of "Trespass by Holder of License to Carry Concealed Handgun."

Criminal Trespass by CHL Holder: Tex. Penal Code § 30.06

a. A license holder commits an offense if the license holder:
1. carries a handgun under the authority of Subchapter H, Chapter 411, Government Code, on property of another without effective consent; and
2. received notice that:
   (A) entry on the property by a license holder with a concealed handgun was forbidden; or
   (B) remaining on the property with a concealed handgun was forbidden and failed to depart.
b. For purposes of this section, a person receives notice if the owner of the property or someone with apparent authority to act for the owner provides notice to the person by oral or written communication.

Under this law, a property owner must give effective legal notice that the carrying of a concealed handgun on the owner's property without permission is prohibited. However, it is important to point out that effective notice may be given orally, in writing, or by sign. All three forms are effective legal notice that a CHL holder is trespassing if he or she carries on that property.

b. What words must be in a 30.06 notice?

The statute allows effective notice to be given not only orally, but by written communication. "Written communication" is: (1) a card or other document on which is written language identical to the following: "Pursuant to Section 30.06, Penal Code (trespass by holder of license to carry a concealed handgun), a person licensed under Subchapter H, Chapter 411, Government Code (concealed handgun law), may not enter this property with a concealed handgun"; or (2) a sign posted on the property that: includes the language described in the preceding sentence in both English and Spanish; appears in contrasting colors with block letters at least one inch in height; and is displayed in a conspicuous manner clearly visible to the public.

Under these specifications, a proper 30.06 sign will often look similar to the one pictured below:

HANDGUNS PROHIBITED

"PURSUANT TO SECTION 30.06, PENAL CODE (TRESPASS BY HOLDER OF A LICENSE TO CARRY A CONCEALED HANDGUN), A PERSON LICENSED UNDER SUBCHAPTER H, CHAPTER 411, GOVERNMENT CODE (CONCEALED HANDGUN LAW), MAY NOT ENTER THIS PROPERTY WITH A CONCEALED HANDGUN"

"CONFORME A LA SECCIÓN 30.06 DEL CÓDIGO PENAL (TRASPASAR PORTANDO ARMAS DE FUEGO) PERSONAS CON LICENCIA BAJO DEL SUB-CAPITULO H, CAPITULO 411, CODIGO DE GOBIERNO (LEY DE PORTAR ARMAS), NO DEBEN ENTRAR A ESTA PROPIEDAD PORTANDO UN ARMA DE FUEGO"

Remember, the 30.06 sign is simply one way to give legal notice that a person carrying a concealed handgun pursuant to a CHL is trespassing.

c. What if I did not see the 30.06 sign?

A very common question with regard to 30.06 signs for CHL holders is "what if I did not see the 30.06 sign—am I breaking the law if I have my concealed handgun?"   A CHL holder possessing a concealed handgun but who does not see a posted 30.06 sign at a place where they are caught carrying may still potentially be charged with the crime of criminal trespass. However, the CHL holder will also have the opportunity to present an argument establishing that he did not see the sign, and, therefore, did not receive effective legal notice that the possession of a concealed handgun was prohibited. The critical element of section 30.06 is that the sign provides "notice" to a CHL holder that the carrying of a concealed handgun is prohibited. A person who does not see the sign because it was not visible, because it was placed in a location where a person would not ordinarily see it, or for any other reason, will have an opportunity to convince a jury that he or she did not receive the notice required under the law. It is important to keep in mind, however, that the purpose of the law is to provide notice, and such notice can be received in three different ways as discussed earlier. Because an oral admonition is sufficient to provide notice (without any of the required language for written notice), it is possible that failing to see a posted sign may not be enough of an argument to prevail.

d. What if the 30.06 sign is defective or does not comply with the law?

Texas law requires under section 30.06 that a sign must be posted conspicuously and clearly visible to the public. Signs must also be presented with contrasting colors between the lettering and background, and the letters must be in block and at least one-inch high. What happens, however, when a CHL holder encounters a sign which he or she does not believe complies with these requirements?

As discussed in the preceding section, the purpose of section 30.06 is to provide notice. If a CHL holder encounters a non-conforming sign and the person chooses to disregard the sign's admonition against carrying a concealed handgun but later finds themselves charged with criminal trespass, then that person will have some strong legal arguments as to why the sign they saw failed to give them adequate statutory notice. Therefore, they are not guilty of criminal trespass. However, they only have a legal argument. This is an issue that has not been decided by the courts, yet.

The lack of case law on this subject makes scenarios where, for instance, a sign is posted using white letters on a clear, glass window difficult to judge beforehand. Is clear glass a sufficient contrasting background from the white letters as required by law? An argument could easily be made either way—which is exactly what will happen should such a case go to trial.

Beware, therefore! If you decide, as a CHL holder, to disregard a posted 30.06 sign because of a technical deficiency, you may be the first "test-case" to help establish the bright-lines of the law. Also, always remember that if a property owner ever gives you oral notice that CHL holders are not welcome to carry on their property, you have been given effective legal notice and must leave the property, otherwise you are criminally trespassing.

e. What happens if I violate 30.06?

Violation of section 30.06 is a class A misdemeanor. A conviction, or order of deferred adjudication for a class A misdemeanor means the suspension of a person's CHL for five years. In addition, a CHL holder convicted of criminal trespass may face up to one year in county jail and/or up to a $4,000 fine or the person may receive a maximum of two years' probation with a minimum of 80 hours of community service.

It is important to point out, however, that violation of 30.06 requires that a property owner who provided valid notice actually press charges to prosecute the crime. One question that is often asked is, "what if I am forced to use my handgun to stop a crime from happening in a place where a 30.06 sign was posted?" One can only speculate what would happen, but if a CHL holder saves the life of another person while violating 30.06, a business owner may be hard-pressed to go forward with charges against a hero.

> *f. Are there property owners who cannot lawfully post a 30.06 sign?*

Yes. According to Texas Penal Code § 30.06(e), buildings and other properties owned or leased by a governmental entity may not lawfully post a 30.06 sign, unless firearms possession on the property is otherwise prohibited by law. A concealed handgun license holder may legally carry their concealed handgun on property owned or leased by a governmental entity even if the government has attempted to post a 30.06 sign that is otherwise compliant with the law. A CHL holder should always be aware if the property is a place where a license holder is prohibited from carrying a handgun under Texas Penal Code § 46.03 (Places Weapons Prohibited) or section 46.035 (Unlawful Carrying of Handgun By License Holder). The Texas Legislature enacted subsection (e) to Texas Penal Code § 30.06 in response to many cities, counties, and other governmental entities that were using the 30.06 law to prohibit CHL holders from carrying on government property where the legislature passively allowed it by not specifically preventing it, such as public libraries, civic centers, and city halls. However, the Texas Legislature did not provide a penalty for a local government that posts an unauthorized 30.06 sign. This oversight has allowed anti-firearm local governments to confuse and intimidate lawful concealed handgun carriers by posting 30.06 signs even though it is prohibited by the statute.

3. Prohibited places

There are a number of places under Texas law where persons are prohibited from carrying a firearm or illegal knife or club, whether or not that person is a CHL holder. We discuss these places in detail in Chapter 10. We also discuss both state and federal "Gun Free School Zones" in Chapter 10 to explain the limits of carrying or possessing a firearm at or near a school. Specific to our discussion on CHL holders, however, under section 46.035, a CHL holder may not legally carry a concealed handgun in the following places:

a. Businesses that receive more than 51% of their income from the sales and service of alcoholic beverages

Concealed Handgun Prohibited in 51% Businesses: Tex. Penal Code § 46.035(b)(1)
A license holder commits an offense if the license holder intentionally, knowingly, or recklessly carries a handgun under the authority of Subchapter H, Chapter 411, Government Code, regardless of whether the handgun is concealed, on or about the license holder's person on the premises of a business that has a permit or license issued under Chapter 25, 28, 32, 69, or 74, Alcoholic Beverage Code, if the business derives 51 percent or more of its income from the sale or service of alcoholic beverages for on-premises consumption, as determined by the Texas Alcoholic Beverage Commission under Section 104.06, Alcoholic Beverage Code.

Texas Penal Code § 46.035(b)(1) makes it a crime for a CHL holder to carry their concealed handgun on the premises of an establishment that derives 51 percent or more of its income from the sale or service of alcoholic beverages for on-premises consumption. How does a person know if an establishment is a "51%" establishment? There is, by law, required to be a 51% sign posted in the establishment. The absence of a 51% sign, even for an establishment that derives the majority of its income from the sale and service of alcoholic beverages, is a defense for any CHL holder who may be charged with the crime of "unlawful carrying of a handgun by [a] license holder." Carefully note: just because an establishment has a bar and sells alcoholic beverages does not necessarily mean that the establishment derives the majority of its income from the sale of the same. A proper 51% sign will give effective notice to a license holder where they may not carry their concealed handgun.

A proper 51% sign will look like this:

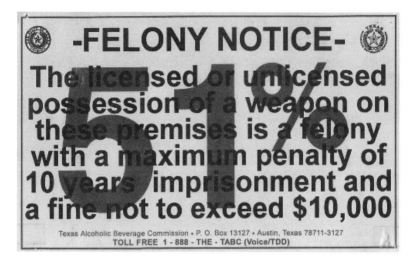

b. *High school, collegiate, and professional sporting games or interscholastic events*

> **Concealed Handgun Prohibited at High School, Collegiate, and Professional Sports Games or Interscholastic Events:**
> **Tex. Penal Code § 46.035(b)(2)**
>
> A license holder commits an offense if the license holder intentionally, knowingly, or recklessly carries a handgun under the authority of Subchapter H, Chapter 411, Government Code, regardless of whether the handgun is concealed, on or about the license holder's person on the premises where a high school, collegiate, or professional sporting event or interscholastic event is taking place, unless the license holder is a participant in the event and a handgun is used in the event.

The issue of sporting events causes much confusion. Texas law prohibits the concealed carry of a handgun on the premises of a high school, collegiate, and professional sporting or interscholastic event. This means, quite obviously, that a CHL holder cannot carry his or her concealed handgun at a high school football game, a college basketball game, a professional baseball game, or similar event. But what about some events that are not so obvious? Some of the confusion comes from the fact that the Penal Code does not define "professional" sporting event. Pro football, baseball, basketball, and so forth, are easy sports to identify. But what about all the flavors of rodeo in Texas?

Professional rodeos
Professional rodeos are events where the concealed carrying of a handgun by a CHL holder is prohibited. This means that a CHL holder is prohibited from carrying in the arena where the rodeo is taking place. Remember, because "premises" includes only the building or structure where the event is taking place, and not the parking lots, sidewalks, fairways, or other similar areas, a CHL holder would only be prohibited from carrying in the arena-proper, unless a proper 30.06 sign is prominently posted at the entrance to those areas. Be careful, however: at many rodeos, high school students from the local FFA or 4H club may have booths or exhibits setup in areas outside of the arena. At those locations, it would be unlawful for a CHL holder to carry a handgun since those areas are hosting "interscholastic" events, which are also prohibited by this statute. It can get legally murky.

Private golf tournaments, sporting events, or rodeos
What about the scenario where a person decides to "host" a rodeo, golf tournament, or other sporting event on his private property? Is such an event prohibited to CHL holders under the statute? It depends on the manner in which the event takes place. If the hosted rodeo, golf tournament, or other sporting event is one of an amateur nature (and not collegiate or interscholastic), rather than a professional nature, then the event likely falls outside the definition of section 46.035(b)(2). On the other hand, if participants are persons that regularly compete in professional competitions; if there is a significant prize or purse associated with the rodeo; if the event is sponsored completely or in-part by outside organizations and companies, then the event begins to look a lot more like a professional sporting event—even though it may not take place at a prominent public venue. It is worth

pointing out that there is no case law on this subject, and it falls squarely within some of the legal "gray area" we see all-too-often in firearms law.

As a general reminder, keep in mind that the statutory definition of the word "premises" makes carrying a weapon in parking lots, sidewalks, and similar areas permissible under the law. This would include events outside the actual venues themselves of high school, collegiate, and professional sporting events such as a tailgate party in the parking lot. As always, however, watch for properly posted 30.06 signs in areas where you wish to carry. If a 30.06 is properly posted, a CHL holder commits a criminal trespass if they continue to carry their concealed handgun past the entrance.

c. Correctional facilities

Concealed Handgun Prohibited in Correctional Facilities: Tex. Penal Code § 46.035(b)(3)
A license holder commits an offense if the license holder intentionally, knowingly, or recklessly carries a handgun under the authority of Subchapter H, Chapter 411, Government Code, regardless of whether the handgun is concealed, on or about the license holder's person on the premises of a correctional facility.

A CHL holder is not permitted to carry a concealed handgun into a correctional facility (the statute makes no distinction between public/private correctional facilities, state prisons, municipal jails, *etc.*) under Texas law. A CHL holder is not prohibited, however, from carrying the handgun in the parking lot or other area not considered the "premises" of the facility. *Note:* Texas Department of Criminal Justice facilities have specific rules about securing a gun in your car when you visit an inmate. *See* Texas Dep't of Criminal Justice, "Offender Rules and Regulations for Visitation" Reference Bulletin BP-03.85, February 2014.

> d. *Hospitals, nursing homes, amusement parks, and places of worship; but only if proper 30.06 notice is given*

A CHL holder may legally be on the premises of a hospital, nursing home, amusement park, or place of worship if 30.06 notice has not been given. Because of the manner in which the law is written, this area of the law causes confusion. It is because one part of the law states it is prohibited only to be trumped by a later section that says it's okay unless a 30.06 sign is present. Under sections 46.035(b)(4)-(6), a CHL holder is prohibited from carrying a concealed handgun into a hospital, nursing home, amusement park, or place of worship.

Concealed Handgun Prohibited in Hospitals, Nursing Homes, Amusement Parks, and Places of Worship Where 30.06 Notice Given: Tex. Penal Code §§ 46.035(b)(4)-(6)

A license holder commits an offense if the license holder intentionally, knowingly, or recklessly carries a handgun under the authority of Subchapter H, Chapter 411, Government Code, regardless of whether the handgun is concealed, on or about the license holder's person: on the premises of a hospital licensed under Chapter 241, Health and Safety Code, or on the premises of a nursing home licensed under Chapter 242, Health and Safety Code, unless the license holder has written authorization of the hospital or nursing home administration, as appropriate; in an amusement park; or on the premises of a church, synagogue, or other established place of religious worship.

However, in 1997, the Texas Legislature added section 46.035(i) to effectively take away the prohibition unless a 30.06 sign is present, or notice is given. They did this by enacting the following language in section 46.035(i):

> *Subsections (b)(4), (b)(5), (b)(6), and (c) do not apply if the actor was not given effective notice under Section 30.06.*

So, the current law is that a CHL holder **is** permitted to carry concealed into a hospital, nursing home, amusement park, or place of worship **unless** a proper 30.06 sign, or other 30.06 notice is provided to the CHL holder.

e. *Meetings of governmental entities where proper 30.06 notice is given*

Concealed Handgun Prohibited at Government Meetings
Where 30.06 Notice Given:
Tex. Penal Code § 46.035(c)

A license holder commits an offense if the license holder intentionally, knowingly, or recklessly carries a handgun under the authority of Subchapter H, Chapter 411, Government Code, regardless of whether the handgun is concealed, at any meeting of a governmental entity.

Just like the prohibition on carrying in hospitals and places of worship, a CHL holder was not permitted to carry in government meetings prior to 1997. However, the 1997 amendment contained in Texas Penal Code § 46.035(i) placed the responsibility for giving notice to prevent handguns on the governmental entity, by requiring the governmental entity to provide notice to CHL holders pursuant to section 30.06 that concealed handguns were not permitted in their meetings. This means that a CHL holder is permitted to carry at a city council meeting or other meetings of governmental entities so long as the city council has not given proper notice under section 30.06 that concealed handguns are prohibited.

f. When a license holder is intoxicated

Handgun Prohibited when Intoxicated Tex. Penal Code § 46.035(d)
A license holder commits an offense if, while intoxicated, the license holder carries a handgun under the authority of Subchapter H, Chapter 411, Government Code regardless of whether the handgun is concealed.

What is intoxication?

This section of the Penal Code states that a person <u>cannot be intoxicated</u> while in the possession of their concealed handgun. It does not say that a person cannot consume alcohol while carrying their gun, merely that the person cannot consume so much alcohol or other substance that they become intoxicated. However, this section of the law does not define what intoxication means, so we have to look elsewhere in the Penal Code for help. Intoxicated is defined in 3 different places in the Texas Penal Code:

(1) § 49.01: intoxicated means not having the normal use of one's mental or physical faculties or having a blood alcohol concentration of .08 grams or more.

(2) § 46.06: intoxicated means the substantial impairment of mental or physical capacity resulting from the introduction of any substance into the body.

(3) § 8.04: intoxicated means a disturbance of mental or physical capacity resulting from the introduction of any substance into the body.

As can be seen from these definitions, intoxication occurs when an individual consumes so much of a substance (commonly alcohol, but could be any substance—legal or otherwise—including prescription and over-the-counter medication) that it has an adverse effect on that person's mental or physical abilities. It is hard to imagine that one beer or glass of wine with dinner would cause someone to lose his or her mental or physical faculties completely. But it should be well-noted that people react to alcohol or medication differently.

Under Texas Government Code Chapter 411 (governing the issuance of CHLs), a CHL cannot be issued to a "chemically dependent person," which is one who repeatedly becomes "intoxicated" as defined by Texas Penal Code § 49.01. *See* Tex. Loc. Gov't Code § 411.172(a)(6). This is the only time in the law governing CHLs that a specific definition of intoxication has been used. Unfortunately, there exists almost no case law on this subject for interpretation in this context.

Practical Legal Tip:

Most people say that the reason they forgot to remove a firearm from their baggage at the airport is because they were in such a hurry to not miss their flight. But, if you do accidentally leave it in your carry-on bags, you can be assured that you will miss your flight! At a very minimum, if TSA finds a gun in your baggage, you will not only cause a scene and miss your flight, but you will also incur a fine from the TSA and possibly be subjected to prosecution by local law enforcement. *-Michele*

B. *Employer/employee parking lot rules*

In addition, under Texas Labor Code § 52.061, most license holders are allowed to conceal their handgun within their locked, privately-owned motor vehicle in an employee parking lot, garage, or other parking area provided by an employer. However, some employers are lawfully allowed to exclude all firearms. Texas Labor Code § 52.062 lists the employers allowed to exclude firearms legally in the parking lot, including:

1. "In a vehicle owned or leased by a public or private employer and used by an employee in the course and scope of the employee's employment, unless the employee is required to transport or store a firearm in the official discharge of the employee's duties;
2. a school district;
3. an open-enrollment charter school, as defined by Section 5.001, Education Code;
4. a private school, as defined by Section 22.081, Education Code;
5. on property owned or controlled by a person, other than the employer, that is subject to a valid, unexpired oil, gas, or other mineral lease that contains a provision prohibiting the possession of firearms on the property; or
6. on property owned or leased by a chemical manufacturer or oil and gas refiner with an air authorization under Chapter 382, Health and Safety Code, and on which the primary business conducted is the manufacture, use, storage, or transportation of hazardous, combustible, or explosive materials, except in regard to an employee who holds a license to carry a concealed handgun under Subchapter H, Chapter 411, Government Code, and who stores a firearm or ammunition the employee is authorized by law to possess in a locked, privately owned motor vehicle in a parking lot, parking garage, or other parking area the employer provides for employees that is outside of a secured and restricted area:
   a. that contains the physical plant;
   b. that is not open to the public; and
   c. the ingress into which is constantly monitored by security personnel."

The law on employer/employee handgun relations is very interesting not because of the rights provided and/or restricted, but because of the fact that there is no penalty for either party who violates this law. Thus, an employer who disciplines an employee for having a firearm in the employee's personal vehicle is not subject to any criminal responsibility or civil liability for doing so. In fact, an employee can be fired for violating company policy in the employee handbook and have no legal recourse against the employer, but the employee does not need to fear criminal prosecution.

C. *Automobiles, watercraft, and other places*
   1. **May a person carry a concealed handgun in an automobile?**

Yes. A CHL holder in Texas can legally carry a concealed handgun in their vehicle. Importantly, however, is the fact that a person does not need a CHL to possess a concealed handgun in their vehicle or a vehicle under their control. Section 46.02(a)(2) provides that a person is entitled to possess a handgun "inside or directly *en route* to" their motor vehicle. A CHL, however, allows you to carry legally in someone else's vehicle that is not under your control. For non-CHL holders, see Chapter 10.

   2. **May a person legally carry a concealed handgun in a commercial vehicle?**

Yes. One question that is often asked is whether a person who operates a commercial shipping vehicle (such as a semi-truck or similar) is entitled to the follow the same rules and regulations governing ordinary CHL holders in Texas. The answer to this question is simple: yes they are. This is because there are no specific Texas or federal regulations regarding carrying in a commercial shipping vehicle beyond those regulations which may be imposed by the operator's employer. This may be a breach of company policy, but not the law and is not a crime.

   3. **May a person carry a concealed handgun on a boat or watercraft?**

Yes. Just like an automobile, however, a person must keep the handgun concealed, and a person does not need to possess a CHL in order to possess the handgun in the watercraft. Under section 46.02(a)(2), a person is allowed to possess a handgun "inside and directly *en route* to" a watercraft that is owned by the person or under the person's control. Section 46.02(a-3) defines watercraft as "any boat, motorboat, vessel, or personal watercraft, other than a seaplane on water, used or capable of being used for transportation on water." For non-CHL holders, see Chapter 10.

4. May a person with a CHL carry a concealed handgun in a state or municipal park?

Yes. State or municipal parks are subject to state law governing public places. A local municipality is preempted by state law from prohibiting the carrying of a concealed handgun by a license holder and is, therefore, not authorized to prevent the legal carrying thereof. It is also permissible for a CHL holder to possess a concealed handgun in a state park.

5. Can a CHL holder carry in a restaurant?

Restaurants are establishments which are subject to the same restrictions discussed earlier in the section governing the use of 51% signs and 30.06 signs. If a restaurant derives more than 51% of its revenue from the sales and service of alcohol, then the carrying of a concealed handgun is prohibited. Likewise, if a restaurant has posted a 30.06 sign, the carrying of a concealed handgun by a license holder is prohibited. However, if neither of these signs is present, then a license holder is legally able to carry their concealed handgun in a restaurant. The bar area of a restaurant is not a separate location. So, if you can carry in the restaurant, you can carry in the bar.

6. Can a person have their gun in a hotel?

Hotels are permitted to follow the same guidelines for other businesses in that they can post a 30.06 sign effectively to prohibit the carrying of a concealed handgun. However, if a hotel has such a restriction—and if a hotel has any other restrictions or policies governing the possession, storage, and transportation of firearms, the hotel is required to provide such information on the hotel's internet reservation website. "If a hotel provides a written confirmation or a written statement of terms and conditions to a consumer after accepting the consumer's hotel reservation by telephone, the hotel shall include information specifying how the consumer may review applicable guest policies. The guest policies must indicate the hotel's policy regarding the possession, storage, and transportation of firearms by guests." Tex. Occ. Code § 2155.103. If a hotel owner or operator fails to follow these laws, the hotel is subject to a $100 civil fine, and a guest is free to cancel their reservations without penalty.

7. The Lower Colorado River Authority

Tucked away in an obscure section of the Parks and Wildlife Code is section 62.081 which states "no person may hunt with, possess, or shoot a firearm, bow, crossbow, slingshot, or any other weapon on or across the land of the Lower Colorado River Authority." This strange law was passed in 1975 and was left apparently unnoticed until 2013 when the legislature amended section 62.082 to exclude CHL holders from the application of this law. Thus, a CHL holder is allowed to possess a concealed handgun on the land of the Lower Colorado River Authority.

D. *Federal Property*

A CHL and its rights are a product of state law and convey no rights to the CHL holder that have been recognized under federal law. However, in certain instances, the federal government recognizes these state rights on certain federal property.

1. Federal buildings: firearms are prohibited

Firearms Prohibited in Federal Facilities: 18 U.S.C. § 930(a)
...whoever knowingly possesses or causes to be present a firearm or other dangerous weapon in a Federal facility (other than a Federal court facility), or attempts to do so, shall be fined under this title or imprisoned not more than 1 year, or both.

Under this statute, a "federal facility" refers to any building or part of a building that is owned or leased by the federal government and is a place where federal employees are regularly present for the purpose of performing their official duties. *See* 18 U.S.C. § 930(g)(1). However, this statute does not apply to "the lawful performance of official duties by an officer, agent, or employee of the United States, a State, or a political subdivision thereof, who is authorized by law to engage in or supervise the prevention, detection, investigation, or prosecution of any violation of law," nor does it apply to federal officials or members of the armed forces who are permitted to possess such a firearm by law, or the lawful carrying of a firearm incident to hunting or "other lawful purposes." 18 U.S.C. § 930(d). This statute does not govern the possession of a firearm in a federal court facility.

2. National parks

CHL holders are permitted to carry in Texas National Parks but not buildings within the park, such as ranger stations because these are federal buildings. Under federal law, for firearms purposes, all federal parks are subject to the state law of the state in which the park is located. *See* 16 U.S.C. § 1a-7b. In 1998, the executive director of the Texas Parks and Wildlife Department issued an executive order stating that the carrying of a concealed handgun in state parks by a CHL holder is governed by the laws concerning concealed handguns and that "nothing in the Public Hunting Lands Proclamation or State Parks Proclamation prohibits a person from possessing a concealed handgun." *See* Exec. Order No. 98-001 (July 8, 1998). A CHL holder may, therefore, carry a handgun concealed in a federal park, but not in federal buildings in the park.

3. VA Hospitals: firearms prohibited

Firearms Prohibited at Veterans Affairs Hospitals: 38 CFR § 1.218(a)(13)
No person while on property shall carry firearms, other dangerous or deadly weapons, or explosives, either openly or concealed, except for official purposes.

One place where many law-abiding CHL holders fall victim is at the VA Hospital. Unlike the Texas laws on hospitals which allow the carrying of a concealed handgun unless a proper 30.06 sign is posted (or notice given), the VA Hospital system is governed by federal law which prohibits the carrying of any firearm while on VA property. This includes the parking lot, sidewalk, and any other area which is the property of the VA.

Under federal law, 38 CFR § 1.218(a)(13) states that "no person while on property shall carry firearms, other dangerous or deadly weapons, or explosives, either openly or concealed, except for official purposes." The "official purposes" specified refer specifically to the VA Hospital Police. The area where this specific law gets good people in trouble is that the Department of Veterans Affairs has its own set of laws and guidelines and is not controlled strictly by the Gun Control Act and the general provisions regarding the prohibition of firearms on federal property. The VA law is much more restrictive, and many veterans have found themselves in trouble when they valet-park their vehicle and the valet discovers a concealed handgun in the console or concealed in the door storage area. How rigidly this law is enforced is determined by the individual hospital administrators as described in 38 CFR § 1.218(a), however, regardless of how strictly the law is enforced firearms are still prohibited under the law and the VA police are very aggressive in enforcing them.

4. United States Post Offices: firearms prohibited

Firearms Prohibited at Post Offices: 39 CFR § 232.1(l)
Notwithstanding the provisions of any other law, rule or regulation, no person while on postal property may carry firearms, other dangerous or deadly weapons, or explosives, either openly or concealed, or store the same on postal property, except for official purposes.

Under this regulation, firearms or other deadly weapons are prohibited on *postal property* which includes not only the building, but all property surrounding the building where a post office is located. This includes the parking lot (*e.g.*, a person's vehicle where a firearm may be stored), as well as the sidewalks and walkways. Earlier in this chapter, we mentioned that parking lots, sidewalks and walkways, and other related areas are generally not included when discussing the premises of a location where the carrying of a weapon is prohibited by law. Like the VA Hospital, United States Post Offices, are another exception to the rule. Recently, there was a decision by a United States District Court addressing this issue in Colorado. However, that case only has application within the states that fall under the jurisdiction of the 10th Circuit Court of Appeals, which does not include Texas, and therefore has no legal bearing on the prohibition to possess firearms on United States Post Office property in Texas.

5. Military bases and installations: firearms generally prohibited

Military bases and installations are treated much like the VA Hospital and US Post Offices in that they have, and are governed by, a separate set of rules and regulations with respect to firearms on the premises of an installation or base and are generally prohibited. Military installations are governed by the federal law under Title 32 of the Code of Federal Regulations. Moreover, the sections covering the laws governing and relating to military bases and installations are exceedingly numerous. There are, in fact, sections which are dedicated to only certain bases such as 32 CFR § 552.98 which only governs the possessing, carrying, concealing, and transporting of firearms on Fort Stewart/Hunter Army Airfield.

E. *Can municipalities restrict firearms rights?*

   1. Can cities or other governmental agencies enact firearms laws or regulations regarding the carrying of a concealed handgun by CHL holders that are more restrictive than state laws?

No, because municipalities are restricted by the Texas Legislature from passing ordinances further restricting the concealed carry of a handgun by a CHL holder. Tex. Loc. Gov't Code § 229.001(b)(6). Under this section, municipalities cannot regulate the carrying of a firearm by a CHL holder at a public park, public meeting of a municipality, county, or other governmental body, political rally, parade, or other political meeting, or non-firearms-related school, college, or professional events. With that in mind, under Texas Penal Code § 46.035(c), a CHL holder can be prohibited from entering the premises of a meeting of a governmental entity with their concealed handgun only if a proper 30.06 sign is posted. However, this ability to prohibit the carrying of a concealed handgun is a function of state law, and not by way of municipal ordinance. For a complete discussion, see Chapter 1.

   2. General preemption laws not specific to CHL holders

In addition, Texas Local Government Code § 229.001(a)(1) prohibits municipalities from enacting regulations relating to the "transfer, private ownership, keeping, transportation, licensing, or registration of firearms" for any person—not just CHL holders. The Texas Government Code does allow a municipality to regulate where a non-CHL holder may carry a weapon under section 229.001(b). However, these laws do not apply to CHL holders.

F. *How big of a handgun can a CHL holder legally carry?*

As we mentioned in Chapter 2, federal law dictates that any firearm which has any barrel with a bore of more than one-half inch in diameter (.50 caliber) is a "destructive device" and is subject to the National Firearms Act (except for certain shotguns). Possession of any such firearm without the proper paperwork associated with NFA firearms is illegal whether a person is a CHL holder or not. For more information on destructive devices and the NFA, see Chapter 14.

III. CHL holders dealing with law enforcement

A. *Do I legally have to present my CHL to a police officer if they ask for my identification and I am carrying my gun?*

Yes, but there is no legal penalty if you fail to present the CHL. Texas CHL law has always required that a person present their CHL along with their identification anytime they are carrying a concealed handgun, and they have been asked for identification by a law enforcement officer or a magistrate. While this is and always has been the law, however, today there is no penalty for a person who fails to present their CHL to law enforcement upon request for identification.

In 2009, the Texas Legislature removed the administrative and criminal penalties for persons who failed to present their CHL upon request for identification by a law enforcement officer. The current state of the law is very unusual, therefore, because a statutory obligation to display the license remains although there is no penalty for failure to do so. Keep in mind that many police officers still believe that failure to present is conduct that can get your CHL suspended and will treat you as such. Additionally, every CHL holder will be identified in the personal data search a police officer runs when they check a CHL holder's driver's license. Even if you do not present your CHL, the officer will know immediately that you have a CHL. If you have failed to identify yourself as a CHL holder who is carrying a concealed handgun, this may alarm the police officer and cause an already stressful situation to become more stressful. In short, you are not gaining anything by not telling the police officer that you are a CHL holder who is carrying a concealed handgun.

B. *Can a police officer legally take a CHL holder's handgun away?*

Yes, police are allowed to disarm CHL holders in the interest of officer safety. Texas Government Code § 411.206 states that a police officer can disarm a CHL holder and confiscate the CHL of a person he has arrested for a criminal offense. In addition, under section 411.207, a police officer may disarm a CHL holder during an encounter with the CHL holder if the officer reasonably believes it is necessary to disarm for the protection of the CHL holder, the police officer, or any other individual.

At the conclusion of the encounter with the officer, if the officer determines that the CHL holder is not a threat and has not committed any violation of the law that results in the person's arrest, then the police officer shall return the firearm to the CHL holder. Keep in mind, however, that the statutes do not dictate the manner in which the officer must return the firearm which means a person may receive their firearm back unloaded, disassembled, or placed in an area of the automobile where it was not originally found.

C. *What are passengers with a CHL in a vehicle legally obligated to do when the driver is stopped by law enforcement?*

If a person is a passenger in a vehicle and is a CHL holder carrying a concealed handgun on their person when law enforcement stops the driver, the passenger is only required to present their CHL if they are asked to identify themselves. Sometimes, police will ask passengers in the vehicle for identification to run a check for outstanding warrants. Passengers who are asked for identification are required to present their CHL (even though, as discussed earlier, there is no penalty for failure to do so) and may be disarmed by police in the interest of safety as described earlier.

Practical Legal Tip:

Having a Concealed Handgun License can make you feel safer as you are out and about. But remember, a CHL is a license to protect against trouble—not to go looking for it! -*Edwin*

IV. Reciprocity

A. *Can I carry a concealed handgun in other states if I have a Texas CHL?*

Yes, in the following states that recognize a Texas CHL:

Alabama	Alaska	Arizona	Arkansas	Colorado*
Delaware	Florida*	Georgia	Idaho	Indiana
Iowa	Kansas	Kentucky	Louisiana	Minnesota
Michigan*	Mississippi	Missouri	Montana	Nebraska
New Mexico	North Carolina	North Dakota	Ohio**	Oklahoma
Pennsylvania	South Carolina*	South Dakota	Tennessee	Utah
Vermont	Virginia	Wisconsin	West Virginia	Wyoming

Indicates only recognizes Texas CHLs for Texas residents
**Indicates only recognizes Texas CHLs while temporarily visiting*

Reciprocity either exists between Texas and these states or they have unilaterally decided to recognize Texas CHLs. Every state has the authority to determine whether or not their state will recognize a carry license or permit issued by another state. Reciprocity is where states enter into an agreement with each other, in this case, to recognize each other's carry licenses. However, states are not required to have reciprocity with one another nor are they required to recognize another state's carry license.

There are many states that issue their own licenses, but refuse to recognize a carry license from another state. Conversely, there are states that choose to recognize some or all other states' carry licenses. Texas gives the governor authority with the assistance of the attorney general, to negotiate reciprocity agreements with other states or to issue proclamations which will unilaterally recognize other states' carry licenses. Since each state is allowed to choose what other states' carry license will be recognized, there are several states that have carry licenses that Texas recognizes, but those states do not recognize Texas. There are also several states that recognize a Texas CHL, but Texas does not recognize their license. As of the date of writing, a Texas CHL is recognized by 34 other states.

B. *What out-of-state handgun licenses does Texas recognize?*
Texas recognizes handgun licenses issued by the following states:

Alabama	Alaska	Arizona	Arkansas	California
Colorado	Connecticut	Delaware	Florida	Georgia
Hawaii	Idaho	Indiana	Iowa	Kansas
Kentucky	Louisiana	Maryland	Massachusetts	Michigan
Mississippi	Missouri	Montana	Nebraska	Nevada
New Jersey	New Mexico	New York	North Carolina	North Dakota
Oklahoma	Pennsylvania	Rhode Island	South Carolina	South Dakota
Tennessee	Utah	Virginia	Washington	West Virginia
Wyoming				

An out-of-state concealed carry license holder must follow Texas law while in Texas just like a Texas CHL holder must follow the laws of the state he or she is located in when traveling. For example, a Florida Concealed Weapons or Firearms License will allow a person to carry a concealed handgun, knife, electric weapon, billy club, and tear-gas gun while in Florida. However, a person with a Florida license will only be allowed to carry a concealed handgun in Texas and not be legally allowed to carry other forms of weapons pursuant to Florida's license.

C. *What state's laws apply to me when using my Texas CHL in another state?*
Anytime a CHL holder is in another state, even if that state recognizes a Texas CHL, the law of the state where the person is currently located will be the law which governs that person's firearms possession and use. If a person is traveling to another state, they must abide by that state's laws. Just like a non-Texan visiting Texas must follow Texas law. Most common laws Texans should be aware of are the requirement to present a license and the places that are off-limits to CHL holders, as most of the time

they vary from state to state. For example, while a CHL holder having a handgun will get a holder quick entry into the Texas Capitol, it will get a person carrying a quick trip to jail in Louisiana and Oklahoma.

D. *Can persons who are not Texas residents obtain a Texas CHL?*
Yes. Texas Government Code § 411.173 authorizes the Texas DPS to issue Texas CHLs to persons who are legal residents of other states or new residents of the State of Texas. The Texas Legislature gave DPS the ability to set out a different procedure for these non-resident licenses. However, the DPS has chosen to use the same application procedure and eligibility requirements for non-resident CHL applicants as they do for Texas resident applicants.

CHAPTER TEN

POSSESSING, CARRYING, AND TRANSPORTING FIREARMS WITHOUT A CHL

This chapter deals with when and where a person may possess, carry, or transport a firearm if they are not a concealed handgun license holder or someone with a Texas-recognized concealed carry permit. One salient fact about Texas firearms law is that in several critical areas of where you can have a firearm, Texas law treats long guns differently from handguns. As a result, under Texas law, handguns must generally be concealed, and the public carrying of a handgun without a concealed handgun license is usually illegal. On the other hand, long guns do not need to be concealed, and no license or permit is required to openly carry a long gun in public.

The laws discussed in this chapter are found primarily in Texas Penal Code Chapter 46, entitled "Weapons." This chapter of the Penal Code governs where and when firearms can be possessed and carried in Texas, and it also contains various exceptions to any such rules. Because handguns and long guns are treated differently under Texas law, this chapter will examine each separately.

I. Where are firearms (long guns or handguns) prohibited under Texas law?

Under Texas law, there are certain places where all firearms including long guns and handguns, as well as other prohibited weapons, such as illegal knives, clubs, and the weapons listed in section 46.05(a) of the Texas Penal Code, are forbidden. Texas Penal Code § 46.03(a) lists six places where a person is prohibited from possessing firearms or prohibited weapons on their premises, regardless of whether a person has a CHL. Remember, "premises" is defined in Texas Penal Code § 46.035(f)(3) as "a building or a portion of a building. The term does not include any public or private driveway, street, sidewalk or walkway, parking lot, parking garage, or other parking area."

A. *Prohibited places for all weapons*

Under section 46.03(a) of the Texas Penal Code, "a person commits an offense if the person intentionally, knowingly, or recklessly possesses or goes with a firearm, illegal knife, club, or prohibited weapon listed in Section 46.05(a)" into any of the following places:

1. Schools and educational institutions

> ### Weapons Prohibited at Schools
> ### Tex. Penal Code § 46.03(a)(1)
>
> A person commits an offense if the person intentionally, knowingly, or recklessly possesses or goes with a firearm, illegal knife, club, or prohibited weapon listed in section 46.05(a) on the physical premises of a school or educational institution, any grounds or building on which an activity sponsored by a school or educational institution is being conducted, or a passenger transportation vehicle of a school or educational institution, whether the school or educational institution is public or private, unless pursuant to written regulations or written authorization of the institution.

It is prohibited for any person to possess or go with a firearm or any other weapon onto the premises of a school or educational institution. This prohibition applies to the physical premises of a school or educational institution, as well as any grounds or building where a school sponsored activity is taking place. This means that if the marching band is practicing in the parking lot of a school—a place where a firearm is otherwise permitted—then while the band is participating in its activity, firearms and other weapons are prohibited. It is important to note that the prohibition on firearms possession can be waived by the institution by giving written permission or creating written regulations. For more information on firearms in Gun-Free School Zones, see Section VII of this chapter.

2. Polling places

Weapons Prohibited at Polling Places Tex. Penal Code § 46.03(a)(2)
A person commits an offense if the person intentionally, knowingly, or recklessly possesses or goes with a firearm, illegal knife, club, or prohibited weapon listed in Section 46.05(a) on the premises of a polling place on the day of an election or while early voting is in progress.

The possession of firearms and other weapons is prohibited at any place where polling for an election is taking place including places where early voting is in progress. Many polling locations are often at places where firearms are not ordinarily prohibited, such as churches, governmental buildings, and libraries. However, while voting is taking place, those locations become off-limits for firearms and other weapons.

3. Courts and court offices

Weapons Prohibited at Court and Court Offices Tex. Penal Code § 46.03(a)(3)
A person commits an offense if the person intentionally, knowingly, or recklessly possesses or goes with a firearm, illegal knife, club, or prohibited weapon listed in Section 46.05(a) on the premises of any government court or offices utilized by the court, unless pursuant to written regulations or written authorization of the court.

Under Texas law, individuals are not permitted to possess firearms or other weapons in court rooms, or in any offices utilized by a court, including the judge's chambers and any court clerk or coordinator offices, unless given explicit written authorization to do so.

4.. Racetracks

Weapons Prohibited at Racetracks
Tex. Penal Code § 46.03(a)(4)

A person commits an offense if the person intentionally, knowingly, or recklessly possesses or goes with a firearm, illegal knife, club, or prohibited weapon listed in Section 46.05(a) on the premises of a racetrack.

Texas law forbids the possession of all firearms and other weapons on the premises of a racetrack. How does the law define racetrack? Article 178e § 1.03(25) of Vernon's Texas Civil Statutes defines racetrack as "a facility that is licensed under this Act for the conduct of pari-mutuel wagering on greyhound racing or horse racing."

5. Secured area of airports

Weapons Prohibited in Secured Area of Airport
Tex. Penal Code § 46.03(a)(5)

A person commits an offense if the person intentionally, knowingly, or recklessly possesses or goes with a firearm, illegal knife, club, or prohibited weapon listed in Section 46.05(a) in or into a secured area of an airport.

No weapons are permitted in the secured area of an airport under Texas law. The "secured area of an airport" refers to all areas in the airport after security and metal detectors. For more information on firearms and air travel, see Section VI of this chapter.

6. Places of execution

Weapons Prohibited at Places of Execution
Tex. Penal Code § 46.03(a)(6)

A person commits an offense if the person intentionally, knowingly, or recklessly possesses or goes with a firearm, illegal knife, club, or prohibited weapon listed in Section 46.05(a) within 1,000 feet of premises the location of which is designated by the Texas Department of Criminal Justice as a place of execution under Article 43.19, Code of Criminal Procedure, on a day that a sentence of death is set to be imposed on the designated premises and the person received notice that:

    (A) going within 1,000 feet of the premises with a weapon listed under this subsection was prohibited; or

    (B) possessing a weapon listed under this subsection within 1,000 feet of the premises was prohibited.

It is prohibited to take a weapon within 1,000 feet of the premises where an execution is scheduled to be carried out as long as the person possessing the weapon was provided with notice that possessing a weapon is prohibited. Note, however, that there is no specific statutory language required to be provided, merely notice that possessing a weapon within 1,000 feet of the premises is prohibited.

B. *Defenses and exceptions to prohibited places*

There are, of course, certain exceptions to possessing firearms and other weapons in the places listed above. Most of these defenses and exceptions are in line with a person acting within the scope of their employment.

1. Defense for possessing a firearm at schools, polling places, courts, and racetracks

There are two clauses in section 46.03 of the Penal Code that provide a defense to prosecution for persons who possess firearms in violation of the law on school, polling place, court or court office, and racetrack premises. First, under section 46.03(b), members of the Armed Forces or National Guard, guards employed by a penal institution, or court officers, all of whom must be acting in the discharge of their official duties, are provided with a defense to prosecution for possessing a firearm in violation of sections 46.03(a)(1) through (4). Second, licensed and commissioned security guards who are wearing an official uniform and are carrying a firearm in plain view traveling to or from the guard's place of assignment or in the actual discharge of duties are provided a defense to prosecution under section 46.03(h).

2. Defense for possessing a firearm or club in the secured areas of an airport

Members of the Armed Forces or National Guard, guards employed by a penal institution, commissioned security officers wearing an official uniform with their firearm in plain view, private security officers authorized under Texas law wearing an official uniform with their firearm in plain view or while wearing plain clothes with their firearm concealed, all of whom must be either traveling to or from a place of assignment or are in the actual discharge of their official duties, are provided a defense to prosecution for possessing a firearm or club under Texas Penal Code § 46.03(d).

Other persons who are traveling and check their firearms as baggage pursuant to all applicable rules and regulations are also provided a defense to prosecution under the provisions of Texas Penal Code § 46.03(e).

3. Exception for places of execution

Under Texas law, persons who possess a firearm or club while driving a vehicle on a public road within 1,000 feet of a place of execution, as well as persons who possess a firearm or club in their own residence or place of employment that happens to be within 1,000 feet of a place of execution are not subject to the statute prohibiting the possession of firearms and clubs within 1,000 feet of the premises of a place of execution as defined under Texas Penal Code § 46.03(i).

C. *Possessing a CHL is not a defense!*

Section 46.03(f) of the Texas Penal Code specifies that persons who violate the provisions of section 46.03 by possessing or carrying a firearm or other prohibited weapon in violation of the statute are not provided a defense to prosecution just because they are a CHL holder. This is why section 46.03 is so important to know: unless a person falls under one of the very limited exceptions discussed earlier—typically in an employment or travel capacity—the possession of a firearm or other prohibited weapon is strictly prohibited.

II. Law concerning handguns

A. *Where are handguns prohibited?*

The possession of handguns is prohibited unless a person is (1) on their own premises or premises under their control, (2) inside of or directly *en route* to a motor vehicle they own or control, (3) traveling, or (4) engaged in lawful sporting activities. Handguns are prohibited everywhere else (unless the person is in possession of a handgun pursuant to a license as discussed in Chapter 9, or an exception as discussed later in this chapter).

Possession and Carrying of Handguns Tex. Penal Code § 46.02(a)
A person commits an offense if the person intentionally, knowingly, or recklessly carries on or about his or her person a handgun, illegal knife, or club if the person is not: (1) on the person's own premises or premises under the person's control; or (2) inside of or directly en route to a motor vehicle or watercraft that is owned by the person or under the person's control.

We start the discussion of the law concerning handguns with section 46.02(a) of the Texas Penal Code. This statute prohibits the carrying of a handgun (and illegal knives or clubs—see Chapter 13 for more information on those weapons) if you are not on your own premises, premises under your control, or your motor vehicle. Individuals who do not possess a CHL (or similar license) are limited in their possession and carrying of a handgun to the places recognized by this statute: on their own premises or premises under their control; or inside of or directly *en route* to a motor vehicle or watercraft owned by the person or under their control.

B. *Places where possession of a handgun is legal*
   1. A person's premises or premises under their control
A person who may legally possess a handgun may possess a handgun on their premises or premises under their control. The handgun may be loaded or unloaded, concealed or unconcealed. How does the law define the term "premises" in this context? Texas Penal Code § 46.02(a-2) states: "For purposes of this section, 'premises' includes real property and a recreational vehicle that is being used as living quarters, regardless of whether that use is temporary or permanent. In this subsection, 'recreational vehicle' means a motor vehicle primarily designed as temporary living quarters or a vehicle that contains temporary living quarters and is designed to be towed by a motor vehicle. The term includes a travel trailer, camping trailer, truck camper, motor home, and horse trailer with living quarters." This definition means that "premises" is more than just a person's habitation; it also includes the land surrounding a habitation and extends to all property which is either owned by a person or is under a person's control. This is a much broader definition than when the term "premises" is used to describe where a CHL holder may or may not carry their concealed handgun. See Chapter 9 for more information on where a CHL can legally carry a concealed handgun.

   a. *What does "premises under the person's control"
      mean?*
In 1913, the Texas Court of Criminal Appeals held in *Gibbs v. State* that premises under a person's control means "to exercise restraint or deciding influence over; to dominate; regulate; to hold

from action; to curb; subject or overpower." *Gibbs v. State*, 70 Tex. Cr. R. 278, 279, 156 S.W. 687 (1913). The Court held in that case that the location of "premises" will mean real property or the building upon it *and* the property or building is owned by the person or the person's employer. If the property is not owned by the person or his employer, then the property should be subject to the control of the person or his employer in some capacity.

Issues involving "premises under a person's control" have been scarcely litigated in the history of Texas jurisprudence. Since the *Gibbs* case in 1913, there has been little commentary on what it means to have premises under a person's control. In 1973, the Texas Attorney General issued an opinion in an attempt to clarify further what this term really means: "While control need not be exclusive of others, it must be a real right to exercise some dominion over the premises. ... The person in question must actually have the right to exercise some control over the conduct of other persons upon the premises although his control need not be exclusive." Op. Tex. Att'y Gen. No. H-185 (1973). Of course, since 1913, and even since 1973, what can be considered a premises has evolved, and today the term also includes recreational vehicles.

In September of 2014, the Texas Court of Criminal Appeals held that this includes the common area of condominiums (not apartments) where a person has an undivided ownership interest in the common areas. *See Chiarini v. State*, 442 S.W.3d 318 (Tex. Crim. App. 2014).

b. When is an RV considered "premises"?
As the Penal Code definition states, an RV is "premises" whenever it is being used as a home (living quarters). Conversely, when an RV is being used as a vehicle, it is a vehicle, and it is not a premises, *i.e.*, when it is actively being driven or towed. This is also an important distinction in whether the handgun must be concealed or not.

c.   Open carrying of handguns on own premises

Texas law does not make it a crime to openly carry a handgun on your own premises; therefore, it is legal. However, as a practical legal matter, a person may not carry the firearm "in a manner calculated to alarm," if the particular area could be argued to be a public place. If a person carries in this manner, the person could be charged with the crime of disorderly conduct under Texas Penal Code § 42.01(a)(8).

2.   <u>Inside of or directly en route to motor vehicle or watercraft owned by the person or under the person's control</u>

What is the legal definition of a motor vehicle? A motor vehicle is defined in Texas Penal Code § 32.34(a)(2) and means "a device in, on, or by which a person or property is or may be transported or drawn on a highway, except a device used exclusively on stationary rails or tracks." This definition is very broad and includes (but is not limited to) vehicles that are not cars or trucks such as:

- Motorcycle;
- Golf carts;
- Motorized scooters;
- ATVs;
- Riding lawnmowers.

One question that is often asked is whether or not a personal mobility scooter (like a Rascal) or some other personal mobility device qualifies as a motor vehicle? Under Texas Transportation Code § 542.009(b), a personal mobility device is not a motor vehicle and is considered to be a pedestrian. This means that a person is not able to legally carry a handgun while traveling in public on such a device without a CHL.

The term "watercraft" is defined in Penal Code § 46.02(a-3) and means "any boat, motorboat, vessel, or personal watercraft, other than a seaplane on water, used or capable of being used for transportation on water." Where watercraft are concerned, the general understanding is that if you can float it, you can boat it. *See* Op. Tex. Att'y Gen. No. DM-169 (1992).

> *a. When is a vehicle under a person's control so as to allow them to possess a concealed handgun legally?*

A person does not have to be the owner of the vehicle or watercraft to carry a concealed handgun legally. For instance, a rental car is the property of the company that rents the car. However, a person who rents the car from a company and takes possession of the car is the person who has control over the vehicle. Where vehicles are concerned, the person "in control" of a vehicle is generally understood to be the driver, as that is the singular individual who has the ability to move the automobile. For that reason, a person may lawfully possess a handgun in a rental vehicle, the same way they can legally possess a handgun in their own vehicle. The same principles would apply to watercraft: whoever drives the boat is the person that has control of the boat. However, there are no appellate cases directly clarifying this issue.

Similar to our discussion on premises, there are no specific laws on the manner in which the gun must be kept (other than concealed) in the vehicle or watercraft such as in a console, under the seat, in the trunk, and so forth, nor is there any statutory law on how the handgun must be stored there—*e.g.*, loaded or unloaded, chambered or unchambered. Unlike the rule on premises, however, Texas Penal Code § 46.02(a-1)(1) requires that the handgun remain "out of plain view," which means it must be concealed.

Practical Legal Tip:

If you carry a handgun in your vehicle, don't allow yourself to be drawn into a road-rage incident, no matter how minor. Someone who calls 911 to report that you pointed a gun at them, even though it was really just your middle finger, may get you arrested and charged with a crime. So, if you carry a gun in the car, forget how to flip the bird! -*Michele*

b. May the handgun be loaded?

Yes. The law allows the handgun to be loaded and accessible—it must only be concealed.

c. What does it mean to be "en route" to a vehicle or watercraft?

Traveling *en route* means to travel directly to a vehicle or watercraft. The more a person strays from a direct route to their vehicle, the less likely it will look like they are in *en route*. There is, however, no case law drawing bright lines in determining this issue.

d. Can a person legally conceal a handgun with their body while in a vehicle?

Yes, because Texas law merely requires that the handgun be "out of plain view." This means that a person could literally conceal a handgun with their body by sitting on the firearm, though this may prove problematic if the person is required to exit the vehicle (such as during a traffic stop). Of course, in addition to the potential problem of a handgun becoming unconcealed when sitting on it, there's also the matter of safety; just because something is legal, does not mean that it's smart!

e. May I keep a handgun in my vehicle if there are children in the car?

Yes, having children in the car does not change the law on whether a person is able to possess a handgun in the vehicle legally. The law requires that the handgun remain concealed. The law does not require the gun to be either loaded or unloaded or separated from the driver (*e.g.*, in the trunk). However, it is a violation of the law if a person allows a child to gain access to a readily dischargeable firearm and with criminal negligence: (1) fails to secure the firearm, or (2) leaves the firearm in a place in which the person knew or should have known the child would gain access. See Chapters 2 and 3 for more information on children and firearms. This requirement that adults take measures so as to prevent children from gaining access to a readily dischargeable firearm is found in section 46.13 of the Penal Code.

f. Is it legal for a passenger in a vehicle or watercraft without a CHL to have a handgun?

The legal requirement is that a person who does not have a CHL may have a handgun in a vehicle or watercraft they own or a vehicle or watercraft under their control. If a passenger in a vehicle is not also the owner or in control of the vehicle, carrying and/or possession of a handgun would not be legal in the vehicle or watercraft under section 46.02 of the Texas Penal Code (although they may qualify under the exceptions for traveling and sporting purposes discussed in Section V later in this chapter). With this in mind, however, there are no appellate cases addressing this issue. The problem is that the term "under control" is not defined anywhere in the penal code. One could certainly envision scenarios where the passenger could be the owner of the vehicle or the person in control.

g. No criminal activity or criminal street gangs

> **Limitations on Handguns in Vehicles**
> **Tex. Penal Code § 46.02(a-1)(2)**
>
> A person commits an offense if the person intentionally, knowingly, or recklessly carries on or about his or her person a handgun in a motor vehicle or watercraft that is owned by the person or under the person's control at any time in which the person is:
> (A) engaged in criminal activity, other than a Class C misdemeanor that is a violation of a law or ordinance regulating traffic or boating;
> (B) prohibited by law from possessing a firearm; or
> (C) a member of a criminal street gang, as defined by Section 71.01.

Individuals who are engaged in criminal activity, other than a class C misdemeanor regulating traffic, who are prohibited from possessing a firearm by law, or are members of a criminal street gang (as defined by Texas Penal Code § 71.01) are not allowed to have a handgun in their vehicle or watercraft. Tex. Penal Code § 46.02(a-1)(2).

If a person is engaged in any crime other than minor traffic or boating offenses, the person will lose the right to possess a handgun in their vehicle or watercraft under Texas law. Similarly, the law does not allow individuals who are prohibited from possessing firearms to have a handgun in their vehicle (for more information on disqualifications from possessing firearms, see Chapter 3).

It should be noted, however, that not all traffic violations are class C misdemeanors. A person who is stopped by law enforcement for changing lanes erratically or running other drivers off the road, for instance, may be charged with reckless driving, which is a crime where jail time is a possible punishment. In that case, possession of a handgun in the vehicle would be illegal. How does the law define "criminal street gang?" Texas Penal Code § 71.01(d) states that a criminal street gang "means three or more persons having a common identifying sign or symbol or an identifiable leadership who continuously or regularly associate in the commission of criminal activities." Members of criminal street gangs are prohibited from possessing a handgun in their vehicle or watercraft even though they may not be otherwise committing a crime.

3. It is legal for an owner of a vehicle to possess a handgun when a passenger in the vehicle is a felon or is otherwise disqualified from possessing firearms?

Yes, so long as the felon (or person disqualified) never possesses the firearm. The law focuses on who has possession, defined as care, custody, or control.

Example:

> Mark arrives at the McDonald's in Huntsville to pick up his brother John who is being released from prison. Mark always keeps a handgun under the driver seat of his vehicle. When John gets in the car, he sits in the front-passenger seat.

Has Mark violated the law? No, Mark still has possession of the handgun. It is a crime to affirmatively *give* a handgun to a disqualified individual—like a felon—but it is not a crime to possess a handgun around such an individual.

The law here revolves around whether the prohibited person possesses the firearm, not whether a firearm is nearby. For instance, if we change the example to a person who hands a recently-released felon a handgun in the car and asks the felon to "put it under the seat," then the person has committed a crime. However, in the real world, the legal fight will be over who was actually in possession of the firearm. This issue may ultimately be for the jury to decide.

4. <u>Cannot "give" a handgun to someone who intends to break the law</u>

Giving a Handgun to Disqualified Individuals Tex. Penal Code § 46.06(a)(1)
A person commits an offense if the person: sells, rents, leases, loans, or gives a handgun to any person knowing that the person to whom the handgun is to be delivered intends to use it unlawfully or in the commission of an unlawful act.

This one is simple. If someone asks you for your gun in order to rob a bank or knock-off a liquor store, it is a crime for you to give them the gun.

5. <u>Handguns allowed if traveling or engaged in sporting activities</u>

Nonapplicability of Section 46.02 Tex. Penal Code § 46.15(b)(2) and (3)
Section 46.02 does not apply to a person who: (2) is traveling; (3) is engaging in lawful hunting, fishing, or other sporting activity on the immediate premises where the activity is conducted, or is en route between the premises and the actor's residence, motor vehicle, or watercraft, if the weapon is a type commonly used in the activity.

The criminal provisions for possession of a weapon under section 46.02 (including firearms) are not applicable if a person is: traveling or engaged in sporting activities.

a. *What is traveling?*

Unfortunately, there is no statutory definition of the term "traveling." In fact, much of the case law on matters addressing traveling is contradictory of what does and does not qualify as traveling. Of note, however, is one case that declares definitively what traveling is not: it is not traveling from a person's place of business to the person's home. *Bergman v. State*, 90 S.W.3d 855, 859 (Tex.App.—San Antonio, 2002). Who, then, determines whether a person was traveling or not? Ultimately, a jury will make the determination. In *Illingworth v. State*, the Fort Worth Court of Appeals held that "the question of whether one is a traveler is a fact question to be resolved by the trier of fact." *Illingworth v. State*, 156 S.W.3d 662 (Tex.App.—Ft. Worth, 2005).

b. *Hunting and sporting activities*

For persons engaged in hunting, fishing, or other lawful sporting activities, a CHL is not required. However, the handgun must be a type commonly used in whatever sporting activity the person engages.

III. Long guns
A. *May be carried openly in public*

Texas law does not require a person to have a permit to carry a long gun, nor does the law require that a long gun be concealed when in public. Texas Penal Code § 46.02 only addresses handguns. There is no statute that addresses the manner in which a long gun may be carried other than that it may not be displayed in a public place in a manner calculated to alarm.

B. *Manner in which long guns may not be displayed in public*

A person may legally display a long gun in public but not intentionally or knowingly in a "manner calculated to alarm."

> ### Disorderly Conduct
> ### Tex. Penal Code § 42.01(a)(8)
>
> A person commits an offense if he intentionally or knowingly displays a firearm or other deadly weapon in a public place in a manner calculated to alarm.

The intention of this statute is to prevent individuals from displaying firearms in a way which would cause some type of panic or scare to others. However, the statute also requires that the person who displays the firearm publicly, do so intentionally or knowingly in a manner calculated to alarm in order to be charged with a crime.

Example:

> *Tim is walking down the street from his home to a shooting range with his AR-15 in a sling pointed down to the ground on his back, coffee in one hand, and range tote bag in the other. Tim is stopped by a police officer.*

Has Tim engaged in disorderly conduct? No. Tim legally carried his rifle down the street in a safe, non-threatening manner. He certainly did not knowingly or intentionally cause alarm to anyone.

The law focuses on Tim's intent and the manner in which the firearm is displayed. However, if Tim (in our example) was engaging in threatening behavior, his conduct might rise to disorderly conduct. A word of caution: this is a subjective standard and is open to interpretation by third parties and law enforcement which could land a person in legal hot water.

C. *May I keep a long gun in my vehicle under Texas law?*
Yes, and the long gun does not have to be concealed or locked in a gun rack. However, openly displaying a long gun in one's vehicle may attract thieves—particularly when it is parked and unattended!

D. *May I possess a long gun while riding in another person's vehicle?*
Yes.

E. *May I have a long gun on a boat or other watercraft?*
Yes, the same rules which allow the possession and carrying of a long gun in a vehicle also apply to boats and other watercraft.

IV. **Possessing and carrying handguns in places other than a person's premises or vehicle without a CHL**
At the beginning of this chapter, we stated that individuals who do not possess a concealed handgun license are generally unable to possess and carry a handgun in places outside of their own premises or motor vehicle. In this section, we will answer some of the common questions about places that are not a person's own premises or their vehicle, and whether or not a person can possess and carry a handgun.

A. *May a person keep a firearm in their hotel room?*
Yes. A hotel room is considered premises, or premises under a person's control and the law allows for the transport to and carry of a firearm in such places under Penal Code § 46.02. However, a hotel, or any private business has the right and ability to prohibit the possession of firearms in or on their property by not just CHL

holders, but also by persons who do not possess a CHL. For individuals who do not possess a CHL, a business is required to provide notice via Texas Penal Code § 30.05 (for unlicensed persons as opposed to Texas Penal Code § 30.06 for licensed persons) that the possession of firearms is prohibited.

If a hotel provides a written confirmation or a written statement of terms and conditions to a consumer after accepting the consumer's hotel reservation by telephone, the hotel shall include information specifying how the consumer may receive applicable guest policies. The guest policies must indicate the hotel's policy regarding the possession, storage, and transportation of firearms by guests. Tex. Occ. Code § 2155.103. If a hotel owner or operator fails to follow these laws, the hotel is subject to a $100 civil fine, and a guest is free to cancel their reservations without penalty.

B. *Signs where alcohol is sold*

In places where alcohol is sold, individuals will often see a sign entitled "Felony Notice" which states that the unlicensed possession of a weapon is a felony under state law. This sign applies to individuals who do not possess a CHL.

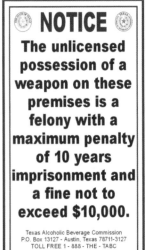

NOTICE

The unlicensed possession of a weapon on these premises is a felony with a maximum penalty of 10 years imprisonment and a fine not to exceed $10,000.

Texas Alcoholic Beverage Commission
P.O. Box 13127 - Austin, Texas 78711-3127
TOLL FREE 1 - 888 - THE - TABC

However, the language of this sign is somewhat misleading. First, because no license is required to possess or carry a long gun, although the sign refers to "weapons," it really only refers to handguns, illegal knives, and clubs. Second, the law the sign refers to is found in Penal Code § 46.02(c), which is a statute that only criminalizes the carrying of handguns and illegal knives and clubs. Thus, a person possessing a long gun may carry that long gun into a place that is licensed by the TABC to sell alcohol, such as a liquor store, without violating Texas law.

With this in mind, pursuant to the Texas Alcoholic Beverage Code and TABC regulations, a business or individual who is licensed by TABC to sell alcohol runs the risk of losing their liquor license if they allow individuals to possess firearms on the premises of the business. That is because the TABC regulation (which applies only to holders of a liquor license) governs all firearms—not just handguns.

V. Traveling across state lines with firearms

Many people vacation and travel outside of Texas. Naturally, no Texan wants to travel unarmed if they can help it, but, unfortunately, not every state shares the same views on gun ownership and gun rights as we do in the Lone Star State. This is especially true in the northeast corner and west coast of the United States. How then does a person pass through states that have restrictive firearms laws or those different from Texas? For example, how does a person legally pass through a state that prohibits the possession of a handgun without a license from that state? The answer: safe-passage legislation.

A. *Federal law: qualifying for firearms "Safe Passage"*

Traveling across state lines with a firearm means that a person may need to use the provisions of the federal law known as the "Safe Passage" provision. Federal law allows individuals who are legally in possession of firearms in their state (the starting point of traveling) to travel through states that are not as friendly. This protection is only available under federal law to transport such firearms across state lines for lawful purposes, as long as they comply with the requirements of the Firearm Owners Protection Act, 18 U.S.C. § 926A, nicknamed the "Safe Passage" provision. The first requirement to qualify for the Federal "Safe Passage" provision is that throughout the duration of the trip through the anti-firearm-state, the firearm must be unloaded and locked in the trunk, or locked in a container that is out of reach or not readily accessible from the passenger compartment. The ammunition also must be locked in the trunk or a container. Note that for the storage of both firearms and ammunition, the glove box and center console compartment are specifically not allowed under the statute.

B. *"Safe Passage" requires legal start to legal finish*
To get protection under federal law, a gun owner's journey must start and end in states where the traveler's possession of the firearm is legal; for instance, a person traveling with their Glock 17 starting in Texas and ending in Vermont. Even though a person must drive through New York or Massachusetts to get to Vermont, as long as the person qualifies under the "Safe Passage" provision then they may legally pass through. However, if the start point was Texas and the end point was New York (a place where the handgun would be illegal), there is no protection under the federal law. Safe-passage requires legal start and legal finish.

Although traveling across state lines naturally invokes federal law, it is important to remember that whenever a person finally completes their journey and reaches their destination state, the laws of that state control the possession, carrying, and use of the firearm. Federal law does not make it legal or provide any protection for possession of a firearm that is illegal under the laws of the destination state (i.e., the end state of your travels).

C. *What is the definition of "traveling" for "Safe Passage" provisions?*
The final requirement for protection under the federal law is that individuals MUST be "traveling" while in the firearm hostile state. The legal definition of "traveling" is both murky and narrow. The "Safe Passage" provision protection has been held in courts to be limited to situations that strictly relate to traveling and nothing more. Traveling is a term that is not defined in the federal statute; however, it has received treatment in the courts that is indicative of what one can expect. Generally speaking, if a person stops somewhere for too long they cease to be "traveling" and, therefore, lose their protection under the "Safe Passage" provision. How long this time limit is has not been determined either statutorily or by case law with any definitiveness.

While stopping for gas or restroom breaks may not disqualify a person from the "traveling" protection, any stop for an activity not directly related to traveling could be considered a destination and thus you would lose the legal protection. For example, in Chicago anyone in the city for more than 24 hours is not considered to be traveling under local policy. In an actual case, stopping for a brief nap in a bank parking lot in New Jersey caused a Texan driving back home from Maine to lose the "traveling" protection. He received 5 years in prison for possession of weapons that are illegal under New Jersey law. Of course, if the driver would have made it to Hershey, Pennsylvania, he would have been safe. The moral of the story is to travel through these gun-unfriendly as fast as you can (without breaking the speed limit, of course)!

D. *Protection under federal law does not mean protection from prosecution in unfriendly states*

To make matters even worse for firearms travelers, even if a person qualifies for protection under the federal "Safe Passage" provision, New Jersey and New York seem quite proud to treat this protection as an affirmative defense. This means that someone can be arrested even though he or she met all of the requirements of the federal statute. Then, they would have to go to court to assert this defense. In other words, while a person could beat the rap, they will not beat the ride! This becomes even more troublesome in the instance of someone who is legally flying with their firearm, and then due to flight complications, must land in New Jersey or New York, as travelers in this position have been arrested or threatened with arrest.

Once again, the "Safe Passage" provision only applies while a person is traveling; as soon as they arrive at their destination and cease their travels, the laws of that state control a person's actions. Remember: check all applicable state firearms laws before you leave for your destination!

VI. **Air travel with a firearm**

A. *How do I legally travel with a firearm as a passenger on a commercial airline?*

It is legal to travel with firearms on commercial airlines so long as the firearms transported are unloaded and in a locked, hard-sided container as checked baggage. Under federal law, the container must be completely inaccessible to passengers. Further, under U.S. Homeland Security rules, firearms, ammunition and firearm parts, including firearm frames, receivers, clips, and magazines, are prohibited in carry-on baggage. The Transportation Safety Administration (TSA) also requires that "realistic replicas of firearms are also prohibited in carry-on bags and must be packed in checked baggage. Rifle scopes are permitted in carry-on and checked bags."

1. Firearms must be inaccessible

Federal law makes it a crime subject to fine, imprisonment for up to 10 years, or both, if a person "when on, or attempting to get on, an aircraft in, or intended for operation in, air transportation or intrastate air transportation, has on or about the individual or the property of the individual a concealed dangerous weapon that is or would be accessible to the individual in flight." 49 U.S.C. § 46505(b). Additionally, under 49 U.S.C. § 46303(a) "[a]n individual who, when on, or attempting to board, an aircraft in, or intended for operation in, air transportation or intrastate air transportation, has on or about the individual or the property of the individual a concealed dangerous weapon that is or would be accessible to the individual in flight is liable to the United States Government for a civil penalty of not more than $10,000 for each violation."

2. Firearms must be checked in baggage

The following guidelines are put out by the TSA for traveling with firearms on airlines:

"To avoid issues that could impact your travel and/or result in law enforcement action, here are some guidelines to assist you in packing your firearms and ammunition:

- All firearms must be declared to the airline during the ticket counter check-in process.
- The term firearm includes: (Please see, for instance, United States Code, Title 18, Part 1, Chapter 44 for information about firearm definitions.)
  - Any weapon (including a starter gun) which will, or is designed to, or may readily be converted to expel a projectile by the action of an explosive.
  - The frame or receiver of any such weapon.
  - Any firearm muffler or firearm silencer.
  - Any destructive device.
- The firearm must be unloaded.
  - As defined by 49 CFR § 1540.5, 'A loaded firearm means a firearm that has a live round of ammunition, or any component thereof, in the chamber or cylinder or in a magazine inserted in the firearm.'
- The firearm must be in a hard-sided container that is locked. A locked container is defined as one that completely secures the firearm from being accessed. Locked cases that can be pulled open with little effort cannot be brought aboard the aircraft.
- If firearms are not properly declared or packaged, TSA will provide the checked bag to law enforcement for resolution with the airline. If the issue is resolved, law enforcement will release the bag to TSA so screening may be completed.
- TSA must resolve all alarms in checked baggage. If a locked container containing a firearm alarms, TSA will contact the airline, who will make a reasonable attempt to contact the owner and advise the passenger to go to the screening

location. If contact is not made, the container will not be placed on the aircraft.

- If a locked container alarms during screening and is not marked as containing a declared firearm, TSA will cut the lock in order to resolve the alarm.
- Travelers should remain in the area designated by the aircraft operator or TSA representative to take the key back after the container is cleared for transportation.
- Travelers must securely pack any ammunition in fiber (such as cardboard), wood or metal boxes or other packaging specifically designed to carry small amounts of ammunition.
- Firearm magazines and ammunition clips, whether loaded or empty, must be securely boxed or included within a hard-sided case containing an unloaded firearm.
- Small arms ammunition, including ammunition not exceeding .75 caliber for a rifle or pistol and shotgun shells of any gauge, may be carried in the same hard-sided case as the firearm, as long as it follows the packing guidelines described above.
- TSA prohibits black powder or percussion caps used with black-powder.
- Rifle scopes are not prohibited in carry-on bags and do not need to be in the hard-sided, locked checked bag."

See www.tsa.gov.

B. *May I have a firearm while operating or as a passenger in a private aircraft flying just in Texas?*

Generally, yes. For purposes of Texas state law, a private aircraft is treated like any other motorized vehicle. For more information concerning firearms in vehicles, see our earlier discussion in this chapter under Sections II and III.

C. *May I have a firearm in a private aircraft that takes off from Texas and lands in another state?*

In situations where a private aircraft is taking off from one state and landing in another, the law will simply view this as traveling interstate with firearms. Where no other statutes apply to the person's flight, the person will be subject to the provisions of 18

U.S.C. § 926A regarding the interstate transportation of a firearm: "any person who is not otherwise prohibited by this chapter from transporting, shipping, or receiving a firearm shall be entitled to transport a firearm for any lawful purpose from any place where he may lawfully possess and carry such firearm to any other place where he may lawfully possess and carry such firearm if, during such transportation the firearm is unloaded, and neither the firearm nor any ammunition being transported is readily accessible or is directly accessible from the passenger compartment of such transporting vehicle."

This statute allows a person to transport firearms between states subject to the following conditions: that the person can lawfully possess the firearm at his or her points of departure and arrival, and that the firearm remain unloaded and inaccessible during the trip. However, what if the person is a CHL holder and wants to carry concealed between states? Fortunately 18 U.S.C. § 927 states that section 926A does not pre-empt applicable state law. Thus, if a person can lawfully carry a concealed weapon in the state in which he or she boards the aircraft and in the state in which he or she lands, the CHL holder is not subject to the unloaded and inaccessible restrictions of section 926A.

For operations of private aircraft within one state, a person will only be subject to the laws of the state within which he or she is operating. The person will need to review their state's statutes to determine whether they impose any restrictions on possession of firearms within non-secure areas of airports. The person will also need to be familiar with the airports he or she will be visiting to determine whether each airport has any restrictions (*e.g.,* posting to prohibit concealed carry, *etc.*).

VII. Understanding gun-free school zone laws

The discussion of gun-free school zones is one that covers many different areas of the law and affects both persons who hold a CHL as well as persons who do not. That is because the "Gun Free School Zone" law and its meaning cause a lot of confusion. Signs warning about being in a "gun free school zone" are common around schools, but what does this mean to people lawfully in possession of firearms? There are actually both Texas and federal "gun free school zone" laws, each with very different meanings and consequences. For this reason, we will explain the applicable rules to individuals who possess and do not possess a CHL in this chapter, although the chapter has been dedicated to possessing or carrying a firearm without a license.

A. *Texas "Gun Free School Zone" law: enhancement statute*
The Texas "Gun Free School Zone" law is part of Texas Penal Code § 46.11. This statute does not create any new crimes or make any rights under other statutes inapplicable, but it is what is legally known as an *enhancement* statute. This means that if a person is already committing a weapons crime in violation of Chapter 46 of the Texas Penal Code, and if it is shown at the trial of the defendant that the crime occurred within 300 feet of a school or a school function, then the range of punishment for that crime is increased.

Since CHL holders as well as other lawful individuals are allowed to carry concealed handguns in their motor vehicles under Texas Penal Code Chapter 46, this law does not prohibit them from carrying a concealed weapon within 300 feet of the premises of a school. The law only applies to people who are committing, or who have committed, a weapons crime near a school.

B. *Federal "Gun Free School Zone" law: 18 U.S.C. § 922(q)*
The text of the federal "Gun Free School Zone" law is found in 18 U.S.C. § 922(q), and, in contrast to Texas law, creates its own independent criminal offense. This law states that it is a federal crime for a person to possess a firearm that has moved through interstate commerce (this includes virtually all firearms), on the grounds of or within 1,000 feet of a public, parochial, or private school. As surprising as it may seem, under this federal law, the mere possession of a firearm by the occupant of a motor vehicle while driving past a school or dropping off a child, is a federal crime.

However, federal law provides seven exceptions:

1. *Exception one*: if the possession is on private property which is not part of the school grounds. This means that a person living within 1,000 feet of a school can keep a firearm in their house.

2. *Exception two*: if the individual possessing the firearm is licensed to do so by the state in which the school zone is located or a political subdivision of the state, and the law of the state or political subdivision requires that, before an individual obtains such a license, the law enforcement authorities of the state or political subdivision verify that the individual is qualified under law to receive the license. This means that a CHL holder may legally carry a concealed firearm into a "gun free school zone." However, there is one important note about the statute: a person can only lawfully carry in a school zone located in the state that issued the firearms license. Therefore, if a person has a Texas CHL they can only carry through Texas school zones. If that Texas CHL holder is traveling through another state, the exception under federal law does not apply to them, and they are in violation of this law. It also means that a Texas resident, who holds a non-resident non-Texas concealed carry license or permit, does not benefit from this exception and is in violation of the law if they take a firearm into a school zone.

3. *Exception three*: if the firearm is not loaded, and is in a locked container, or a locked firearms rack that is on a motor vehicle. This means that if a firearm is unloaded and carried in a locked case, or other type of locked container, such as a glove box or trunk, there is no violation of the federal law.

4. *Exception four*: if the firearm is carried by an individual for use in a program approved by a school in the school zone. This exception covers school-sponsored shooting activities, such as an ROTC program.

5. *Exception five*: if the firearm is carried by an individual in accordance with a contract entered into between a school

in the school zone and the individual or an employer of the individual. This means that school security guards can carry firearms while on the job.

6. *Exception six*: if the firearm is carried by a law enforcement officer acting in his or her official capacity. This exception covers police officers while on-duty only. It does not appear to cover them while they are off-duty, even if they are required by state law to carry while off-duty.

7. *Exception seven*: if the firearm is unloaded and is in the possession of an individual while traversing school property for the purpose of gaining access to public or private lands open to hunting, if the entry on school premises is authorized by school authorities. This means that if a hunter must cross school property to get to a lawful hunting ground, they must have the permission of the school, and the firearm must be unloaded.

C. *Reconciling Texas and federal laws on gun-free school zones*

The law puts a vast number of unknowing and unsuspecting people in conflict with federal law while being in full compliance with state law. As a result, it is likely that this law is violated thousands of times a day. However, while this has been federal law since 1996 and its predecessor was the law since 1990, there does not appear to be a wave of federal prosecutions for the mere possession of a firearm by a person who is only driving through a school zone or picking up or dropping off their child. Nevertheless, even though it appears that the Feds are not inclined to enforce some of the provisions of this statute today, the law is on the books right now.

D. *"School Marshals:" teachers with guns*

Generally, while a teacher or administrator is not permitted to possess a handgun inside a school building, schools can allow it through a written regulation or with written authorization. In 2013, Texas enacted a law creating a new type of licensee in the form of a school marshal. Texas Code of Criminal Procedure article 2.127. In order for a teacher or administrator to become a school marshal, the person must:

(1) Obtain permission from the superintendent or board of trustees;
(2) Complete an 80 hour training course conducted by a law enforcement academy administering the school marshal curriculum;
(3) Complete a psychological examination; and
(4) Possess a valid concealed handgun license.

The Commission on Law Enforcement Officer Standards and Education states that a school marshal's "sole purpose is to prevent the act of murder or serious bodily injury on the school premises" and that school marshals are "not peace officers." For more information, see the TCLEOSE website.

E. *Is a person legally permitted to possess a firearm in their vehicle in the parking lot of a college or university?*

Yes, all individuals may possess a firearm in a vehicle the person owns or is under their control in a college or university parking lot as the parking lot does not constitute the "premises" of the institution. Some colleges and universities passed their own rules and regulations to prevent employees, visitors, and students from having firearms in their cars. A recent law, Texas Government Code § 411.2032, now prevents an institution of higher learning from creating a disciplinary policy preventing CHL holders from storing firearms and ammunition in their locked motor vehicles on campus parking lots.

CHAPTER ELEVEN
RESTORATION OF FIREARMS RIGHTS:
THE LAW OF PARDONS AND EXPUNGEMENTS

I. Is it possible to restore a person's right to bear arms?

What happens after a person has been convicted of a crime, is it possible to later clear their name and/or criminal record? If possible, then what is the process for removing a conviction and restoring a person's right to purchase and possess firearms? This chapter will explain how a person under very limited circumstances can have arrest records, criminal charges, and even criminal convictions removed or nullified. But words of caution, success in this arena may be rare. Further, each state has different rules concerning these issues as well as a completely different set of rules under federal law. Before we begin a meaningful discussion, it is important to explain two terms and concepts: clemency and expungement.

A. *What is clemency?*

Clemency is the action the government, usually the chief executive (*e.g.,* the President on the federal level or a governor on the state level), takes in forgiving or pardoning a crime or canceling the penalty of a crime, either wholly, or in part. Clemency can include full pardons after a conviction, full pardons after completion of deferred adjudication community supervision, conditional pardons, pardons based on innocence, commutations of a sentence, emergency medical reprieves, and family medical reprieves. Clemency can be granted at both the federal and state level.

B. *What is expungement?*

Expungement is the physical act of destroying or purging government criminal records, unlike sealing which is simply hiding the records from the public. Under certain circumstances, a person may have their criminal record either expunged or sealed.

Practical Legal Tip:

While our intention is to provide you with as much information as possible as to how you can have your firearms rights restored if you are convicted of a crime, it's also important to make sure you are aware of how rarely pardons, expungements, and restorations of firearms rights are granted. While it's certainly worth the effort to apply for a pardon in the event you receive one, be careful not to get your hopes, because they are seldom granted. -*Edwin*

II. Federal law

A. *Presidential pardon*

Under Article II, Section 2 of the United States Constitution, the President of the United States has the power "to grant reprieves and pardons for offenses against the United States, except in cases of impeachment." The President's power to pardon offenses has also been interpreted to include the power to grant conditional pardons, commutations of sentence, conditional commutations of sentence, remission of fines and forfeitures, respites, and amnesties. However, the President's clemency authority only extends to federal offenses; the President cannot grant clemency for a state crime.

1. How does a person petition for federal clemency or a pardon?

Under federal law, a person requesting executive clemency must petition the President of the United States and submit the petition to the Office of the Pardon Attorney in the Department of Justice. The Office of the Pardon Attorney can provide petitions and other required forms necessary to complete the application for clemency. *See* 28 CFR § 1.1. Petition forms for commutation of sentence may also be obtained from the wardens of federal penal institutions. In addition, a petitioner applying for executive clemency with respect to military offenses should submit his or her petition directly to the Secretary of the military branch that had original jurisdiction over the court-martial trial and conviction of the petitioner.

The Code of Federal Regulations requires an applicant to wait five years after the date of the release of the petitioner from confinement, or in a case where no prison sentence was imposed, an applicant is required to wait five years after the date of conviction prior to submitting a petition for clemency. The regulation further states that "generally, no petition should be submitted by a person who is on probation, parole, or supervised release." 28 CFR § 1.2. With that in mind, the President can grant clemency at any time, whether an individual has made a formal petition or not. For example, President Gerald Ford granted a full and unconditional pardon to former President Richard Nixon prior to any indictment or charges being filed related to his involvement in Watergate.

2. What should a petition for clemency include?

Petitions for executive clemency should include the information required in the form prescribed by the United States Attorney General. This includes information:

1. that the person requesting clemency must state specifically the purpose for which clemency is sought, as well as attach any and all relevant documentary evidence that will support how clemency will support that purpose;
2. that discloses any arrests or convictions subsequent to the federal crime for which clemency is sought;
3. that discloses all delinquent credit obligations (whether disputed or not), all civil lawsuits to which the applicant is a party (whether plaintiff or defendant), and all unpaid tax obligations (whether local, state, or federal);
4. that includes three character affidavits from persons not related to the applicant by blood or marriage.

In addition, acceptance of a Presidential pardon generally carries with it an admission of guilt. For that reason, a petitioner should include in his or her petition a statement of the petitioner's acceptance of responsibility, an expression of remorse, and atonement for the offense. All of the requirements are contained in 28 CFR §§ 1.1-1.11.

3. What happens after a petition for executive clemency is submitted?

All petitions for federal clemency are reviewed by the Office of the Pardon Attorney in the Department of Justice. A non-binding recommendation on an application is made to the President. Federal regulations also provide for guidelines and requirements to notify victims of the crimes, if any, for which clemency is sought. The President will either grant or deny a pardon. There are no hearings held on the petition, and there is no appeal of the President's decision.

4. What is the effect of a Presidential pardon?

A pardon is the forgiveness of a crime and the cancelation of the penalty associated with that crime. While a Presidential pardon will restore various rights lost as a result of the pardoned offense, it will not expunge the record of your conviction. This means that even if a person is granted a pardon, the person must still disclose their conviction on any form where such information is required, although the person may also disclose the fact that the offense for which they were convicted was pardoned.

B. *Expungement of federal convictions*

1. No law exists for general federal expungement

Congress has not provided federal legislation that offers any comprehensive authority or procedure for expunging criminal offenses. There exist only statues that allow expungement in certain cases for possession of small amounts of controlled substances (see below) and interestingly, a procedure to expunge DNA samples of certain members of the military wrongfully convicted. Because there is no statutory guidance, federal courts have literally made up the rules and procedures themselves, often coming to different conclusions. Some federal court circuits have stated they have no power to expunge records. However, other federal courts have indicated that they do have the power to expunge. The federal Fifth Circuit, which includes Texas, has held that under certain limited circumstances, federal courts may order expungement both of records held by other branches of the government (*e.g.*, executive branch), and its own court records. *See Sealed Appellant v. Sealed Appellee*, 130 F.3d 695 (5th Cir. 1997). The Supreme Court has passed on hearing cases that would have resolved the split between the circuits. This issue remains legally murky.

2.   Possible procedure for federal expungement

There are no statutory guidelines for how to seek an expungement under federal law, however, the place to start would be to file a motion with the federal court that issued the conviction that a person wants to be expunged. However, federal judges very rarely grant these types of motions. Some circuits, including the Fifth Circuit have adopted a balancing test to decide if a record held by the court may be expunged: "if the dangers of unwarranted adverse consequences to the individual outweigh the public interest in maintenance of the records, then expunction is appropriate." Further, these same courts have freely stated that this balancing test "rarely tips in favor of expungement," and that expungement should be granted in only the most extreme cases. *United States v. Flowers*, 389 F.3d 737 (7th Cir. 2004). Some of the areas where expungement has worked are in incidents of extreme police misconduct, or where the conviction is being misused against the person. Unless there exist compelling reasons, a federal judge is highly unlikely to grant expungement.

3.   Expungement for drug possession: statutory authority

Under a federal law entitled "special probation and expungement procedures for drug possessors," certain persons are allowed to request a federal court to issue an expungement order from all public records. 18 U.S.C. § 3607. Congress intended this order to restore the person to the status he or she "occupied before such arrest or institution of criminal proceedings." 18 U.S.C. § 3607(c).

In order to qualify for the expungement, you must have been under the age of 21 when you were convicted, you must have no prior drug offenses, and your conviction must have been for simple possession of a small amount of a controlled substance.

4. How does a person have firearms rights restored under federal law?

Under the Gun Control Act of 1968, a person who has received a Presidential pardon is not considered convicted of a crime preventing the purchase and possession of firearms subject to all other federal laws. *See* 18 U.S.C. §§ 921(a)(20) and (a)(33). In addition, persons who had a conviction expunged or set aside, or who have had their civil rights restored are not considered to have been convicted for purposes of the GCA "unless the pardon, expungement, or restoration of civil rights expressly provides the person may not ship, transport, possess, or receive firearms." 18 U.S.C. §§ 921(a)(20) and (a)(33).

The GCA also provides the United States Attorney General with the authority to grant relief from firearms disabilities where the Attorney General determines that the person is not likely to act in a manner dangerous to the public safety and where granting relief would not be contrary to the public interest. 18 U.S.C. § 925(c). The Attorney General has delegated this authority to the ATF. Unfortunately, the ATF reports that it has been prohibited from spending any funds in order to investigate or act upon applications from individuals seeking relief from federal firearms disabilities. This means that until the ATF's prohibition has been lifted, a person's best—and most likely—option to have their firearms rights restored is through a Presidential pardon. *See* www.atf.gov.

III. Texas law

A. *Clemency by Governor and Board of Pardons and Paroles*

The Governor of Texas possesses the authority to grant executive clemency under Article IV, Section 11 of the Texas Constitution except in cases of treason and impeachment. Unlike federal clemency where the President is free to pardon whomever the President chooses, the Governor of Texas can only grant clemency if a majority of the members of the Texas Board of Pardons and Paroles makes such a recommendation. However, the Board is required to consider any request of the Governor for clemency under section 508.050 of the Texas Government Code.

1. Who is eligible for executive clemency in Texas?

Executive clemency can be granted to any person who has been convicted of a felony or misdemeanor, or any person who has successfully completed a term of deferred adjudication community supervision under Texas Administrative Code § 143 for a criminal offense. In addition, a full pardon may be granted to a person based on "innocence." A pardon for innocence requires the "written recommendation of at least two of the current trial officials of the sentencing court, with one trial official submitting documentary evidence of actual innocence; or a certified order or judgment of a court having jurisdiction accompanied by a certified copy of the findings of fact and conclusions of law where the court recommends that the Court of Criminal Appeals grant state habeas relief on the grounds of actual innocence." Tex. Admin. Code § 143.2(a).

2. How does a person seek executive clemency in Texas?

A person seeking executive clemency in Texas is required to complete an application which is available from the Texas Board of Pardons and Paroles. Once properly submitted, the file of any applicant eligible for clemency will be reviewed by the Board of Pardons and Paroles.

The Board will review the application in a public hearing, however, the hearing is actually a review of the applicant's file rather than a formal hearing. The Board members vote on case files individually, and an applicant must obtain a majority number of votes of the Board before the application will be sent to the Governor for a final determination. Applicants are not able to appeal the decision of the Board, but applicants may re-apply for clemency once two years after the Board's decision have passed, if denied. If the majority of the Board recommends clemency be extended to an applicant, the file is sent to the Governor, who may accept the Board's recommendation and grant clemency, or reject the recommendation. For more information on the process, please visit http://www.tdcj.state.tx.us/bpp/faq/ClemencyProcess.html.

1. What is the effect of executive clemency in Texas?

Similar to federal clemency, unless the person receiving clemency has their records expunged, the records of the original conviction continue to exist. A person granted clemency must still disclose the conviction on any relevant form seeking such information, however, the person may also state the nature of the clemency received. The result of executive clemency in Texas depends on the type of clemency granted by the Governor.

B. *Texas expungement*

Chapter 55 of the Texas Code of Criminal Procedure controls expungement under Texas law. This chapter provides for when a person is entitled to expungement. Note that the technical term under Texas law is expunction, but we will use these terms interchangeably. The chapter allows expungement for persons who were acquitted or pardoned, had charges dismissed or were no-billed by a grand jury, were convicted as a juvenile for being delinquent or for an alcohol-related offense, or were victims of identity theft (where a criminal gave the innocent person's name as their own to law enforcement). *See* Tex. Code Crim. Proc. art. 55.01.

However, not all individuals are entitled to an expungement of their record. For instance, if a person was acquitted of one offense, but was convicted or remains subject to prosecution for another offense relating to or arising out of the charge for which they were acquitted, that person is not entitled to an expungement of their record. Additionally, adults who were convicted of a felony within five years of the arrest the person seeks to be expunged from their record are not eligible.

Expungement petitions under chapter 55 can become adversarial proceedings involving one or more party, including the State, which may object to the court granting an order of expungement. Under Texas law, prosecutors and law enforcement officers may object to the expungement of arrest records if the statute of limitations has not expired for a charge that was previously dismissed and they plan on re-filing, or if they wish to reserve the right to re-file charges against a person in the future.

To obtain an expunction, a petitioner is required to file a petition for expungement in a state civil district court. Even though expungement proceedings are governed by the Code of Criminal Procedure, expungement itself is a civil matter and, therefore, is a matter addressed by civil district courts. Individuals who apply for expungement within 30 days of an acquittal are not required to pay the filing fees associated with the expungement petition. If an individual was acquitted and files a petition for expungement more than 30 days after the date of acquittal, the normal fees for filing in the civil district court will apply.

C. *How does a person have firearms rights restored under Texas law?*

First, after five years, some rights are automatically restored. Texas Penal Code § 46.04(a) allows a convicted felon to possess a firearm in their residence after "the fifth anniversary of the person's release from confinement following conviction of the felony or the person's release from supervision under community supervision, parole, or mandatory supervision, whichever date is later."

Further, for a person seeking executive clemency, the person or the Governor may petition the Board of Pardons and Paroles to grant a "Pardon with Restoration of Firearms Rights" pursuant to Texas Administrative Code Rule 143.12. In addition to qualifying for a pardon, in order to also have the Board recommend that one's firearms rights be restored, the provisions of Rule 143.12 must be met which state:

> *The board will consider recommending restoration of the right to receive, possess, bear, and transport in commerce a firearm only in extreme and unusual circumstances which prevent the applicant from gaining a livelihood, and only if the applicant: (1) provides either proof of clearance by a previously granted full pardon or a request for such express restoration in a pending application for a full pardon from jurisdiction(s) of the relevant conviction(s) or successful completion of a punishment similar to a term of deferred adjudication community supervision; and (2) provides proof of application under the United States Code, Title 18, Section 925(c), for exemption, relief from disabilities to the Director of Alcohol. Tobacco, Firearms, and Explosives, and furnishes copies of all relevant applications and responses thereto by the Director of Alcohol, Tobacco, Firearms and Explosives including any final actions by said Director...*

The process for obtaining a restoration of firearms rights is essentially the same as receiving a grant of executive clemency in Texas and is subject to the non-appealable decisions of the Governor and the Board of Pardons and Paroles.

CHAPTER TWELVE
I'M BEING SUED FOR WHAT?
CIVIL LIABILITY IF YOU HAVE USED YOUR GUN

I. What does it mean to be sued?

The term "lawsuit" refers to one party's assertion in a written filing with a court and that another party has violated the law. In the context of firearms, typically the party suing has been injured and wants a ruling or judgment from the court to that effect, that most likely will entitle the person suing to receive money.

A. *What is a civil claim or lawsuit?*

A civil "lawsuit" or "suit" refers to the actual filing of written paperwork with a court (1) asserting that another party violated the law, and (2) seeking some type of redress. A "claim" can exist without the filing of a lawsuit. A claim is simply the belief or assertion that another party has violated the law. Many parties have claims they never assert, or sometimes parties informally assert the claim in hopes of resolving the disputes without the filing of a lawsuit. Also, another term commonly used is "tort" or "tort claim." A tort is a civil claim arising out of a wrongful act, not including a breach of contract or trust, that results in injury to another's person, property, reputation, or the like. The claims described below are all tort claims.

B. *Difference between "civil claims" and "criminal charges"*

To start with the basics, there are two different aspects of the legal system that gun owners may face after the use of a firearm: criminal and civil. There are several names and descriptive terms used for each (*e.g.*, civil lawsuit, criminal actions, civil claims, criminal proceedings, etc.), but regardless of the terms, the same breakdown applies; most cases are either criminal or civil. There is another subgroup of proceedings called administrative actions. Those actions are not covered by this chapter but can sometimes impact CHL holders. For example, appealing the denial of a CHL is an administrative act. See Chapters 8 and 9 for more information.

With that said, the three primary differences between a criminal action and a civil proceeding are: (1) who or what is bringing the action or lawsuit, (2) what are they seeking, and (3) what is the burden of proof? These differences are fairly straightforward:

1. State versus individual bringing claims

In a criminal case, the party bringing the action is the "sovereign," meaning the United States, state, municipality, county, *etc.* that believes that a person violated their laws. Even if an individual calls the police, fills out a criminal complaint, or even asks the district attorney to file charges, the party that actually brings a criminal action is the state, county, *etc.*, not the individual.

However, a civil action may be filed by any individual, business or other entity (partnership, LLC, trust, *etc.*). The entity bringing the claim is called the "plaintiff." Even governmental entities can bring civil claims; *i.e.*, if you negligently shoot a county propane tank causing a fire, the county can sue you civilly for those damages. The typical gun case, though, will involve an individual filing a lawsuit against another individual for damages caused by the firearm. If the incident occurs at a place of business, the plaintiff may also sue the business claiming that it is in some way at fault for the incident. The party being sued is typically called the "defendant."

2. Relief sought/awarded

In a criminal case, the entity prosecuting the case is usually seeking to imprison or fine you. Most crimes are punishable by "X" number or days/months/years in prison or jail, and a fine not to exceed "X" dollars.

By contrast, the plaintiff in the civil case is almost always seeking a monetary award. Several other types of relief are available (declaratory, injunctive, specific performance), but for the most part, gun cases will involve the plaintiff seeking monetary damages.

3. Burden of proof

In a criminal case, the standard is "beyond a reasonable doubt." In civil cases, however, a plaintiff must prove a person is liable for damages by a "preponderance of the evidence" standard. A preponderance of the evidence is a much lower standard than the criminal standard of beyond a reasonable doubt. It generally means that the party with the greater weight of credible evidence wins that issue. The preponderance of the evidence has been described as more than half, that is, if the evidence demonstrates that something "more likely occurred than not," this meets the burden of proof. Whereas in a criminal case, if there exists any "reasonable doubt," the burden of proof is not met. It does not mean the party with the most exhibits or greater number of witnesses will prevail. One highly credible witness can prevail over the testimony of a dozen biased, shady witnesses.

Example:

>   *John mistakes a utility meter reader for a burglar due to his disheveled appearance, tool bag, and because he looks to be snooping around John's house. John fires a shot without warning and injures the meter reader.*

Possible criminal liability: the State of Texas could bring criminal charges against John for a number of crimes (aggravated assault, attempted murder, deadly conduct, discharge of a firearm inside the city limits, and so forth). The State would be seeking to imprison or fine John for his conduct, and it would be required to prove that John committed the crime at issue "beyond a reasonable doubt."

Possible civil liability: the meter reader could also file a civil lawsuit against John alleging that John was negligent or committed the tort of assault. The meter reader would seek monetary damages and be required to prove his claims by a "preponderance of the evidence."

C. *Impact of result in one court upon the other*
    1. <u>Can a result in a criminal trial be used in a civil trial?</u>
Yes, because of the legal doctrines of *res judicata* and collateral estoppel. These two legal doctrines govern the impact of a ruling or judgment in one case, upon a separate case involving the same set of facts and circumstances. For the present discussion, if a person is found guilty of a crime in a criminal proceeding, because that court uses a higher standard of "beyond a reasonable doubt" than the civil requirement of "preponderance of the evidence," the finding of the criminal court may be used for purposes of establishing civil liability. Entire chapters in law books have been written on these topics, so, suffice to say, this section is a brief overview of these laws.

The criminal concept of *nolo contendere* or "no contest" often generates confusion in this area. In a criminal case, a plea of *nolo contendere* or no contest means that the defendant does not admit guilt. The plea, however, still results in a judgment that the defendant is guilty of the crime and that judgment can be used to establish the defendant's liability in a separate civil case.

Example:
> *Phil and Jeremy become involved in a road rage incident, and an altercation follows. Phil shoots Jeremy, wounding him. When all is sorted out, Phil is found guilty of criminal assault and receives punishment from the court (remember, criminal trials use the "beyond a reasonable doubt" standard).*

If Jeremy later sues Phil from the injuries he received when Phil shot him, Jeremy, in his civil action, will very likely be allowed to use the finding of guilt in the criminal case (because it used the higher standard of reasonable doubt) to establish his burden in the civil case (the lower preponderance of the evidence standard) that he is owed damages or money in the civil case. This is an example of collateral estoppel; Phil will not be permitted to re-litigate his guilt in the civil case.

Both doctrines are based on the concept that a party to a legal proceeding should not be able to endlessly litigate issues that have already been decided by the legal system. At its most basic level, it means that a party to a legal proceeding who receives a final ruling on a particular issue, win or lose, cannot attempt to have another trial court or even the same court decide the same issue.

Note about appeals: this is a different concept than an appeal, or asking the court in the first proceeding to reconsider its ruling, or grant a new trial. An appeal is a request to a higher court to review the decision of a lower court. Likewise, in any given case, the parties will have numerous opportunities to ask the current court to reconsider its rulings, or even ask for a new trial after a trial is completed. Collateral estoppel and *res judicata* come into play after a final judgment that is no longer subject to appeal or revision by the trial court.

Example:

> *Michele is sued for accidentally shooting Nancy.*
> *Nancy wins a judgment of $350 against Michele,*
> *much less than Nancy believed she was damaged.*

In that case, Nancy can appeal the decision, or even ask that trial court for a new trial. However, Nancy cannot file another, or new, lawsuit regarding the same incident and attempt to recover more in the second case because of the doctrine of *res judicata*. In order for the doctrine to apply, the facts, circumstances and issues must be the same.

Example:

> *Justin fires his hunting rifle from his deer blind,*
> *hitting Peter with one round. Peter files a civil suit*
> *against Justin and loses at trial. The court awards*

Peter no damages. Peter appeals and loses the appeal also.

Peter is legally barred from recovering in another lawsuit against Justin involving the same incident. However, Peter is not barred from filing suit against Justin for damages arising out of another set of facts and circumstances, for example, if the two are involved in a car wreck on a different day.

2. <u>Civil case result impact on criminal case</u>

Suppose you lose a civil suit and a judgment is entered against you arising out of a shooting incident. Can that judgment be used to establish that you committed a crime? No. The burden of proof is much higher in the criminal context than the civil case. The plaintiff proved his civil case by a "preponderance of the evidence." This does not mean that he proved his case "beyond a reasonable doubt," meaning a separate criminal trial is required to make that determination.

The one area where a civil case can impact a criminal case is the potential overlapping use of evidence and testimony. Your admission in one case can almost always be used against you in another case. Meaning, your sworn testimony in the civil case ("yes, I shot the guy") can almost always be used against you in the criminal case, and vice versa.

> ## Practical Legal Tip:
>
> Unlike criminal cases where a unanimous jury verdict is required to convict someone, to prevail in a civil suit in Texas, only ten of the twelve jurors (or five out of six, depending upon the court where your case is pending) must agree to render a verdict. In a criminal case, many times the goal of the defendant is to avoid conviction by convincing a single juror that the State cannot prove its case at the higher "beyond a reasonable doubt" standard. By contrast, in a civil lawsuit a plaintiff can prevail and recover damages, even if two of the jurors vehemently believe the defendant should prevail, as long as the remaining ten jurors believe that the plaintiff has proven his case by the lower "preponderance of the evidence" standard. -*Kirk*

II. What might you be sued for? Gun related claims in civil courts

A. *Liability for unintentional discharge*

This section deals with accidental or unintentional discharges of your firearm. Common unintentional discharges are associated with hunting and cleaning accidents or the mishandling of a weapon. Intentional shootings are addressed in the following section.

With that said, the following are the types of civil claims that may be asserted in connection with an unintentional discharge:

1. Negligence/gross negligence

Most civil cases for damages resulting from an accidental discharge will include a negligence or gross negligence claim. What does this mean and what does a plaintiff have to prove before they can win? Under Texas law, negligence is defined as the failure to use ordinary care, that is, failing to do that which a person of ordinary prudence would have done under the same or similar circumstances, or doing that which a person of ordinary prudence would not have done under the same or similar circumstances. If a person fails to use ordinary care, then they have acted negligently and will be liable for damages resulting from their conduct. "Ordinary care" means that degree of care that would be used by a person of ordinary prudence under the same or similar circumstances. This is an "objective standard," meaning, the test is not whether you believed you acted prudently, but whether the judge or jury believes you acted as a person of ordinary prudence would have acted. Of course, this is the definition of negligence in the civil context. There is actually a different definition of criminal negligence, which is beyond the scope of this book's discussion.

What is gross negligence and how is it different than "regular" negligence? Many gun cases will include a claim for "gross negligence" by the plaintiff. The primary reason for this is that if a plaintiff establishes gross negligence by a defendant, the plaintiff may be entitled to additional types or amounts of money that are legally available if mere negligence is established. The Texas Supreme Court and the Texas Legislature have defined gross negligence as an act or omission involving the subjective awareness of an extreme degree of risk, indicating conscious indifference to the rights, safety, or welfare of others. Tex Civ. Prac. & Rem. Code § 41.001(11)(A)-(B); *State v. Shumake*, 199 S.W.3d 279, 287 (Tex. 2006). The Texas Legislature has defined gross negligence as follows:

> "Gross negligence" means an act or omission:
>
> (A) which when viewed objectively from the standpoint of the actor at the time of its occurrence involves an extreme degree of risk, considering the probability and magnitude of the potential harm to others; and

(B) of which the actor has actual, subjective awareness of the risk involved, but nevertheless proceeds with conscious indifference to the rights, safety, or welfare of the others.

The defendant's state of mind is also a key difference between negligence and gross negligence. Negligence involves an objective standard—how would a reasonable person have acted? Gross negligence applies a subjective component—was this particular person actually aware of the risk involved?

Example:

Jessica has practiced her shooting at a private range on her country property for 20 years, without incident. Jessica shoots towards an area where she has never seen another person, and she believes the range of her guns cannot reach her property line. One day, a neighbor is hit by a shot as he is strolling through the woods just off of Jessica's property.

Result: Jessica might be liable for negligence if a jury determines, for example, that a reasonably prudent person would have acted differently, tested the range of her guns, or built a different type of back stop or berm, *etc.* However, Jessica was not subjectively aware of an extreme degree of risk so there would be no evidence of gross negligence. However, change Jessica's awareness and it changes the result.

Example:

Jessica has received several complaints over the years about bullets leaving her property and hitting her neighbor's property. Nevertheless, Jessica ignores the complaints and continues practicing in the direction that she typically shoots. One day while practicing, her bullet leaves her property and hits her neighbor. She is later sued by the neighbor for gross negligence.

Result: Jessica may very well be liable for gross negligence because she was subjectively aware that her shots were reaching the neighbor's property and that there were people in the same area (*i.e.*, the folks who reported the shots), and despite that knowledge, she continued to shoot without changing direction or building a back stop or berm and someone was injured as a result.

2. <u>Negligent entrustment of a firearm</u>

Texas recognizes a claim for entrusting (*e.g.*, giving, lending, transferring) a firearm to another person. To prove that a person or entity negligently entrusted a firearm, the plaintiff must show that (1) the owner entrusted the gun (2) to a person who was incompetent or reckless, (3) whom the owner knew or should have known was incompetent or reckless, (4) the person with the gun was negligent, and (5) and the person's negligence proximately caused the incident and the plaintiff's injuries.

Example:

Shaun lets his adult grandson Gordon borrow a shotgun to take on a fishing trip because he knows there are water moccasins in the spot where they plan to fish. Gordon has never been in trouble with the law, has repeatedly been trained in firearms safety, and has never had an incident with a gun. However, while on the trip, Gordon accidentally shoots a fellow fishing buddy with Shaun's shotgun. The fishing buddy, now turned plaintiff, sues Gordon for negligence and Shaun for negligent entrustment of a firearm.

Can the plaintiff win his claim for negligent entrustment? Probably not. Shaun might get sued for giving the shotgun to his grandson, but the facts described do not meet the elements necessary to establish negligent entrustment under Texas law; and Shaun should prevail in any lawsuit. First, there are no facts that suggest Gordon was incompetent or reckless. Further, there are no facts showing knowledge by Shaun that Gordon was either incompetent or reckless. Thus, the negligent entrustment claim would legally fail.

Many plaintiffs have urged Texas appellate courts to adopt a "strict liability" standard when looking at gun cases. In other words, if you give someone your gun, you are automatically liable for whatever happens. Texas appellate courts have, to-date, uniformly rejected a strict liability standard.

3. Is negligent storage of a firearm recognized in Texas?

A question commonly asked by gun owners is "if someone steals my gun, am I liable if they shoot someone?" In other words, if I store my gun and a criminal or another less-than-responsible person gets the gun, am I liable if they shoot someone? As of the date of this publication, the answer in Texas is "probably not." A Texas appellate court has affirmatively stated that the claim of negligent storage of a firearm is not recognized in Texas. *Richardson v. Crawford*, No. 10-11-00089-CV, 2011 LEXIS 6578 (Tex.App.—Waco 2011). What does this mean? If someone accesses your gun and you did not intend for them to access your gun, Texas does not currently recognize this claim, and a plaintiff should not be able to recover if the person who accesses your gun injures himself or others.

Several caveats to this exist: (1) many other states *do* recognize this claim; (2) until the Texas Supreme Court rules on this issue, it is possible that another appellate court in Texas could decide differently; and (3) there are severe criminal consequences for storing your gun where it can be accessed by a minor. *See* Tex. Penal Code § 46.13.

As a result, while no civil claim exists in Texas today, it remains extraordinarily important to exercise care in the storage of your firearms.

B. *Intentional discharge: a person intended to shoot*
1. Negligence/gross negligence

Just because you intend to shoot someone, or otherwise "use" your gun, does not necessarily mean that the plaintiff will not assert negligence or gross negligence claims. In other words, you may have fully intended to pull the trigger, but the plaintiff may claim that you were negligent for any number of reasons; for example, you mistook the mailman for a burglar, or the criminal was retreating and you were negligent in using deadly force. The negligence and gross negligence claims, as defined above, can be brought even if you intended to pull the trigger.

2. Assault and battery

If a person has shot at or shot someone, if they are sued, it may include a claim for assault and battery. This is an intentional act, not an accident or a claim based on a deviation from a standard of care. An assault occurs if a person:

> (1) intentionally, knowingly, or recklessly causes bodily injury to another, including the person's spouse;

> (2) intentionally or knowingly threatens another with imminent bodily injury, including the person's spouse; or

> (3) intentionally or knowingly causes physical contact with another when the person knows or should reasonably believe that the other will regard the contact as offensive or provocative.

Tex. Penal Code § 22.01(a) (West Supp. 2013); *see Loaisiga v. Cerda*, 379 S.W.3d 248, 256 (Tex. 2012) (recognizing civil assault elements mirror criminal assault).

Example:

> *Bill is startled while driving. Martha is standing next to his passenger window at a light screaming that he cut her off in traffic, but taking no action to indicate she intends to harm Bill or do anything besides verbally lodge her complaints. In response, Bill fires a shot at Martha to make her go away, and hits her in the leg.*

Bill has committed a civil assault. He intended to and did cause serious bodily injury to Martha with no legal justification. Therefore, a civil jury would likely find Bill liable and award damages to Martha.

Example:

> *Bill is startled while driving. Martha is standing next to his passenger window at a light screaming that he cut her off in traffic, but taking no action to indicate she intends to harm Bill or do anything besides verbally lodge her complaints. In response, Bill points his gun at Martha and says "You're dead!" He fires his gun but misses.*

Bill has committed a civil assault. He knowingly threatened Martha with imminent bodily injury with no legal justification.

3. <u>False imprisonment: being sued for detaining people</u>

What if a gun owner detains someone at gun point? If the person who was detained later decides to sue, it will likely include a claim for "false imprisonment." Texas recognizes a civil claim for false imprisonment. This claim can arise when someone detains persons waiting for police, *e.g.* homeowners detaining burglars, *etc.* However, it can also come up commonly in shoplifting cases (see Chapter 7). The elements of false imprisonment are: (1) a willful detention, (2) without consent, and (3) without justification or authority of law. *Dangerfield v. Ormsby*, 264 S.W.3d 904, 909 (Tex.App.—Fort Worth 2008, no pet.).

Example:

> *Emily fears she is about to be attacked in a grocery store parking lot by Randall. Randall follows her step-by-step through the parking lot and stops right next to Emily's car. Emily draws her .380 and tells Randall to "stay right there while I call the police." Randall complies, and Emily holds him at gunpoint until the police arrive. When the police arrive, they determine that Randall was an out-of-uniform store employee tasked with rounding up the grocery carts in the parking lot and was no threat to Emily.*

If a jury determines that Emily acted without justification (*i.e.*, she was not reasonably in fear of death or bodily injury), Emily could be civilly liable for falsely imprisoning Randall and owe him damages, if any.

4. Wrongful death

If a person is in the unfortunate position that they have shot and killed another individual and a civil suit occurs because of the shooting, it likely will include a claim for wrongful death. In Texas, "[a] person is liable for damages arising from an injury that causes an individual's death if the injury was caused by the person's or his agent's or servant's wrongful act, neglect, carelessness, unskillfulness, or default." Tex. Civ. Prac. & Rem. Code § 71.002.

A wrongful death claim can be proven by establishing that one of the other claims described in this chapter caused the death of another person. In other words, the "wrongful act, neglect, carelessness, unskillfulness, or default" needed to establish a wrongful death claim, can be established by proving that the defendant was liable for a tort such as battery or negligence and that the tort caused the death of a person.

III. What can the plaintiff recover?

If a person is sued in civil court and the plaintiff convinces a jury that the defendant was liable for damages, what and how much can a plaintiff get? There are scores of cases discussing the details of each category of damages that a plaintiff can recover in a civil lawsuit. The following is a brief description of two very important concepts: (1) "proximate cause," which is essential to recover damages in most circumstances, and (2) the basic types of damages that a plaintiff may typically seek in a gun case.

A. *Proximate cause*

One basic concept that is important to most civil claims, and is usually required to recover damages, is "proximate cause." Virtually every tort claim will require the plaintiff to prove that his damages were proximately caused by the defendant. "Proximate cause" is defined as cause that was a substantial factor in bringing about an event and without which the event would not have occurred. This concept has few bright-line tests.

For a gun owner, the most obvious cases of proximate cause are pulling the trigger on a firearm and hitting the person or thing you aimed at. The law will hold that your action proximately caused whatever physical damage the bullet did to persons or property. But what about those circumstances where the use of the gun is so far removed from the damages claimed? This is where the doctrine of proximate cause will cut off liability. If the damage is too far removed from the act, then the act cannot be a proximate cause of that damage.

Example:

> *Anthony is cleaning his AR-15 one night in his apartment and is negligent in his handling of the rifle. He has an accidental discharge and the bullet goes through the wall of his apartment and strikes his neighbor, Ray, in the leg. Ray, although in massive pain, received prompt medical care from his wife, Gail, and made a speedy recovery.*

If Anthony is later sued by Ray and his wife Gail, Anthony's negligence undoubtedly "proximately caused" damages for things like Ray's medical bills, hospital stay, and perhaps even lost wages. But what if Gail claims that because of her having to treat Ray's wounds that she missed a big job interview and lost out on a big raise in pay and that she wants Anthony to pay that as a component of damages? The law would hold that Gail likely could not recover damages for her lost raise in pay because the loss would not be "proximately caused" by the act being sued for. To put it another way, it is reasonably foreseeable that the negligent discharge of a firearm will cause medical bills, *etc.* for someone struck by a bullet. Therefore, this is recoverable. However, the law would say that the loss of a possible job opportunity for the wife who treated the person who was actually shot is not a reasonably foreseeable consequence of negligently discharging a firearm and, therefore, was not proximately caused by the act of negligence. In that case, there will be no recovery for the plaintiff, Gail. Proximate cause must be established in every case and may appear to be arbitrary legal line drawing because it is.

As discussed below, Texas law also recognizes a doctrine that unforeseen criminal conduct breaks the causal link between an action and a third-party's injuries.

B. *What types of damages can a plaintiff recover?*
The following is merely a brief snapshot of the types of damages recoverable in a firearms case. To recover any of the damages

below, the plaintiff must first prove one of the claims above by a preponderance of the evidence. For example, if the jury determines a defendant was not negligent, a plaintiff cannot recover his or her medical costs, no matter how severe the plaintiff's injuries. Some of the damages a plaintiff can try to recover include:

- Lost Wages
- Medical Costs
- Disability
- Pain & Suffering (Physical, Mental & Emotional)
- Funeral and Burial Costs
- Disfigurement
- Loss of Companionship
- Loss of Household Services
- Lost Future Wages
- Future Medical Costs
- Punitive or exemplary damages (Note, the standard of proof for punitive/exemplary damages is "clear and convincing evidence," which is higher than a "preponderance of the evidence." Punitive damages are also only available in cases of intentional or reckless conduct, or gross negligence.)

A court can find the defendant 100% at fault, but award no damages because the plaintiff failed to prove damages by a preponderance of the evidence. For example, a plaintiff who seeks reimbursement for medical expenses but has no evidence that they ever went to a doctor or hospital, will very unlikely be able to recover those medical expenses.

Practical Legal Tip:

Most people don't know that civil courts in Texas have no independent means of sifting through the thousands of lawsuits filed every year to determine which are frivolous and which are meritorious and should go forward. The civil justice system is "user driven," meaning that unless one side or the other asks the judge to rule on a particular issue (usually called a "motion"), no one at the courthouse, including the judge, is going to take any action to examine the merit, or lack thereof, of a lawsuit. -*Kirk*

IV. How good are Texas civil immunity laws for gun owners?

A. *No immunity from lawsuits*

There is a common misunderstanding that there exists a law that if you are legally justified in using your gun that you can't be sued. This is just not the case. First, if a person has the filing fee, anyone can sue anyone else in the State of Texas. There is no one stopping anyone else from filing a lawsuit. Winning a lawsuit is a different issue entirely. If someone files the lawsuit, no matter how frivolous, it still must be dealt with, and it still must be shown to the court that this or that defense bars this lawsuit. This process can take significant time, money, and legal energy even for the most loser of cases. In short, lawyers get paid and even if you beat the "rap," you still have to take the civil "ride." So, if there is no immunity to lawsuits for gun owners, what protection is there?

B. *Immunity for certain claims*

Most important for gun owners if they find themselves included in a civil suit after a justified use of force will be Texas Civil Practice and Remedies Code § 83.001.

> **Immunity from Damages**
> **Tex. Civil Practice and Remedies Code § 83.001**
>
> A defendant who uses force or deadly force that is justified under Chapter 9, Penal Code, is immune from civil liability for personal injury or death that results from the defendant's use of force or deadly force, as applicable.

This section provides that a person who uses force or deadly force that is justified under Chapter 9 of the Texas Penal Code is immune from civil <u>liability</u> for personal injury or death that results from the defendant's use of force or deadly force, as applicable. This statute does not prevent lawsuits; it just makes the ones filed harder to win. Immunity from liability is an affirmative defense, and, as such, this defense will be considered only after a plaintiff is well into the pain a civil suit may cause an innocent defendant. Texas courts have ruled that immunity from suit would be a violation of the "Open Courts Doctrine" of Article 1, § 13 of the Texas Constitution. A Texas intermediate appellate court ruled in *In re Smith* that section 83.001 does not mean immunity from suit. *In re Smith*, 262 S.W.3d 463 (Tex.App.—Beaumont 2008) It means immunity from damages if the defense is proven during the case.

Also, note the language in section 83.001 is "liability for personal injury or death." While it has not yet been interpreted by the appellate courts, this language likely means that property damage is not covered. What could that mean?

Example:

> *John is the victim of a home invasion. He fires several shots at the intruder. The intruder is hit and stopped. One shot, however, misses the intruder and hits a propane tank at the house across the street. The propane tank explodes and burns down the neighbor's home.*

The resulting damage is neither personal injury nor death. It is very unlikely that the immunity statute will provide John with any protection from a civil suit by the neighbor for the damages to the house.

C. *Justification*

All of the justifications under Chapter 9 of the Texas Penal Code can also be asserted as affirmative defenses in a civil action. This means, for example, if you shoot someone in defense of yourself, others, or your property and are sued as a result, you may assert the applicable sections of the Penal Code as a defense to the civil claims. If the judge or jury agrees that you acted in self-defense, or properly used force to defend others or property, the plaintiff will be barred from recovery. See Chapters 4 through 7.

D. *Statute of limitations for civil claims*

The statute of limitations is a doctrine in Texas (and almost every other jurisdiction) that requires civil claims to be brought within a certain period of time after the incident. If the claim is not brought within the statute of limitations period, it is barred. There are a number of issues relating to *when* the statute of limitations starts to run in many cases, but for the most part, limitations will start to run immediately after a shooting incident. The statute of limitations can vary from claim to claim, most, however, are between one and four years. In Texas, the limitations period most likely to apply to gun cases is going to be two years. Assault and battery, negligence, wrongful death, and false imprisonment claims all provide two-year limitations periods.

What does this mean for gun owners? If you "use" your gun, the plaintiff must bring a civil suit against within two years of the incident in almost all cases or else the claim will be barred.

E. *Superseding or intervening criminal conduct*

Texas law recognizes a doctrine that absolves someone from responsibility for conduct that might otherwise be a tort (*e.g.*, negligence) if a criminal act breaks the causal connection between the tort and the injury. Generally, a third party's criminal conduct is a superseding cause which relieves the negligent actor from liability. However, the actor's negligence will not be excused where the criminal conduct is a foreseeable result of the actor's negligence. *Byrd v. Woodruff*, 891 S.W.2d 689, 701 (Tex.App.— Dallas 1994); *Nixon v. Mr. Prop. Mgmt. Co.*, 690 S.W.2d 546, 550 (Tex. 1985).

Example:

> *Justin allows his nephew Randall to use his handgun for protection. Justin knows Randall has been in trouble with the law repeatedly and has been accused of armed robbery. While Randall has the handgun, his apartment is burglarized, and the gun is stolen and used in a crime spree. During the crime spree, Melanie is shot and injured.*

Melanie would not be able to recover from Justin, even though Justin may have been negligent in giving his gun to Randall, because the criminal act of burglarizing Randall's apartment and subsequent crime spree were superseding causes that broke the link between Justin's actions and the resulting injuries.

F. *Contributory negligence/proportionate responsibility*

Texas has a doctrine called proportionate responsibility. If this defense is applicable and properly raised, either the judge or the jury will be asked to determine the percentage of fault or responsibility of the parties involved in the incident. The damages are then apportioned based upon the percentages assigned by the judge or jury.

Example:

> *Richard is a young adult trick-or-treater. He uses a fake gun as a part of his costume and knocks loudly on Nancy's door at 11:30 p.m. on October 31. Nancy, having forgotten about Halloween, is*

frightened by the knock, the fake gun, and the
late hour of Richard's arrival. She fires through
the door, injuring Richard.

In the civil suit that follows by Richard against Nancy, the jury will be permitted to consider whether Richard's negligence, if any, contributed to cause the resulting injuries. The jury could determine that Richard was 0% at fault, 100%, or anything in between. By way of example only, if the jury awarded Richard $100,000.00 in damages, but found he was 30% at fault, and Nancy 70%, Richard would only be able to recover $70,000 of his damages.

In Texas, this rule only applies where the damaged party is 50% or less at fault. In other words, if the plaintiff bringing the lawsuit is determined to be more than 50% responsible for the injuries, he or she cannot recover any damages. This can be important for the average gun owner in that a carjacker/home invader/general troublemaker who is the overwhelming cause of an incident cannot recover just because the judge or jury finds you made a slight misstep in defending yourself or your home.

V.   What about third-parties?

Texas law provides a different standard when it comes to injuries to third parties. In this section, a "third-party" generally means someone who is not a party to the encounter with the firearm; *e.g.*, bystanders, witnesses, folks nearby who were not the intended target, etc.

"Acts of self-defense or in defense of one's property have always been in accord with the public policy of Texas, and those persons having sufficient courage to so act legally enjoy the privilege. It is only when acts in self-defense or in defense of one's property are committed under circumstances where the actor should realize that such acts create an unreasonable risk of causing harm to innocent third parties that such third parties may subject the actor to liability." *Helms v. Harris*, 281 S.W.2d 770, 771 (Tex. Civ. App.

1955). Likewise, the Texas Penal Code also provides in sections 9.05 and 9.06 that a person cannot use justification as a defense where they injure a third party by their reckless acts.

This means that even if you defend yourself, others or property, but you create an unreasonable risk to others in doing so, you can be liable if one of those third-parties is injured.

Example:
> Mel shoots Anthony as he unlawfully breaks into Mel's occupied home at night. She fires a single shot with her .22 that narrowly misses Anthony but hits a man washing his car down the street.

Mel is probably not liable to the man down the street, because her conduct did not unreasonably place third-parties at risk.

Example:
> Ben shoots at Anthony as he unlawfully breaks into Ben's occupied home at night. Ben fires 30 shots with his fully-automatic M-16, missing with the initial burst. Anthony turns and runs. Ben continues to fire haphazardly at Anthony as he runs down the street. One shot hits a man washing his car four houses away.

Ben could very likely be liable to the man washing his car because he unreasonably placed third-parties at risk by firing a fully automatic weapon down a neighborhood street.

VI. Traps and spring guns
Texas Penal Code § 9.44 governs the use of "devices" to protect land or tangible movable property. Non-lethal devices are completely permissible in Texas as long as they are not designed to cause death or serious bodily injury and must be reasonable under all circumstances at the time installed.

However, a "trap" or "spring gun" that discharges a firearm may cause death or serious bodily injury and is illegal. Basically, any "device" with a loaded firearm capable of discharging will be prohibited by section 9.44.

What types of "devices" are permitted? Anything "reasonable" at the time installed and not designed to cause death or serious bodily injury.

Examples:

1. *Barbed wire around a business in the warehouse district of town*
Likely permitted. Barbed wire is typically a reasonable security measure and usually not capable of, or designed to, cause death or serious bodily injury.

2. *Razor wire around a playground across from an elementary school*
Likely unlawful. While probably not designed to cause death, it is arguably unreasonable to install such a "device" near an elementary school, particularly around a playground likely to attract children.

Also, note that warnings, notices, and the like are not included in the wording of the statute, meaning that using a warning sign is unlikely to shield you from liability. Notice, warning, or knowledge of the maintenance of a spring gun or similar device has been held not to constitute a defense to a criminal prosecution and are unlikely to shield a person from liability for such a device. In the criminal context, courts around the country have held that even if a deceased knew of the spring gun, this alone did not justify his killing.

VII. Will insurance cover it if I shoot someone?

A. *Homeowners' insurance*

With few exceptions, almost every homeowner's insurance policy excludes coverage for intentional acts. The act of using your firearm in self-defense is almost always an intentional act. You intended to stop the threat. Plaintiffs' attorneys will very likely assert a negligence claim against a homeowner in an attempt to fall within the coverage, but at the end of the day, if the only evidence is that you intentionally shot the plaintiff because you intended to stop a threat, it is likely that any policy with an intentional act exclusion will not provide coverage for any damages awarded.

B. *Auto insurance*

Scores of cases around the country exist where the parties allege that a gun incident is covered by automobile insurance merely because the use of the firearm occurs in the auto or involves an auto. Almost universally, courts have held that these incidents are not covered merely because the discharge occurs in a car or involves a car.

Example:

> *Justin is cleaning his 9mm handgun in the car. It accidentally discharges causing his passenger Edwin severe injuries.*

This event will almost certainly not be covered by auto insurance.

Example:

> *Justin discharges his 9mm handgun in the car at Edwin during an attempted carjacking, causing Edwin severe injuries and also hitting a bystander.*

This event will almost certainly not be covered by auto insurance. For an injury to fall within the "use" coverage of an automobile policy (1) the accident must have arisen out of the inherent nature of the automobile, as such, (2) the accident must have arisen within the natural territorial limits of an automobile, and the actual use must not have terminated, (3) the automobile must not merely contribute to cause the condition which produces the injury, but must itself produce injury.

Two Texas courts of appeals have used these factors to conclude that a drive-by shooting does not arise out of the use of a vehicle. Also, if the injury occurs when purposefully handling a gun (e.g. playing with it or intentionally shooting it), not in order to place or remove it from the vehicle, there is no causal connection between the injury and the use of the vehicle; the vehicle is merely the *situs* of the injury and its use incidental to the injury-producing act. *See Texas Farm Bureau Mut. Ins. Co. v. Sturrock*, 65 S.W.3d 763 (Tex.App.—Beaumont 2002)

Texas recognizes one minor exception. While a gun is resting in or being removed from a gun rack permanently attached to a vehicle, the presence of the permanently attached gun rack in the vehicle establishes a significant causal connection between the accident and the "use" of the vehicle. In other words, if a gun discharges while resting on or being removed from a gun rack attached to a vehicle, auto insurance will likely cover the event under existing Texas law. *Mid-Century Ins. Co. v. Lindsey*, 997 S.W.2d 153 (Tex. 1999).

VIII. What civil liability does a person face if their children access their firearms?

A. *Parents are not responsible for minor children's actions merely because they are parents!*

As a general rule, minors are civilly liable for their own torts (that is, their wrongful actions such as negligence, gross negligence, assault, *etc.*). The mere fact of paternity or maternity does not make a parent liable to third parties for the torts of his or her minor children. Under this general rule, parents are not responsible for their minor children's tortious actions when the minor child commits a tort and the parent had no direct relationship to the child's action, such as providing a firearm in a negligent manner, failing to supervise the child, or allowing the child to engage in behavior the parent knows is dangerous or risky.

B. *Parents who fail to "parent" may become responsible for minor children's actions*

While a parent who has no direct relationship to a minor child's tortious actions is generally not liable for that child's actions, if the parent negligently allows his child to act in a manner likely to harm another, if he gives his child a dangerous instrumentality, or if he does not restrain a child known to have dangerous tendencies, the parent may be liable.

Another issue related to negligent storage is whether or not the storage of a gun in violation of Texas Penal Code § 46.13 could result in civil liability, in addition to the severe criminal penalties in the statute. No appellate court has decided this issue as of this writing. However, one appellate judge in a dissenting opinion (dissenting opinions are not binding on other courts) has suggested that a claim for negligence *per se* might exist for violation of Section 46.13. *Perez v. Lopez*, 74 S.W.3d 60, 73 (Tex.App.—El Paso 2002) (dissenting opinion). Negligence *per se* means that liability is automatically established due to the violation of the statute, while damages and proximate cause must still be proven. Regardless, all gun owners should exercise great care to avoid unintended access to guns by minors.

Example:
> *Your 17-year-old son Jon has been hunting since he was 11 and has taken several firearms training courses.*

If you take Jon hunting, and for some reason Jon accidentally discharges his shotgun, injuring another person, it is highly unlikely that you, the parent, will be civilly liable for an accident that occurs while hunting.

Example:

> *Your 12-year-old son Gordon has never handled a gun or taken a firearms training course. You decide to take him to the range for the first time, but you are both asked to leave the range after Gordon repeatedly fires into the ceiling and the floor. Fed up, you take Gordon to another range with no additional instruction or training.*

If Gordon shoots and injures someone at the second range, it is likely that you will be liable, because you allowed him to act in a manner likely to harm another, and you did not restrain him despite his dangerous conduct.

C. *Parents have a duty to control and discipline children*

In addition to the situations described in the preceding section where parents may become liable for a minor child's actions when the parent's own actions (or lack, thereof) played a role, Texas has a statute that also provides limited parental liability. Texas Family Code § 41.001 provides that a parent or other person who has the duty of control and reasonable discipline of a child is liable for any property damage proximately caused by:

> (1) the negligent conduct of the child if the conduct is reasonably attributable to the negligent failure of the parent or other person to exercise that duty; or

> (2) the willful and malicious conduct of a child who is at least 10 years of age but under 18 years of age (recovery for damage caused by willful and malicious conduct is limited to actual damages, not to exceed $25,000 per occurrence, plus court costs and reasonable attorney's fees).

The first subsection mirrors the standard for parental liability in Texas, meaning a parent is liable for the negligence of a child, if the parent was negligent in failing to control or discipline the child. For example, if your child has previously injured someone in a gun incident, and you fail to better supervise, discipline, or take control of his shooting, you will almost certainly be liable for subsequent shooting incidents.

Example:

> In preparation for the annual family hunting trip, Frank took his 16-year-old son Billy to the outdoor shooting range. As happens every year, while at the range, Billy was haphazard and intentionally unsafe in his handling of his firearm. Billy, who refuses to take anything seriously, repeatedly pointed his firearm in the direction of other persons, and even discharged his gun into the air three times while ululating. Frank scolded Billy by telling him that it is "not nice" to point guns at other people. During the hunting trip, Billy randomly fired his shotgun for no apparent reason at all into the trees. Billy's last shot hit a fellow hunter standing among the trees.

Is Frank liable for his minor son Billy's acts? Probably yes. Frank was well-aware of the fact that Billy handles firearms in a dangerous manner, and Frank failed to take any reasonable measures to prevent Billy injuring another person. The law would very likely find that Frank's failure to reasonably discipline and supervise his child proximately caused the injury to the other hunter.

The second subsection provides *per se* (*i.e.*, automatic), but limited, liability for willful and malicious damages caused by a child age 10-17. This will commonly cover incidents of vandalism but could also encompass intentional (but not negligent) shootings. The damages under this subsection are capped at $25,000.

Example:

> *Bobby, a 14-year-old boy, does not like his neighbor. One day, he retrieves the family 12-gauge shotgun and decides to shoot the neighbor's fence. Bobby's parents know nothing about this behavior and Bobby has never had trouble with a firearm in the past. As a result of the shooting, a number of pickets from the fence were destroyed, three windows were broken, and numerous pockmarks were left in the brick façade of the home.*

Under the second subsection of Texas Family Code § 41.001, Bobby's parents would be liable for the damage Bobby caused to his neighbor's property up to $25,000.00 plus court costs and reasonable attorneys' fees because Bobby's actions were willful and malicious.

CHAPTER THIRTEEN
BEYOND FIREARMS:
KNIVES, CLUBS, AND TASERS

I. Introduction

In addition to Texas' many firearms laws, there also exist state laws governing the possession and use of "other weapons." This includes any object that is not a firearm, but could be used as a weapon. This chapter will briefly discuss the laws governing these other weapons, including weapons that are absolutely illegal under the law, weapons that are illegal to carry, and exceptions to the laws prohibiting the carrying of illegal weapons.

II. Absolutely prohibited weapons

A. *What is an absolutely prohibited weapon?*

Texas Penal Code § 46.05, which is entitled "Prohibited Weapons," states that it is a crime if a person "intentionally or knowingly possesses, manufactures, transports, repairs, or sells" certain prohibited weapons. As opposed to many laws which merely prohibit the *carrying* of a weapon in a public place, this section of the Penal Code prohibits a person from even *possessing* such a weapon—including in their home or on any property under their control or influence.

B. *What weapons are absolutely prohibited under Texas law?*

The list of absolutely prohibited weapons is found in Texas Penal Code § 46.05. This section prohibits the possession, manufacturing, transporting, repair, or sale of nine different weapons or classes of weapon:

1. Knuckles are absolutely prohibited

The term "knuckles" is defined in Texas Penal Code § 46.01(8) as "any instrument that consists of finger rings or guards made of a hard substance and that is designed, made, or adapted for the purpose of inflicting serious bodily injury or death by striking a person with a fist enclosed in the knuckles." The common use of "knuckles" typically refers to "brass knuckles." However, the statute covers more than just "brass knuckles."

Traditional "Brass Knuckles"

There are three general requirements for an object to be considered knuckles: (1) the object must be made of a hard substance, (2) the object must have some form of a finger-ring or guard, and (3) it must be designed, made, or adapted for the purpose of inflicting serious bodily injury or death when striking another person with a fist enclosed in the knuckles.

Other objects which may be held in the hand used to augment the strength of a punch as an offensive weapon, such as a "fist filler" (pictured below), are not "knuckles" as defined by Texas law and should not be considered prohibited weapons. "Knuckles" are very strictly defined, and an object must meet the legal definition in order to be a prohibited weapon.

Commercial "Fist Filler"   *Roll of Coins*

2. Chemical dispensing devices are prohibited with an exception

A chemical dispensing device means a "device, other than a small chemical dispenser sold commercially for personal protection, that is designed, made, or adapted for the purpose of dispensing a substance capable of causing an adverse psychological or physiological effect on a human being." Tex. Penal Code § 46.01(14). Because this definition of chemical dispensing device specifically excludes "small chemical dispenser[s] sold commercially for personal protection," items such as personal mace or pepper-spray, as well as bear or wasp spray, are not prohibited. Instead, a chemical dispensing device includes items that cause "adverse psychological or physiological effect[s]" on people such as tear gas, including items available to the military or law enforcement and not the general public.

3. Tire deflation devices

Texas law prohibits tire deflation devices which are defined as "a device, including a caltrop or spike strip, that, when driven over, impedes or stops the movement of a wheeled vehicle by puncturing one or more of the vehicle's tires." Tex. Penal Code § 46.01(17).

What is a caltrop? A caltrop is a weapon made up of two or more sharp nails arranged in a way that one always points up from a stable base. Anciently, caltrops were used as a way to slow the advance of horses, war elephants, camels, and human troops and were used as early as 331 BC. Today, caltrops (pictured below) are used to deflate automobile tires. Since 2008, there have been approximately 94 illegal caltrop-related incidents near the Texas-Mexico border. *See* "Cartel Crime Statistics" on the Texas DPS website.

Caltrops

Personal-use, mobile spike strips are also prohibited. These strips should not be confused with permanent traffic control devices that are "designed to puncture one or more of a vehicle's tires when driven over in a specific direction; and [have] a clearly visible sign posted in close proximity to the traffic control device that prohibits entry or warns motor vehicle operators of the traffic control device." Tex. Penal Code § 46.01(17). These types of traffic control devices are often seen at airports and other secured facilities to prevent the unauthorized entry or exit from the facility such as the one pictured below.

C. *Additional weapons prohibited by Texas Penal Code § 46.05 unless NFA compliance is met*

Section 46.05 also prohibits the following weapons and devices which are discussed in greater detail in Chapter 14, "National Firearms Act." Possession of these weapons and devices remains prohibited, however, Texas law provides a defense if possession of one of these weapons "was pursuant to registration pursuant to the National Firearms Act." Tex. Penal Code § 46.05(c).

- Explosive weapons
- Machine guns
- Short-barreled firearms
- Firearm silencers
- Zip guns

D. *Defense for members of the military or law enforcement*
Under section 46.05(b), persons who are members of the armed forces or National Guard, a governmental law enforcement agency, or a correctional facility who use one of these prohibited weapons in the course of their official duties, are provided a defense to prosecution. This explains why, most commonly, one would see a police officer use a spike strip in the course of a high-speed chase down the highway but not be charged with a crime for breaking the law regarding prohibited weapons.

E. *Affirmative defenses for antique weapons, and use of or sales of tire deflation devices to military or law enforcement agencies*
In addition, Texas law provides an affirmative defense to prosecution for individuals whose conduct was incidental to dealing with a tire deflation device solely as an antique or curio. This means that persons who possess ancient caltrops, such as those described earlier are subject to the affirmative defense. Tex. Penal Code § 46.05(d)(1).

Moreover, individuals whose conduct was incidental to dealing with a tire deflation device solely for the purpose of making them available to an organization, agency, or institution within the armed forces or National Guard, a governmental law enforcement agency, or a correctional facility, are also provided with an affirmative defense. Tex. Penal Code § 46.05(d)(3).

III. Generally prohibited weapons
As opposed to Texas Penal Code § 46.05 which strictly prohibits the possession, manufacture, transport, or sale of certain weapons, section 46.02 prohibits the *carrying* of other weapons. This section of the Penal Code makes it a crime when a person intentionally, knowingly, or recklessly carries on or about his person an illegal knife or club when not: (1) on his own premises or premises under his control, or (2) inside of or directly *en route* to a vehicle or watercraft owned by or under the control of the person. Tex. Penal Code § 46.02(a).

Note, however, that this section does not prohibit the possession, manufacture, or sale of such weapons—merely the carrying (and transport) of them at any place other than the person's premises or motor vehicle (including watercraft).

A. *Illegal knives*
What is an illegal knife? Under Texas Penal Code § 46.01(6), an illegal knife means:
- A knife with a blade over five and one-half inches;
- A hand instrument designed to cut or stab another by being thrown;
- A dagger, including but not limited to a dirk, stiletto, and poniard;
- A bowie knife;
- A sword; or
- A spear.

Bowie Knife   *Throwing Knives*

Note: many knives similar to bowie knives are perfectly legal so long as only one side of the blade is sharpened.

How does the law define dagger? The term dagger is not defined in the Penal Code. However, the Texas Court of Criminal Appeals provided a definition of a weapon that is (1) equipped with a double guard, (2) with a fixed blade, and (3) which is sharpened on both edges as being a dagger. *Armendariz v. State*, 396 S.W.2d 132 (Tex. Crim. App. 1965). Because a dagger may come in a variety of forms, however, section 46.01(6) includes some variations of thrusting knives which also qualify as a dagger, though they may not possess each of the characteristics listed above. Regardless, the carrying of one of these illegal knives is prohibited under section 46.02 as described above.

Dagger   Dirk

Stiletto   Poniard

1.   <u>Switchblades are no longer illegal!</u>

Once listed as a prohibited weapon, switchblades were removed from the list in 2013. Texas Penal Code § 46.01(11) defines a switchblade as "any knife that has a blade that folds, closes, or retracts into the handle or sheath and that opens automatically by pressure applied to a button or other device located on the handle or opens or releases a blade from the handle or sheath by the force of gravity or by the application of centrifugal force. The term does not include a knife that has a spring, detent, or other mechanism designed to create a bias toward closure and that requires exertion applied to the blade by hand, wrist, or arm to overcome the bias toward closure and open the knife."

However, while switchblades are not generally prohibited, if a knife fits the definition of a switchblade, but also possesses characteristics of some of the other illegal knives listed earlier, then it would become an illegal knife as well. For instance, if a switchblade possessed a double-sided blade, then it would be an illegal knife as it also meets the definition of a "dagger."

2. Local knife ordinances *may* be more restrictive than the general state law!

Unlike firearms, there is no preemption by state law of local knife ordinances. This means that local municipalities, government agencies, and other regulatory bodies are free to enact laws, ordinances, and rules which are more restrictive than Texas law. As a result, there are currently two basic divisions in the local knife laws enacted by counties, cities, and towns throughout Texas: municipalities that prohibit the carrying of knives while in public, and municipalities that prohibit the carrying of knives while on government-owned or controlled property.

a. Municipalities that prohibit the public carry of knives

At the time of publication, the following three cities have their own laws restricting the possession and carrying of certain knives in public places—note that some of the local law is identical to and repetitive of Texas law and that this list may change with the law; be sure to check the particular municipal ordinances:

Corpus Christi
- Does not allow blades greater than 3 inches that can be used for offensive or defensive purposes at the Corpus Christi International Airport;
- Does not allow the carrying of straight razors, unpackaged safety razor blades, any knives having a blade of more than 3 inches in length, any knife that will not shut, any knife that will open and lock by the press of a button, ice picks,

bowie knives, dirks, daggers, spears, machetes, hand sickles, stilettos, or any sword cases made of any metal or any hard substance, or any dangerous weapon;
Corpus Christi, Tex. Code §§ 33-73 and 9-38.

Jacksonville
- Does not allow a person to knowingly sell, offer to sell, give, or barter, or cause to be sold, given or bartered, any switchblade, springblade, or throw blade knife, unless the knife is an antique or curio;
- Does not allow a person to knowingly sell, give, barter or cause to be sold, given, or bartered a dirk, dagger, sword cane, spear, bowie knife, or knife with a blade over 5 ½ inches long to any minor without the written consent of the parent or guardian;
- Does not allow a person to knowingly carry on his or her person any dirk, dagger, sword cane, spear, bowie knife, switchblade, springblade, or throwblade knife, or any knife with a blade over 5½ inches, or any other knife manufactured or sold for offensive or defensive purposes;

Jacksonville, Tex. Code §§ 12-20 and 12-21.

San Antonio
- Does not allow persons under the age of 17 to possess any knives on public roadways or public right-of-ways, or on any other property in which a governmental entity has an interest, or on private property without the permission of the owner;
- Does not allow a person to intentionally or knowingly carry any knives with blades that are **less** than 5 ½ inches that can lock in place to become fixed, except for law enforcement officers, persons on their own premises or on premises under their control, persons traveling, persons lawfully hunting, fishing, or engaging in sporting activities, or persons engaged in a lawful occupation where such knives are used (such as a chef).

San Antonio, Tex. Code §§ 21-17 and 21-155.

b. *Municipalities that prohibit the carrying of knives while on government owned or controlled property, or similar municipal events*

The following municipalities have enacted local laws beyond the Texas Penal Code which restrict the carrying of certain knives in government-owned or controlled premises, or at certain municipal functions:

Alice
- No carrying of knives allowed at the Alice International Airport if the knife is manufactured for offensive or defensive purposes.

Alice, Tex. Code § 14-98.

Clear Lake Shores
- No knives or weapons in the gated or fenced pool areas of Shell Bottom Park or Jarboe Bayou Park.

Clear Lake Shores, Tex. § 66-140.

Denton and Decatur
- The city can prohibit the carrying of knives during a declared public crisis or emergency.

Denton, Tex. Code § 9-1;
Decatur, Tex. Code § 2-294.

Dallas County
- Possession of knives longer than 4 inches, or any other hand instrument designed to cut or stab, including daggers, dirks, stilettos, poniards, bowie knives, swords, spears, or switchblades is prohibited on county property.

Dallas County, Tex. Code § 106-52.

Jacinto City
- No carrying of knives allowed in the municipal courtroom or municipal court offices.

Jacinto City, Tex. Code § 37.

Laredo
- No carrying of illegal knives allowed at or in public parks, public meetings, political rallies, parades, or non-weapons-related school, collegiate, or professional athletic events.

Laredo, Tex. Code § 21-152.

Magnolia
- No possession of knives or other weapons capable of inflicting injury is allowed in any park area or facility.

Magnolia, Tex. Code § 78-79.

Melissa
- No carrying of knives, or any bladed cutting utensil of any length is allowed for peddlers, solicitors, or handbill distributors.

Melissa, Tex. Code § 4.614.

Richland Hills
- No possession of knives or weapons of any kind is allowed in city parks or other city recreational facilities.

Richland Hills, Tex. Code § 70-162.

Robinson
- No possession of illegal knives or switchblades is allowed in city-owned or controlled buildings or property.

Robinson, Tex. Code § 12-30.

Shenandoah
- No possession of knives or any other weapon that can inflict injury is allowed in any park area or facility.

Shenandoah, Tex. Code § 54-40.

Texarkana
- No knives or any deadly weapons may be carried on a person on public transportation or in public transportation facilities.

Texarkana, Tex. Code § 15-66.

3. Exception for bowie knives and swords

> **Exception for Bowie Knives and Swords:**
> **Tex. Penal Code § 45.15(e)**
>
> The provisions of Section 46.02 prohibiting the carrying of an illegal knife do not apply to an individual carrying a bowie knife or a sword used in a historical demonstration or in a ceremony in which the knife or sword is significant to the performance of the ceremony.

Texas Penal Code § 46.15(e) provides a specific exception to the law prohibiting the illegal carrying or transportation of bowie knives and swords if the weapon is used in a historical demonstration, or in a ceremony in which the knife or sword is significant to the performance of the ceremony.

Under this exception, individuals who are historical re-enactors demonstrating a historical battle where a sword is a part of the re-enactment are not guilty of the crime of carrying an illegal knife. Likewise, persons participating in a ceremony, such as a wedding where the bride and groom walk under a steeple of swords, would also not be guilty of carrying an illegal knife since this exception states that the provisions of section 46.02 do not apply in such a situation.

B. *Clubs*

Section 46.01(1) of the Texas Penal Code defines a "club" as "an instrument that is specifically designed, made, or adapted for the purpose of inflicting serious bodily injury or death by striking a person with the instrument, and includes but is not limited to the following: (a) blackjack; (b) nightstick; (c) mace; (d) tomahawk."

Examples of these clubs are pictured below:

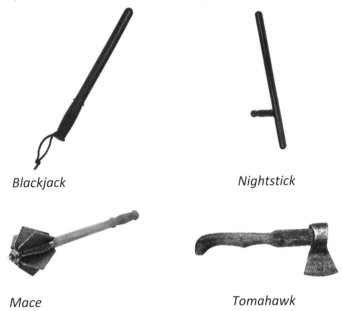

Blackjack   Nightstick

Mace   Tomahawk

The carrying of a club on one's person at a place that is not the person's premises or premises under the person's control, or at any place outside of or not directly *en route* to the person's motor vehicle or watercraft, is prohibited by Texas Penal Code § 46.02. However, clubs are weapons which are often utilized in various jobs. For that reason, the legislature has crafted four exceptions specific to the carrying of a club.

1. When do ordinary items become illegal clubs?

The legal definition of an illegal club includes any instruments that are "adapted for the purpose of inflicting serious bodily injury or death by striking the person with the instrument." Tex. Penal Code § 46.01(1). This means that many ordinary items that a person may find in the home or vehicle may be considered to be an illegal club if the item has been adapted to serve a different purpose than originally intended.

For instance, a baseball bat is designed to be used for playing baseball. However, if a person takes a baseball bat and hammers a few nails through the end of the bat, the baseball bat has been adapted to become a mace.

Baseball Bat adapted as a Mace

Practical Legal Tip:

Some weapons are combinations of some of the items we've talked about throughout this chapter such as polymer knuckles combined with a taser, or a taser-baton. Even though such a weapon includes a legal item such as a taser, if it incorporates any illegal item (such as knuckles, or illegal knives or clubs), it is still illegal! *-Edwin*

2. <u>Specific exceptions to the law prohibiting the carrying of a club</u>

Texas Penal Code § 46.15 also contains a number of exceptions for other persons who have, as a result of their employment, the need to carry a club. For those individuals, Texas law provides an exception to the prohibition of carrying an illegal club so long as the person meets the specific requirements of each exception.

University or college security guards

Exception for University or College Security Guards: Tex. Penal Code § 46.15(c)
The provision of Section 46.02 prohibiting the carrying of a club does not apply to a noncommissioned security guard at an institution of higher education who carries a nightstick or similar club, and who has undergone 15 hours of training in the proper use of the club, including at least seven hours of training in the use of the club for nonviolent restraint. For the purposes of this section, "nonviolent restraint" means the use of reasonable force, not intended and not likely to inflict bodily injury.

The training requirements, in addition to the employment requirement, of this exception are very specific and strict. Noncommissioned security guards (security guards possessing a Level 2 security license), must have been trained for a minimum of 15 hours in the proper use of the club, and 7 of those hours must have dealt with using the club in a nonviolent manner.

Public security officers

Exception for Public Security Officers: Tex. Penal Code § 46.15(d)
The provision of Section 46.02 prohibiting the carrying of a firearm or carrying of a club do not apply to a public security officer employed by the adjutant general under Section 437.053, Government Code, in performance of official duties or while traveling to or from a place of duty.

This exception refers specifically to state military forces and security guards who are employed by the adjutant general of the state military force as a guard at a base or other state military installation.

Members of the armed forces and employees of penal institutions

> ### Exception for Members of the Armed Forces and Employees of Penal Institutions at Places of Execution: Tex. Penal Code § 46.15(f)
>
> Section 46.03(a)(6) does not apply to a person who possesses a firearm or club while in the actual discharge of official duties as:
> (1) a member of the armed forces or state military forces, as defined by Section 437.001, Government Code; or
> (2) an employee of a penal institution.

The exception provided in this portion of the statute is specific to places of execution and those members of the armed forces or employees of a penal institution who are present at or within 1,000 feet of the place of execution in an official capacity as they carry out their duties.

Animal control officers

> ### Exception for Animal Control Officers: Tex. Penal Code § 46.15(g)
>
> The provisions of Section 46.02 and 46.03 prohibiting the possession or carrying of a club do not apply to an animal control officer who holds a certificate issued under Section 829.006, Health and Safety Code, and who possesses or carries an instrument used specifically for deterring the bite of an animal while the officer is in the performance of official duties under the Health and Safety Code or is traveling to or from a place of duty.

The exception for animal control officers may be slightly misleading. First, it is important to point out that this only provides an exception for licensed animal control officers. Second, and more importantly, however, the exception is also only for the use of a club which is specific to the catching of an animal, such as a "catchers pole" or snare. Animal control officers who attempt to use a mace, for instance, are unlikely to avail themselves of this exception.

IV. Tasers

There is no Texas statutory law governing the carrying or use of tasers. As such, it is perfectly legal for persons to purchase, sell, carry, and use tasers under Texas law. Of course, the use of tasers is not without controversy. Most frequently, tasers are used by law enforcement officers as a method of subduing a suspect without the use of a firearm. Unfortunately, is some instances, the use of a taser has amounted to lethal force.

The Texas Penal Code does not provide a blanket definition for a taser. In fact, the term taser is not used anywhere in the Penal Code. The term "stun gun" is defined, however, in section 38.14(a)(2) as "a device designed to propel darts or other projectiles attached to wires that, on contact, will deliver an electrical pulse capable of incapacitating a person." Unfortunately, this definition applies specifically to a law which prohibits a criminal or suspect from taking or attempting to take the device from a peace officer. The statute does not cover any type of taser beyond the one that expels darts.

Handheld "Stun Gun"   Cartridge Taser

In addition, at the time of writing, there are fewer than 20 Texas appellate cases that even mention the words taser or stun gun. None of these cases involve when or how a taser may be used. For that reason, it is important to be aware that the use of a taser will subject a person to the same standards of self-defense as outlined in Chapters 4 through 6 of this book, in that a person will likely need to be justified in using either force or deadly force before the use of a taser will also be justified. Because the law does not clearly classify or define a taser in any way, and because there are no cases on this subject addressing it, how a prosecutor, judge, or jury will view a person's use of a taser as being either mere force or deadly force is unknown. Although a taser is not designed to kill, you should be aware that under certain circumstances, and when used in a manner other than designed (such as prolonged use), a taser may play a part in a person's cause of death.

CHAPTER FOURTEEN
SILENCERS, SHORT-BARRELED WEAPONS, AND MACHINE GUNS: THE NATIONAL FIREARMS ACT

Can an individual in Texas legally own a silencer or suppressor, short-barreled shotgun, short-barreled rifle, machine gun, or "destructive device?" Yes, if all NFA regulations are satisfied. This chapter deals with the laws regarding the possession and use of firearms that are subject to the provisions of the National Firearms Act (NFA) codified in 26 U.S.C. Chapter 53, specifically, silencers, short-barreled firearms, machine guns, and firearms that are otherwise illegal. These firearms are illegal to purchase or possess without possessing the proper paperwork and a "tax stamp." In this chapter, we will discuss the purpose behind the NFA, what firearms are regulated by the Act, as well as the process and procedure for legally possessing weapons that are subject to the Act's provisions.

I. What is the National Firearms Act?
The National Firearms Act was enacted in 1934 in response to gangster crimes. Prior to the Act's passage, any person could go to the local hardware store and purchase a Thompson Submachine Gun or shorten the barrel on their rifle or shotgun. President Roosevelt pushed for the passage of the NFA in an attempt to diminish a gangster's ability to possess and carry dangerous and/or easily concealable firearms, such as machine guns and short-barreled rifles and shotguns.

NFA is firearms regulation using a registration and tax requirement
The NFA requires both the registration of and tax on the manufacture and transfer of certain firearms. The law created a tax of $200 on the transfer of the following firearms: short-barreled shotguns, short-barreled rifles, machine guns, silencers, and destructive devices. The tax is only $5 for firearms that are classified as "Any Other Weapons" or AOWs. Back in 1934, a $200 tax was the approximate equivalent to about $3,500 today!

Five years after the NFA's passage, the Supreme Court held in *United States v. Miller* that the right to bear arms can be subject to federal regulation. Miller brought suit against the government stating that the NFA infringed upon his Constitutional right to bear arms under the Second Amendment. While the Court agreed that the Constitution does guarantee *a right* to bear arms, it held that the right does not extend to every firearm. *See United States v. Miller*, 307 U.S. 174 (1939).

II. What firearms does the NFA regulate?
A. *Short-barreled rifles and shotguns*
In order to be legal, short-barreled shotguns and rifles must be registered, and a tax paid on the firearm. What is a short-barreled shotgun? Under both federal and Texas law, short-barreled shotguns have one or more barrels less than 18 inches in length and the overall length of the shotgun is less than 26 inches. What is a short-barreled rifle? It is any rifle with one or more barrels less than 16 inches in length, and the overall length of the rifle is less than 26 inches. *See* 27 CFR § 478.11 and Tex. Penal Code § 46.01(10).

Short-barreled shotguns and rifles may be purchased from an FFL that deals in NFA items. Also, short-barreled firearms are very popular for individuals to build and/or modify on their own. This is legal if the person has properly registered the firearm to be modified into a short-barreled firearm with the ATF and paid the tax before it is modified. Once approved, a person may alter or produce a short-barreled firearm and must engrave legally required information on the receiver of the firearm such as manufacturer, location, *etc. See discussion later in this chapter for detailed requirements.*

B. *Machine guns*
Machine guns are illegal under federal and state law. However, if the requirements of the NFA are satisfied, machine guns may be legally owned by individuals. First, what is a machine gun? Federal law defines a machine gun as "any weapon which shoots, is

designed to shoot, or can be readily restored to shoot, automatically more than one shot, without manual reloading, by a single function of the trigger. The term shall also include the frame or receiver of any such weapon, any part designed and intended solely and exclusively, or combination of parts designed and intended, for use in converting a weapon into a machine gun, and any combination of parts from which a machine gun can be assembled if such parts are in the possession or under the control of a person." 27 CFR § 478.11. As a result of this definition, the individual metal components that make up a whole machine gun, such as a full-auto sear, individually meet the federal definition of machine gun. The parts for the machine gun do not have to be assembled.

Similarly, under Texas law, a machine gun is defined as "any firearm that is capable of shooting more than two shots automatically, without manual reloading, by a single function of the trigger." Tex. Penal Code § 46.01(9). Texas law lists machine guns as prohibited weapons under section 46.05 of the Texas Penal Code unless the possessor holds the proper paperwork under the NFA. In other words, if more than two bullets come out of a firearm with only one pull of the trigger, the firearm is a machine gun.

No new manufacturing of machine guns for private ownership
Because of a federal law that effectively disallows private ownership (not military, police department, etc.) of any machine gun manufactured after May 19, 1986, machine gun available for private ownership are limited to the legally registered machine guns that existed prior to May 19, 1986. Thus, the private market is very limited and prices, as a result, are very high.

C. *Firearm suppressors*
What is a suppressor? It is just a muffler for a firearm and is legal if all NFA requirements are met. In legal terms, a firearm suppressor is defined in 27 CFR § 478.11 as "any device for silencing, muffling, or diminishing the report of a portable firearm,

including any combination of parts, designed or redesigned, and intended for use in assembling or fabricating a firearm silencer or firearm muffler, and any part intended only for use in such assembly or fabrication." The Texas definition is contained within the federal one as "any device designed, made, or adapted to muffle the report of a firearm." Tex. Penal Code § 46.01(4).

Firearm suppressors are very practical instruments. They are great for hunting and recreational shooting not only because it suppresses gunshots in a way so as to not alarm other animals being hunted nearby, but also because it lessens the impact on the shooter's ears. However, firearms owners should be carefully aware that the definition of a suppressor is very broad whether under federal or Texas law. Suppressors do not need to be items manufactured specifically for use as a suppressor. There are some ordinary, every-day items that could be easily converted into a suppressor such as a water bottle or an automotive oil filter. Possession of otherwise legal items when used or modified to be used as a suppressor is illegal.

D. *Destructive devices*

The term "destructive device" is a legal term given to certain firearms, objects, and munitions that are illegal under the NFA.

Destructive Devices – Part A 27 C.F.R. § 478.11
Any explosive, incendiary, or poison gas (1) bomb, (2) grenade, (3) rocket having a propellant charge of more than 4 ounces, (6) missile having an explosive or incendiary charge of more than one-quarter ounce, (5) mine, or (6) device similar to any of the devices described in the preceding paragraphs of this definition.

Destructive Devices – Part B 27 C.F.R. § 478.11
Any type of weapon (other than a shotgun or shotgun shell which the Director finds is generally recognized as particularly suitable for sporting purposes) by whatever name known which will, or which may be readily converted to, expel a projectile by the action of an explosive or other propellant, and which has any barrel with a bore of more than one-half inch in diameter.

Destructive Devices – Part C 27 C.F.R. § 478.11
Any combination of parts either designed or intended for use in converting any destructive device described in [part] (A) and (B) of this section and from which a destructive device may be readily assembled.

The "destructive devices" as defined in the statute are effectively broken down into three categories: explosive devices, large caliber weapons, and parts easily convertible into a destructive device.

The first portion of the definition of a destructive device deals with explosive, incendiary and poison gas munitions. The definition specifies that any explosive, incendiary, or poison gas bomb, grenade, mine or similar device is a destructive device. In addition, the definition includes a rocket having a propellant charge of more than four ounces and a missile (projectile) having an explosive or incendiary charge of more than one-quarter ounce. These topics and the regulations thereof are beyond the scope of this book's discussion.

The second section of the definition addresses large caliber weapons and states that any type of weapon that has a bore diameter of <u>more than one-half inch</u> in diameter is a destructive device with the exception of shotguns (and shotgun shells) that are suitable for sporting purposes. Thus, any caliber in a rifle or handgun more than .5 inches or fifty caliber is classified as a destructive device. Shotguns are exempt from this prohibition on size <u>unless</u> the ATF rules it is not for "sporting purposes." How do you know if a shotgun is suitable for sporting purposes? The ATF keeps a list, and has issued rulings classifying specific shotguns as destructive devices because they are not considered to be particularly "suitable for sporting purposes" including the USAS-12, Striker-12, Streetsweeper, and 37/38mm Beanbags. The ATF does not provide any specific definition of what constitutes being "suitable for sporting purposes" nor does it specify the methodology in which it determines what makes a particular shotgun suitable for sporting purposes. Ultimately, one will have to check with the ATF lists to see whether a particular shotgun with a larger bore-diameter is classified as a destructive device or not.

Finally, a destructive device does not need to be a completed and assembled product to fall under the federal definition and regulation under the NFA. Much like machine guns, if a person possesses parts that can be readily assembled into a destructive device, then whether or not the device has actually been constructed is irrelevant—by law it's already a destructive device.

Although these firearms, munitions, and devices are prohibited by the law on its face pursuant to the National Firearms Act, a person may nevertheless receive permission to possess them so long as they possess the correct legal authorization.

E. *"Any Other Weapons" or AOWs*

The AOW category under the NFA pertains to firearms and weapons that may not fit the traditional definition of some of the firearms discussed elsewhere in this book due to the way in which they are manufactured or modified. Under federal law, an AOW is "any weapon or device capable of being concealed on the person from which a shot can be discharged through the energy of an explosive, a pistol or revolver having a barrel with a smooth bore designed or redesigned to fire a fixed shotgun shell, weapons with combination shotgun and rifle barrels 12 inches or more, less than 18 inches in length, from which only a single discharge can be made from either barrel without manual reloading, and shall include any such weapon which may be readily restored to fire. Such term shall not include a pistol or a revolver having a rifled bore, or rifled bores, or weapons designed, made, or intended to be fired from the shoulder and not capable of firing fixed ammunition." 26 U.S.C. § 5845(e).

1. Concealable weapons and devices

Weapons which are capable of being concealed from which one shot can be discharged are AOWs. This includes such weapons as a pengun, knife gun, or umbrella gun. Texas law does not use the term AOW but rather makes "zip guns" illegal. A "zip gun" is defined in Texas Penal Code § 46.01 as "a device or combination of devices that was not originally a firearm and is adapted to expel a projectile through a smooth-bore or rifled-bore barrel by using the energy generated by an explosion or burning substance." Tex. Penal Code § 46.01(16). This is the legal equivalent to an AOW.

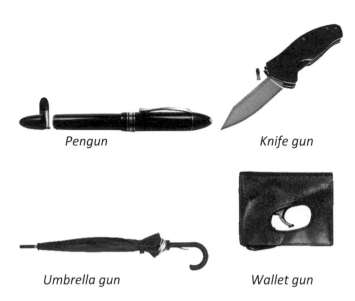

Pengun   Knife gun

Umbrella gun   Wallet gun

2. <u>Pistols and revolvers having a smooth-bore barrel for firing shotgun shells</u>

Pistols and revolvers that have a smooth bore (no rifling) that are designed to shoot shotgun ammunition are defined as an AOW. The ATF cites firearms such as the H&R Handy Gun or the Ithaca Auto & Burglar Gun as firearms which fall under the AOW category. *Note:* handguns with partially rifled barrels such as The Judge do not fall under this category due to the rifling of the barrel.

H&R Handy Gun   Ithaca Auto & Burglar Gun

3. <u>Weapons with barrels 12 inches or longer and lengths 18 inches or shorter</u>

The definition of Any Other Weapon also includes any weapon which has a shotgun or rifle barrel of 12 inches or more but is 18 inches or less in overall length from which only a single discharge can be made from either barrel without manual reloading. The ATF identifies the "Marble Game Getter" as the firearm most commonly associated with this definition (excluding the model with an 18" barrel and folding shoulder stock).

4. Pistols and revolvers with vertical handgrips

If a pistol is modified with a vertical grip on the front, it will now be legally classified as an AOW and require registration and a paid tax. Note, vertical grips are readily available and are legal to own as long as they are not placed on a handgun. The definition of a handgun is a weapon which is intended to be fired by one hand, the addition of the vertical foregrip makes it so the weapon now is intended to be used with two hands to fire. This modification changes the weapon from a handgun to what is known as an "AOW" and is now a prohibited weapon without the proper documentation.

F. *Antique firearms*

Firearms that are defined by the NFA as "antique firearms" are <u>not</u> regulated by the NFA. The NFA definition of antique firearm is found in 26 U.S.C. § 5845(g) as "any firearm not designed or redesigned for using rim fire or conventional center fire ignition with fixed ammunition and manufactured in or before 1898 (including any matchlock, flintlock, percussion cap, or similar type of ignition system or replica thereof, whether actually manufactured before or after the year 1898) and also any firearm using fixed ammunition manufactured in or before 1898, for which ammunition is no longer manufactured in the United States and is not readily available in the ordinary channels of commercial trade." Under this statute and for NFA purposes, the only firearms that are antiques are firearms which were both actually manufactured in or before 1898 and ones for which fixed ammunition is no longer manufactured in the United States and is not readily available in the ordinary channels of commercial trade.

With this in mind, the ATF states in its NFA guidebook that "it is important to note that a specific type of fixed ammunition that has been out of production for many years may again become available due to increasing interest in older firearms. Therefore, the classification of a specific NFA firearm as an antique can change if ammunition for the weapon becomes readily available in the ordinary channels of commerce."

Practical Legal Tip:

Some of the items regulated by the NFA simply don't make as much sense as the other things it regulates. Suppressors are really nothing more than mufflers for your firearm—they aren't really firearms themselves (notwithstanding the legal definition). Thinking about the utility of the suppressor, if the firearm was invented today, you can be sure that not only would the government not prohibit them, OSHA would probably require them for safety purposes! -*Michele*

G. *NFA curio firearms and relics*
Under federal law, curios or relics are defined in 27 CFR § 478.11 as "firearms which are of special interest to collectors by reason of some quality other than is associated with firearms intended for sporting use or as offensive or defensive weapons." Persons that collect curios or relics may do so with a special collector's license although one is not required. The impact of an NFA item being classified as a curio or relic, however, is that it allows the item to be transferred interstate to persons possessing a collector's

license. The collector's license does not allow the individual to deal in curios or relics, nor does it allow the collector to obtain other firearms interstate as those transactions still require an FFL.

To be classified as a curio or relic, federal law states that the firearm must fall into one of the following three categories:

1. Firearms which were manufactured at least 50 years prior to the current date, but not including replicas thereof;
2. Firearms which are certified by the curator of a municipal, State, or Federal museum which exhibits firearms to be curious or relics of museum interest; or
3. Any other firearms which derive a substantial part of their monetary value from the fact that they are novel, rare, bizarre, or because of their association with some historical figure, period, or event.

See 27 CFR § 478.11.

The ATF maintains a list of firearms that are classified as curios or relics.

H. *How can some after-market gun parts make your firearm illegal?*

A number of companies manufacture and sell gun products or parts that alter the appearance or utility of a firearm (*i.e.* shoulder stocks, forward hand grips, *etc.*). However, some of these after-market products can actually change the firearm you possess from one type of a weapon to another type of weapon for legal purposes whether you realize it or not. As a result, many individuals make the modifications to their firearms thinking that because there was no special process for purchasing the accessory, any modification would be in compliance with the law. Unfortunately, this is not always the case. Consider the example of short-barreled uppers for AR-15s: selling, buying, or possessing AR-15 "uppers" with barrels less than 16 inches is legal. However, it is illegal to put the upper on a receiver of an AR-15 because this would be the act of manufacturing a short-barreled rifle and is legally prohibited. This is equally true of vertical forward grips on a handgun. Vertical foregrips are legal to buy or possess, however, if you actually install one on a handgun, you have manufactured an AOW, and it is illegal, unless registered and a tax paid. *Note:* there are other types of braces that are permissible in their proper application and illegal in any application or adaptation that would alter the classification of the weapon. For example, the Sig Arm Brace is legal to attach to an AR Pistol when used as an arm brace, but illegal when used as a shoulder stock.

III. Process and procedure for obtaining NFA firearms
A. *Who can own and possess an NFA firearm?*
Any person may own and possess an NFA firearm as long as they are legally not disqualified to own or possess firearms and live in a state that allows possession of NFA items. See Chapters 2 and 3. The ATF also allows for a non-person legal entity to own these items, such as corporations, partnerships, and trusts, *etc.*

Practical Legal Tip:

Even if you don't own a machine gun today, that doesn't mean you won't be the intended owner of one later. A person could always leave you their NFA items in a will. If this happens, you must file the appropriate paperwork with the ATF as soon as possible, or at least before probate is closed. *-Michele*

B. *What are the usual steps for buying or manufacturing NFA items?*
Whether a person is buying or making (manufacturing) an NFA firearm, there are several steps in the process. The transfer or manufacture of an NFA firearm requires the filing of an appropriate transfer form with the ATF, payment of any federally-mandated

transfer tax, approval of the transfer by the ATF, and registration of the firearm to the transferee. Only after these steps have occurred may a buyer legally take possession of the NFA item, or may a person legally assemble or manufacture the NFA item. In this section, we will walk through the process, step-by-step, of (1) purchasing an NFA item that already exists, and (2) manufacturing an NFA firearm.

Steps for buying an existing NFA item (for example, a suppressor)
1. Select and purchase the item (suppressor) from a dealer;
2. Assemble appropriate paperwork (ATF Form 4, see Appendix B) and tax ($200.00);
   a. If the buyer is an individual: must secure Chief Law Enforcement Officer signature on ATF Form 4, a photograph, and fingerprints;
   b. If the buyer is a corporation/trust: no Chief Law Enforcement Officer signature, photograph, or fingerprints are required;
3. Submit paperwork, fingerprints, and tax to the ATF → ATF review and approval;
4. ATF sends approval (tax stamp affixed to Form 4) to the dealer;
5. Pick up suppressor from the dealer.

Steps for manufacturing an NFA item (such as a short-barreled rifle)
1. Select the item to manufacture or modify, *i.e.*, short-barreled AR-15;
2. Assemble appropriate paperwork (ATF Form 1, see Appendix B) and tax ($200.00);
   a. If the buyer is an individual: must secure Chief Law Enforcement Officer signature on ATF Form 1, a photograph, and fingerprints;
   b. If the buyer is a corporation/trust: no Chief Law Enforcement Officer signature, photograph, or fingerprints are required;
3. Submit paperwork and tax to the ATF → ATF review and approval;

4. ATF sends you the approval (tax stamp affixed to Form 1);
5. You may then legally assemble the AR-15, *i.e.*, put upper with a barrel length of less than 16 inches on a lower receiver, *etc.* The item must now be engraved and identified, see below.

When purchasing an NFA firearm from a dealer, the dealer is required to have the purchaser fill out ATF Form 4473 when the purchaser goes to pick up the item from the dealer.

C. *How must an NFA item be engraved and identified if I make it myself?*
Once you receive ATF approval to manufacture your own NFA item (such as the short-barreled AR-15 in the previous section), federal law requires that you engrave, cast, stamp, or otherwise conspicuously place or cause to be engraved, cast, stamped, or placed on the frame, receiver, or barrel of the NFA item the following information:
1. The item's serial number;
2. The item's model (if so designated);
3. Caliber or gauge;
4. The name of the owner whether individual, corporation, or trust; and
5. The city and state where the item was made.

This information must be placed on the item with a minimum depth of .003 inch and in a print size no smaller than 1/16 inch. *See* 27 CFR § 479.102.

D. *Which way should I own my NFA item? Paperwork requirements for individuals, trusts, or business entities to own NFA items*
Form 4 and Form 1
The appropriate paperwork that must be assembled and submitted to the ATF under the NFA varies depending on whether an individual, or a legal entity such as a trust, corporation, or partnership is purchasing or manufacturing the NFA item. The paperwork generally starts either with an ATF Form 4 (used for

purchasing an existing item), or an ATF Form 1 which is used if a person wishes to manufacture a new NFA item. All relevant portions of the Form must be completed. Both Form 4 and Form 1 have a requirement that a Chief Law Enforcement Officer for the applicant must sign the ATF Form. However, this requirement only applies to living, breathing individuals; it does <u>not</u> apply to applicants who are legal entities like trusts, corporations, *etc*. Therefore, a Chief Law Enforcement Officer signature is not necessary. The signature of the Chief Law Enforcement Officer is difficult or impossible to obtain for an individual

Who may sign a Form 4 or Form 1 as a Chief Law Enforcement Officer?
For the purposes of Form 4, "the chief law enforcement officer is considered to be the Chief of Police for the transferee's city or town of residence, the Sheriff for the transferee's county of residence; the Head of the State Police for the transferee's State of residence; a State or local district attorney or prosecutor having jurisdiction in the transferee's area of residence; or another person whose certification is acceptable to the Director, Bureau of Alcohol, Tobacco and Firearms." ATF Form 1, *Instructions*.

Photograph and fingerprints only required for individual applicants
In addition, if an individual is purchasing or manufacturing an NFA item, the applicant must submit an appropriate photograph and their fingerprints. Neither fingerprints nor photographs are required if the applicant is not an individual. Conversely, an entity such as a trust or corporation must submit the appropriate documents showing its existence, such as the trust or corporate formation documents.

E. *Why are trusts so popular to own NFA items?*
There are three major reasons trusts are very popular to own NFA items: paperwork, control, and ease of ownership. A trust is a legal entity that can hold property. On the paperwork side, trusts are beneficial because they, as of the time of writing, do not require the signature of the Chief Law Enforcement Officer on Form 1 or

Form 4. In addition, unlike individuals seeking ownership of an NFA item, no fingerprints or photographs are required. The only paperwork required to own an NFA item under a trust is the trust agreement and the appropriate ATF form or forms. *Note:* as of the time of publication, there are currently proposed regulations that may alter the requirement for a Chief Law Enforcement Officer signature for trusts and corporations.

A second major reason for having a trust own an NFA item is that it makes owning and using the NFA item easier if more than one person wishes to use the item. If an individual owns the item, then only the individual can ever "possess" it. On the other hand, if the item is owned by a trust, all trustees, including co-trustees, are able to possess and use the items contained in the trust. Therefore, co-trustees may be added or removed.

Third, unlike other entities such as corporations, LLCs, *etc.*, a trust requires no filings with a government to create, which saves expenses. Further, these expense savings continue because there are no continuing government fees or compliance requirements. Thus, trusts are one of the best ways currently to own an NFA item.

F. *The Tax Stamp*

Once the ATF has an applicant's materials in hand, they will be reviewed and checked by NFA researchers and an examiner. The application will then either be approved or denied. A denial will be accompanied by an explanation of why the application was denied and how to remedy it, if possible. If the application is approved, the examiner will affix a tax stamp on one of the submitted Form 1 or Form 4 and send the newly-stamped Form to the applicant.

This tax stamp on the appropriate form is a person's evidence of compliance with the NFA's requirements and is a very important document. A copy should always be kept with the NFA item. *See below.*

G. *What documents should I have with me when I am in actual possession of my suppressor, short-barreled firearm, or other NFA item?*

If you have an NFA item, always have the proper documentation with you to prove that you legally possess the item. Again, if you are in possession of your suppressor, short-barreled firearm, destructive device, or if you are lucky enough, your machine gun— always have your paperwork showing you are legal, or it may be a long day with law enforcement. To show you are legal, always keep a copy of your ATF Form 4 or Form 1 (whichever is applicable) with the tax stamp affixed for every NFA item in your possession, personal identification, and if the item is held in a trust or corporation, a copy of the trust or articles of incorporation, and the authorization for possession. Care should be given to make sure these documents name the individual so as to show legal ownership, *i.e.,* trust and/or amendments showing the person is a co-trustee or an officer of the corporation.

Practically, individuals should not carry around the original documents as they could be destroyed by wear and tear, rain, or be misplaced, effectively destroying the required evidence of compliance. Photocopies of the stamp and any other pertinent documents are generally enough to satisfy inquisitive law enforcement officials. The more technologically advanced may take pictures on their phone or other mobile device, or even upload them to a cloud database. Keep in mind that if the phone dies or the cloud cannot be reached, and you have no way to access the documents, your proof is gone and you may have a very bad day ahead of you! We recommend keeping photocopies of the ATF form with the tax stamp affixed and appropriate documents to avoid any problems with technology.

H. *Why is the paperwork necessary?*

According to Texas Penal Code § 46.05, explosive weapons, machine guns, short-barreled firearms, and firearm silencers (also referred to as suppressors) are illegal to possess. However, Texas Penal Code § 46.05(c) states that it is a defense to prosecution that possession was pursuant to the National Firearms Act. This defense is what is known as an affirmative defense; a defense which, if proven, defeats or mitigates the legal consequences of otherwise unlawful conduct. In other words, even though you meet the elements of committing a crime (possessing the listed items), the law provides a defense you can prove to defeat the criminal charges (proving possession pursuant to the NFA). In theory, law enforcement officers could arrest individuals, who would then be forced to show up to court to prove this affirmative defense; practically, however, simply showing the proper paperwork to the law enforcement officer is likely sufficient to avoid any further entanglement in the legal system.

APPENDICES

APPENDIX A: SELECTED TEXAS STATUTES

TEXAS PENAL CODE CHAPTER 9:
JUSTIFICATION EXCLUDING CRIMINAL RESPONSIBILITY

Texas Penal Code § 9.02
JUSTIFICATION AS A DEFENSE.
It is a defense to prosecution that the conduct in question is justified under this chapter.

Texas Penal Code § 9.04
THREATS AS JUSTIFIABLE FORCE.
The threat of force is justified when the use of force is justified by this chapter. For purposes of this section, a threat to cause death or serious bodily injury by the production of a weapon or otherwise, as long as the actor's purpose is limited to creating an apprehension that he will use deadly force if necessary, does not constitute the use of deadly force.

Texas Penal Code § 9.22
NECESSITY.
Conduct is justified if:
(1) the actor reasonably believes the conduct is immediately necessary to avoid imminent harm;
(2) the desirability and urgency of avoiding the harm clearly outweigh, according to ordinary standards of reasonableness, the harm sought to be prevented by the law proscribing the conduct; and
(3) a legislative purpose to exclude the justification claimed for the conduct does not otherwise plainly appear.

Texas Penal Code § 9.31

SELF-DEFENSE.

(a) Except as provided in Subsection (b), a person is justified in using force against another when and to the degree the actor reasonably believes the force is immediately necessary to protect the actor against the other's use or attempted use of unlawful force. The actor's belief that the force was immediately necessary as described by this subsection is presumed to be reasonable if the actor:

    (1) knew or had reason to believe that the person against whom the force was used:

        (A) unlawfully and with force entered, or was attempting to enter unlawfully and with force, the actor's occupied habitation, vehicle, or place of business or employment;

        (B) unlawfully and with force removed, or was attempting to remove unlawfully and with force, the actor from the actor's habitation, vehicle, or place of business or employment; or

        (C) was committing or attempting to commit aggravated kidnapping, murder, sexual assault, aggravated sexual assault, robbery, or aggravated robbery;

    (2) did not provoke the person against whom the force was used; and

    (3) was not otherwise engaged in criminal activity, other than a Class C misdemeanor that is a violation of a law or ordinance regulating traffic at the time the force was used.

(b) The use of force against another is not justified:

    (1) in response to verbal provocation alone;

    (2) to resist an arrest or search that the actor knows is being made by a peace officer, or by a person acting in a peace officer's presence and at his direction, even though the arrest or search is unlawful, unless the resistance is justified under Subsection (c);

    (3) if the actor consented to the exact force used or attempted by the other;

(4) if the actor provoked the other's use or attempted use of unlawful force, unless:

    (A) the actor abandons the encounter, or clearly communicates to the other his intent to do so reasonably believing he cannot safely abandon the encounter; and

    (B) the other nevertheless continues or attempts to use unlawful force against the actor; or

(5) if the actor sought an explanation from or discussion with the other person concerning the actor's differences with the other person while the actor was:

    (A) carrying a weapon in violation of Section 46.02; or

    (B) possessing or transporting a weapon in violation of Section 46.05.

(c) The use of force to resist an arrest or search is justified:

    (1) if, before the actor offers any resistance, the peace officer (or person acting at his direction) uses or attempts to use greater force than necessary to make the arrest or search; and

    (2) when and to the degree the actor reasonably believes the force is immediately necessary to protect himself against the peace officer's (or other person's) use or attempted use of greater force than necessary.

(d) The use of deadly force is not justified under this subchapter except as provided in Sections 9.32, 9.33, and 9.34.

(e) A person who has a right to be present at the location where the force is used, who has not provoked the person against whom the force is used, and who is not engaged in criminal activity at the time the force is used is not required to retreat before using force as described by this section.

(f) For purposes of Subsection (a), in determining whether an actor described by Subsection (e) reasonably believed that the use of force was necessary, a finder of fact may not consider whether the actor failed to retreat.

Texas Penal Code § 9.32
DEADLY FORCE IN DEFENSE OF PERSON.
(a) A person is justified in using deadly force against another:
    (1) if the actor would be justified in using force against the other under Section 9.31; and
    (2) when and to the degree the actor reasonably believes the deadly force is immediately necessary:
        (A) to protect the actor against the other's use or attempted use of unlawful deadly force; or
        (B) to prevent the other's imminent commission of aggravated kidnapping, murder, sexual assault, aggravated sexual assault, robbery, or aggravated robbery.
(b) The actor's belief under Subsection (a)(2) that the deadly force was immediately necessary as described by that subdivision is presumed to be reasonable if the actor:
    (1) knew or had reason to believe that the person against whom the deadly force was used:
        (A) unlawfully and with force entered, or was attempting to enter unlawfully and with force, the actor's occupied habitation, vehicle, or place of business or employment;
        (B) unlawfully and with force removed, or was attempting to remove unlawfully and with force, the actor from the actor's habitation, vehicle, or place of business or employment; or
        (C) was committing or attempting to commit an offense described by Subsection (a)(2)(B);
    (2) did not provoke the person against whom the force was used; and
    (3) was not otherwise engaged in criminal activity, other than a Class C misdemeanor that is a violation of a law or ordinance regulating traffic at the time the force was used.
(c) A person who has a right to be present at the location where the deadly force is used, who has not provoked the person against whom the deadly force is used, and who is not engaged in criminal activity at the time the deadly force is used is not

required to retreat before using deadly force as described by this section.

(d) For purposes of Subsection (a)(2), in determining whether an actor described by Subsection (c) reasonably believed that the use of deadly force was necessary, a finder of fact may not consider whether the actor failed to retreat.

Texas Penal Code § 9.33
DEFENSE OF THIRD PERSON.

A person is justified in using force or deadly force against another to protect a third person if:

(1) under the circumstances as the actor reasonably believes them to be, the actor would be justified under Section 9.31 or 9.32 in using force or deadly force to protect himself against the unlawful force or unlawful deadly force he reasonably believes to be threatening the third person he seeks to protect; and

(2) the actor reasonably believes that his intervention is immediately necessary to protect the third person.

Texas Penal Code § 9.34
PROTECTION OF LIFE OR HEALTH.

(a) A person is justified in using force, but not deadly force, against another when and to the degree he reasonably believes the force is immediately necessary to prevent the other from committing suicide or inflicting serious bodily injury to himself.

(b) A person is justified in using both force and deadly force against another when and to the degree he reasonably believes the force or deadly force is immediately necessary to preserve the other's life in an emergency.

Texas Penal Code § 9.41
PROTECTION OF ONE'S OWN PROPERTY.

(a) A person in lawful possession of land or tangible, movable property is justified in using force against another when and to the degree the actor reasonably believes the force is immediately necessary to prevent or terminate the other's trespass on the land or unlawful interference with the property.

(b) A person unlawfully dispossessed of land or tangible, movable property by another is justified in using force against the other when and to the degree the actor reasonably believes the force is immediately necessary to reenter the land or recover the property if the actor uses the force immediately or in fresh pursuit after the dispossession and:
   (1) the actor reasonably believes the other had no claim of right when he dispossessed the actor; or
   (2) the other accomplished the dispossession by using force, threat, or fraud against the actor.

Texas Penal Code § 9.42
DEADLY FORCE TO PROTECT PROPERTY.
A person is justified in using deadly force against another to protect land or tangible, movable property:
(1) if he would be justified in using force against the other under Section 9.41; and
(2) when and to the degree he reasonably believes the deadly force is immediately necessary:
   (A) to prevent the other's imminent commission of arson, burglary, robbery, aggravated robbery, theft during the nighttime, or criminal mischief during the nighttime; or
   (B) to prevent the other who is fleeing immediately after committing burglary, robbery, aggravated robbery, or theft during the nighttime from escaping with the property; and
(3) he reasonably believes that:
   (A) the land or property cannot be protected or recovered by any other means; or
   (B) the use of force other than deadly force to protect or recover the land or property would expose the actor or another to a substantial risk of death or serious bodily injury.

Texas Penal Code § 9.43
PROTECTION OF THIRD PERSON'S PROPERTY.

A person is justified in using force or deadly force against another to protect land or tangible, movable property of a third person if, under the circumstances as he reasonably believes them to be, the actor would be justified under Section 9.41 or 9.42 in using force or deadly force to protect his own land or property and:

(1) the actor reasonably believes the unlawful interference constitutes attempted or consummated theft of or criminal mischief to the tangible, movable property; or

(2) the actor reasonably believes that:

(A) the third person has requested his protection of the land or property;

(B) he has a legal duty to protect the third person's land or property; or

(C) the third person whose land or property he uses force or deadly force to protect is the actor's spouse, parent, or child, resides with the actor, or is under the actor's care.

Texas Penal Code § 9.44
USE OF DEVICE TO PROTECT PROPERTY.

The justification afforded by Sections 9.41 and 9.43 applies to the use of a device to protect land or tangible, movable property if:

(1) the device is not designed to cause, or known by the actor to create a substantial risk of causing, death or serious bodily injury; and

(2) use of the device is reasonable under all the circumstances as the actor reasonably believes them to be when he installs the device.

Texas Penal Code § 9.51
ARREST AND SEARCH.

(a) A peace officer, or a person acting in a peace officer's presence and at his direction, is justified in using force against another when and to the degree the actor reasonably believes the force is immediately necessary to make or assist in making an arrest or search, or to prevent or assist in preventing escape after arrest, if:

(1) the actor reasonably believes the arrest or search is lawful or, if the arrest or search is made under a warrant, he reasonably believes the warrant is valid; and

(2) before using force, the actor manifests his purpose to arrest or search and identifies himself as a peace officer or as one acting at a peace officer's direction, unless he reasonably believes his purpose and identity are already known by or cannot reasonably be made known to the person to be arrested.

(b) A person other than a peace officer (or one acting at his direction) is justified in using force against another when and to the degree the actor reasonably believes the force is immediately necessary to make or assist in making a lawful arrest, or to prevent or assist in preventing escape after lawful arrest if, before using force, the actor manifests his purpose to and the reason for the arrest or reasonably believes his purpose and the reason are already known by or cannot reasonably be made known to the person to be arrested.

(c) A peace officer is justified in using deadly force against another when and to the degree the peace officer reasonably believes the deadly force is immediately necessary to make an arrest, or to prevent escape after arrest, if the use of force would have been justified under Subsection (a) and:

(1) the actor reasonably believes the conduct for which arrest is authorized included the use or attempted use of deadly force; or

(2) the actor reasonably believes there is a substantial risk that the person to be arrested will cause death or serious bodily injury to the actor or another if the arrest is delayed.

(d) A person other than a peace officer acting in a peace officer's presence and at his direction is justified in using deadly force against another when and to the degree the person reasonably believes the deadly force is immediately necessary to make a lawful arrest, or to prevent escape after a lawful arrest, if the use of force would have been justified under Subsection (b) and:

(1) the actor reasonably believes the felony or offense against the public peace for which arrest is authorized included the use or attempted use of deadly force; or

(2) the actor reasonably believes there is a substantial risk that the person to be arrested will cause death or serious bodily injury to another if the arrest is delayed.

(e) There is no duty to retreat before using deadly force justified by Subsection (c) or (d).

(f) Nothing in this section relating to the actor's manifestation of purpose or identity shall be construed as conflicting with any other law relating to the issuance, service, and execution of an arrest or search warrant either under the laws of this state or the United States.

(g) Deadly force may only be used under the circumstances enumerated in Subsections (c) and (d).

TEXAS PENAL CODE CHAPTER 30:
BURGLARY AND CRIMINAL TRESPASS

Texas Penal Code § 30.05
CRIMINAL TRESPASS.

(a) A person commits an offense if the person enters or remains on or in property of another, including residential land, agricultural land, a recreational vehicle park, a building, or an aircraft or other vehicle, without effective consent and the person:

(1) had notice that the entry was forbidden; or

(2) received notice to depart but failed to do so.

(b) For purposes of this section:

(1) "Entry" means the intrusion of the entire body.

(2) "Notice" means:

(A) oral or written communication by the owner or someone with apparent authority to act for the owner;

(B) fencing or other enclosure obviously designed to exclude intruders or to contain livestock;

(C) a sign or signs posted on the property or at the entrance to the building, reasonably likely to come to the attention of intruders, indicating that entry is forbidden;

(D) the placement of identifying purple paint marks on trees or posts on the property, provided that the marks are:

(i) vertical lines of not less than eight inches in length and not less than one inch in width;

(ii) placed so that the bottom of the mark is not less than three feet from the ground or more than five feet from the ground; and

(iii) placed at locations that are readily visible to any person approaching the property and no more than:

(a) 100 feet apart on forest land; or

(b) 1,000 feet apart on land other than forest land; or

(E) the visible presence on the property of a crop grown for human consumption that is under cultivation, in the process of being harvested, or marketable if harvested at the time of entry.

(3) "Shelter center" has the meaning assigned by Section 51.002, Human Resources Code.

(4) "Forest land" means land on which the trees are potentially valuable for timber products.

(5) "Agricultural land" has the meaning assigned by Section 75.001, Civil Practice and Remedies Code.

(6) "Superfund site" means a facility that:

(A) is.on the National Priorities List established under Section 105 of the federal Comprehensive Environmental Response, Compensation, and Liability Act of 1980 (42 U.S.C. Section 9605); or

(B) is listed on the state registry established under Section 361.181, Health and Safety Code.

(7) "Critical infrastructure facility" means one of the following, if completely enclosed by a fence or other physical barrier that is obviously designed to exclude intruders:

(A) a chemical manufacturing facility;

(B) a refinery;

(C) an electrical power generating facility, substation, switching station, electrical control center, or electrical transmission or distribution facility;

(D) a water intake structure, water treatment facility, wastewater treatment plant, or pump station;

(E) a natural gas transmission compressor station;

(F) a liquid natural gas terminal or storage facility;

(G) a telecommunications central switching office;

(H) a port, railroad switching yard, trucking terminal, or other freight transportation facility;

(I) a gas processing plant, including a plant used in the processing, treatment, or fractionation of natural gas; or

(J) a transmission facility used by a federally licensed radio or television station.

(8) "Protected freshwater area" has the meaning assigned by Section 90.001, Parks and Wildlife Code.

(9) "Recognized state" means another state with which the attorney general of this state, with the approval of the governor of this state, negotiated an agreement after determining that the other state:

    (A) has firearm proficiency requirements for peace officers; and

    (B) fully recognizes the right of peace officers commissioned in this state to carry weapons in the other state.

(10) "Recreational vehicle park" has the meaning assigned by Section 13.087, Water Code.

(11) "Residential land" means real property improved by a dwelling and zoned for or otherwise authorized for single-family or multifamily use.

(c) Repealed by Acts 2009, 81st Leg., R.S., Ch. 1138, Sec. 4, eff. September 1, 2009.

(d) An offense under this section is:

    (1) a Class B misdemeanor, except as provided by Subdivisions (2) and (3);

    (2) a Class C misdemeanor, except as provided by Subdivision (3), if the offense is committed:

        (A) on agricultural land and within 100 feet of the boundary of the land; or

        (B) on residential land and within 100 feet of a protected freshwater area; and

    (3) a Class A misdemeanor if:

        (A) the offense is committed:

            (i) in a habitation or a shelter center;

            (ii) on a Superfund site; or

            (iii) on or in a critical infrastructure facility; or

        (B) the person carries a deadly weapon during the commission of the offense.

(e) It is a defense to prosecution under this section that the actor at the time of the offense was:

(1) a firefighter or emergency medical services personnel, as defined by Section 773.003, Health and Safety Code, acting in the lawful discharge of an official duty under exigent circumstances;

(2) a person who was:

(A) an employee or agent of:

(i) an electric utility, as defined by Section 31.002, Utilities Code;

(ii) a telecommunications provider, as defined by Section 51.002, Utilities Code;

(iii) a video service provider or cable service provider, as defined by Section 66.002, Utilities Code;

(iv) a gas utility, as defined by Section 101.003, Utilities Code, which for the purposes of this subsection includes a municipally owned utility as defined by that section;

(v) a gas utility, as defined by Section 121.001, Utilities Code;

(vi) a pipeline used for the transportation or sale of oil, gas, or related products; or

(vii) an electric cooperative or municipally owned utility, as defined by Section 11.003, Utilities Code; and

(B) performing a duty within the scope of that employment or agency; or

(3) a person who was:

(A) employed by or acting as agent for an entity that had, or that the person reasonably believed had, effective consent or authorization provided by law to enter the property; and

(B) performing a duty within the scope of that employment or agency.

(f) It is a defense to prosecution under this section that:

(1) the basis on which entry on the property or land or in the building was forbidden is that entry with a handgun was forbidden; and

(2) the person was carrying a concealed handgun and a license issued under Subchapter H, Chapter 411, Government Code, to carry a concealed handgun.

(g) It is a defense to prosecution under this section that the actor entered a railroad switching yard or any part of a railroad switching yard and was at that time an employee or a representative of employees exercising a right under the Railway Labor Act (45 U.S.C. Section 151 et seq.).

(h) At the punishment stage of a trial in which the attorney representing the state seeks the increase in punishment provided by Subsection (d)(3)(A)(iii), the defendant may raise the issue as to whether the defendant entered or remained on or in a critical infrastructure facility as part of a peaceful or lawful assembly, including an attempt to exercise rights guaranteed by state or federal labor laws. If the defendant proves the issue in the affirmative by a preponderance of the evidence, the increase in punishment provided by Subsection (d)(3)(A)(iii) does not apply.

(i) This section does not apply if:

(1) the basis on which entry on the property or land or in the building was forbidden is that entry with a handgun or other weapon was forbidden; and

(2) the actor at the time of the offense was a peace officer, including a commissioned peace officer of a recognized state, or a special investigator under Article 2.122, Code of Criminal Procedure, regardless of whether the peace officer or special investigator was engaged in the actual discharge of an official duty while carrying the weapon.

Texas Penal Code § 30.06
TRESPASS BY HOLDER OF LICENSE TO CARRY CONCEALED HANDGUN.
(a) A license holder commits an offense if the license holder:
  (1) carries a handgun under the authority of Subchapter H, Chapter 411, Government Code, on property of another without effective consent; and
  (2) received notice that:
    (A) entry on the property by a license holder with a concealed handgun was forbidden; or
    (B) remaining on the property with a concealed handgun was forbidden and failed to depart.
(b) For purposes of this section, a person receives notice if the owner of the property or someone with apparent authority to act for the owner provides notice to the person by oral or written communication.
(c) In this section:
  (1) "Entry" has the meaning assigned by Section 30.05(b).
  (2) "License holder" has the meaning assigned by Section 46.035(f).
  (3) "Written communication" means:
    (A) a card or other document on which is written language identical to the following: "Pursuant to Section 30.06, Penal Code (trespass by holder of license to carry a concealed handgun), a person licensed under Subchapter H, Chapter 411, Government Code (concealed handgun law), may not enter this property with a concealed handgun"; or
    (B) a sign posted on the property that:
      (i) includes the language described by Paragraph (A) in both English and Spanish;
      (ii) appears in contrasting colors with block letters at least one inch in height; and
      (iii) is displayed in a conspicuous manner clearly visible to the public.
(d) An offense under this section is a Class A misdemeanor.

(e) It is an exception to the application of this section that the property on which the license holder carries a handgun is owned or leased by a governmental entity and is not a premises or other place on which the license holder is prohibited from carrying the handgun under Section 46.03 or 46.035.

TEXAS PENAL CODE CHAPTER 46:
WEAPONS

Texas Penal Code § 46.01

DEFINITIONS. In this chapter:

(1) "Club" means an instrument that is specially designed, made, or adapted for the purpose of inflicting serious bodily injury or death by striking a person with the instrument, and includes but is not limited to the following:
(A) blackjack;
(B) nightstick;
(C) mace;
(D) tomahawk.

(2) "Explosive weapon" means any explosive or incendiary bomb, grenade, rocket, or mine, that is designed, made, or adapted for the purpose of inflicting serious bodily injury, death, or substantial property damage, or for the principal purpose of causing such a loud report as to cause undue public alarm or terror, and includes a device designed, made, or adapted for delivery or shooting an explosive weapon.

(3) "Firearm" means any device designed, made, or adapted to expel a projectile through a barrel by using the energy generated by an explosion or burning substance or any device readily convertible to that use. Firearm does not include a firearm that may have, as an integral part, a folding knife blade or other characteristics of weapons made illegal by this chapter and that is:
(A) an antique or curio firearm manufactured before 1899; or
(B) a replica of an antique or curio firearm manufactured before 1899, but only if the replica does not use rim fire or center fire ammunition.

(4) "Firearm silencer" means any device designed, made, or adapted to muffle the report of a firearm.

(5) "Handgun" means any firearm that is designed, made, or adapted to be fired with one hand.

(6) "Illegal knife" means a:

    (A) knife with a blade over five and one-half inches;

    (B) hand instrument designed to cut or stab another by being thrown;

    (C) dagger, including but not limited to a dirk, stiletto, and poniard;

    (D) bowie knife;

    (E) sword; or

    (F) spear.

(7) "Knife" means any bladed hand instrument that is capable of inflicting serious bodily injury or death by cutting or stabbing a person with the instrument.

(8) "Knuckles" means any instrument that consists of finger rings or guards made of a hard substance and that is designed, made, or adapted for the purpose of inflicting serious bodily injury or death by striking a person with a fist enclosed in the knuckles.

(9) "Machine gun" means any firearm that is capable of shooting more than two shots automatically, without manual reloading, by a single function of the trigger.

(10) "Short-barrel firearm" means a rifle with a barrel length of less than 16 inches or a shotgun with a barrel length of less than 18 inches, or any weapon made from a shotgun or rifle if, as altered, it has an overall length of less than 26 inches.

(11) "Switchblade knife" means any knife that has a blade that folds, closes, or retracts into the handle or sheath and that opens automatically by pressure applied to a button or other device located on the handle or opens or releases a blade from the handle or sheath by the force of gravity or by the application of centrifugal force. The term does not include a knife that has a spring, detent, or other mechanism designed to create a bias toward closure and that requires exertion applied to the blade by hand, wrist, or arm to overcome the bias toward closure and open the knife.

(12) "Armor-piercing ammunition" means handgun ammunition that is designed primarily for the purpose of penetrating metal or body armor and to be used principally in pistols and revolvers.

(13) "Hoax bomb" means a device that:
   (A) reasonably appears to be an explosive or incendiary device; or
   (B) by its design causes alarm or reaction of any type by an official of a public safety agency or a volunteer agency organized to deal with emergencies.
(14) "Chemical dispensing device" means a device, other than a small chemical dispenser sold commercially for personal protection, that is designed, made, or adapted for the purpose of dispensing a substance capable of causing an adverse psychological or physiological effect on a human being.
(15) "Racetrack" has the meaning assigned that term by the Texas Racing Act (Article 179e, Vernon's Texas Civil Statutes).
(16) "Zip gun" means a device or combination of devices that was not originally a firearm and is adapted to expel a projectile through a smooth-bore or rifled-bore barrel by using the energy generated by an explosion or burning substance.
(17) "Tire deflation device" means a device, including a caltrop or spike strip, that, when driven over, impedes or stops the movement of a wheeled vehicle by puncturing one or more of the vehicle's tires. The term does not include a traffic control device that:
   (A) is designed to puncture one or more of a vehicle's tires when driven over in a specific direction; and
   (B) has a clearly visible sign posted in close proximity to the traffic control device that prohibits entry or warns motor vehicle operators of the traffic control device.

Texas Penal Code § 46.02
UNLAWFUL CARRYING WEAPONS.
(a) A person commits an offense if the person intentionally, knowingly, or recklessly carries on or about his or her person a handgun, illegal knife, or club if the person is not:
   (1) on the person's own premises or premises under the person's control; or

(2) inside of or directly en route to a motor vehicle or watercraft that is owned by the person or under the person's control.

(a-1) A person commits an offense if the person intentionally, knowingly, or recklessly carries on or about his or her person a handgun in a motor vehicle or watercraft that is owned by the person or under the person's control at any time in which:

(1) the handgun is in plain view; or

(2) the person is:

    (A) engaged in criminal activity, other than a Class C misdemeanor that is a violation of a law or ordinance regulating traffic or boating;

    (B) prohibited by law from possessing a firearm; or

    (C) a member of a criminal street gang, as defined by Section 71.01.

(a-2) For purposes of this section, "premises" includes real property and a recreational vehicle that is being used as living quarters, regardless of whether that use is temporary or permanent. In this subsection, "recreational vehicle" means a motor vehicle primarily designed as temporary living quarters or a vehicle that contains temporary living quarters and is designed to be towed by a motor vehicle. The term includes a travel trailer, camping trailer, truck camper, motor home, and horse trailer with living quarters.

(a-3) For purposes of this section, "watercraft" means any boat, motorboat, vessel, or personal watercraft, other than a seaplane on water, used or capable of being used for transportation on water.

(b) Except as provided by Subsection (c), an offense under this section is a Class A misdemeanor.

(c) An offense under this section is a felony of the third degree if the offense is committed on any premises licensed or issued a permit by this state for the sale of alcoholic beverages.

Texas Penal Code § 46.03

PLACES WEAPONS PROHIBITED.

(a) A person commits an offense if the person intentionally, knowingly, or recklessly possesses or goes with a firearm, illegal knife, club, or prohibited weapon listed in Section 46.05(a):

(1) on the physical premises of a school or educational institution, any grounds or building on which an activity sponsored by a school or educational institution is being conducted, or a passenger transportation vehicle of a school or educational institution, whether the school or educational institution is public or private, unless pursuant to written regulations or written authorization of the institution;

(2) on the premises of a polling place on the day of an election or while early voting is in progress;

(3) on the premises of any government court or offices utilized by the court, unless pursuant to written regulations or written authorization of the court;

(4) on the premises of a racetrack;

(5) in or into a secured area of an airport; or

(6) within 1,000 feet of premises the location of which is designated by the Texas Department of Criminal Justice as a place of execution under Article 43.19, Code of Criminal Procedure, on a day that a sentence of death is set to be imposed on the designated premises and the person received notice that:

(A) going within 1,000 feet of the premises with a weapon listed under this subsection was prohibited; or

(B) possessing a weapon listed under this subsection within 1,000 feet of the premises was prohibited.

(b) It is a defense to prosecution under Subsections (a)(1)-(4) that the actor possessed a firearm while in the actual discharge of his official duties as a member of the armed forces or national guard or a guard employed by a penal institution, or an officer of the court.

(c) In this section:

(1) "Premises" has the meaning assigned by Section 46.035.

(2) "Secured area" means an area of an airport terminal building to which access is controlled by the inspection of persons and property under federal law.

(d) It is a defense to prosecution under Subsection (a)(5) that the actor possessed a firearm or club while traveling to or from the actor's place of assignment or in the actual discharge of duties as:

(1) a member of the armed forces or national guard;

(2) a guard employed by a penal institution; or

(3) a security officer commissioned by the Texas Private Security Board if:

(A) the actor is wearing a distinctive uniform; and

(B) the firearm or club is in plain view; or

(4) a security officer who holds a personal protection authorization under Chapter 1702, Occupations Code, provided that the officer is either:

(A) wearing the uniform of a security officer, including any uniform or apparel described by Section 1702.323(d), Occupations Code, and carrying the officer's firearm in plain view; or

(B) not wearing the uniform of a security officer and carrying the officer's firearm in a concealed manner.

(e) It is a defense to prosecution under Subsection (a)(5) that the actor checked all firearms as baggage in accordance with federal or state law or regulations before entering a secured area.

(f) It is not a defense to prosecution under this section that the actor possessed a handgun and was licensed to carry a concealed handgun under Subchapter H, Chapter 411, Government Code.

(g) An offense under this section is a third degree felony.

(h) It is a defense to prosecution under Subsection (a)(4) that the actor possessed a firearm or club while traveling to or from the actor's place of assignment or in the actual discharge of duties as a security officer commissioned by the Texas Board of Private Investigators and Private Security Agencies, if:

    (1) the actor is wearing a distinctive uniform; and
    (2) the firearm or club is in plain view.

(i) It is an exception to the application of Subsection (a)(6) that the actor possessed a firearm or club:
    (1) while in a vehicle being driven on a public road; or
    (2) at the actor's residence or place of employment.

Texas Penal Code § 46.035
UNLAWFUL CARRYING OF HANDGUN BY LICENSE HOLDER.

(a) A license holder commits an offense if the license holder carries a handgun on or about the license holder's person under the authority of Subchapter H, Chapter 411, Government Code, and intentionally displays the handgun in plain view of another person in a public place.

(b) A license holder commits an offense if the license holder intentionally, knowingly, or recklessly carries a handgun under the authority of Subchapter H, Chapter 411, Government Code, regardless of whether the handgun is concealed, on or about the license holder's person:
    (1) on the premises of a business that has a permit or license issued under Chapter 25, 28, 32, 69, or 74, Alcoholic Beverage Code, if the business derives 51 percent or more of its income from the sale or service of alcoholic beverages for on-premises consumption, as determined by the Texas Alcoholic Beverage Commission under Section 104.06, Alcoholic Beverage Code;
    (2) on the premises where a high school, collegiate, or professional sporting event or interscholastic event is taking place, unless the license holder is a participant in the event and a handgun is used in the event;
    (3) on the premises of a correctional facility;
    (4) on the premises of a hospital licensed under Chapter 241, Health and Safety Code, or on the premises of a nursing home licensed under Chapter 242, Health and Safety Code, unless the license holder has written authorization of the hospital or nursing home administration, as appropriate;
    (5) in an amusement park; or

(6) on the premises of a church, synagogue, or other established place of religious worship.

(c) A license holder commits an offense if the license holder intentionally, knowingly, or recklessly carries a handgun under the authority of Subchapter H, Chapter 411, Government Code, regardless of whether the handgun is concealed, at any meeting of a governmental entity.

(d) A license holder commits an offense if, while intoxicated, the license holder carries a handgun under the authority of Subchapter H, Chapter 411, Government Code, regardless of whether the handgun is concealed.

(e) A license holder who is licensed as a security officer under Chapter 1702, Occupations Code, and employed as a security officer commits an offense if, while in the course and scope of the security officer's employment, the security officer violates a provision of Subchapter H, Chapter 411, Government Code.

(f) In this section:

(1) "Amusement park" means a permanent indoor or outdoor facility or park where amusement rides are available for use by the public that is located in a county with a population of more than one million, encompasses at least 75 acres in surface area, is enclosed with access only through controlled entries, is open for operation more than 120 days in each calendar year, and has security guards on the premises at all times. The term does not include any public or private driveway, street, sidewalk or walkway, parking lot, parking garage, or other parking area.

(2) "License holder" means a person licensed to carry a handgun under Subchapter H, Chapter 411, Government Code.

(3) "Premises" means a building or a portion of a building. The term does not include any public or private driveway, street, sidewalk or walkway, parking lot, parking garage, or other parking area.

(g) An offense under Subsection (a), (b), (c), (d), or (e) is a Class A misdemeanor, unless the offense is committed under

Subsection (b)(1) or (b)(3), in which event the offense is a felony of the third degree.

(h) It is a defense to prosecution under Subsection (a) that the actor, at the time of the commission of the offense, displayed the handgun under circumstances in which the actor would have been justified in the use of force or deadly force under Chapter 9.

Text of subsection as added by Acts 2007, 80th Leg., R.S., Ch. 1214 (H.B. 1889), Sec. 2

(h-1) It is a defense to prosecution under Subsections (b) and (c) that the actor, at the time of the commission of the offense, was:

(1) an active judicial officer, as defined by Section 411.201, Government Code; or

(2) a bailiff designated by the active judicial officer and engaged in escorting the officer.

Text of subsection as added by Acts 2007, 80th Leg., R.S., Ch. 1222 (H.B. 2300), Sec. 5

(h-1) It is a defense to prosecution under Subsections (b)(1), (2), and (4)-(6), and (c) that at the time of the commission of the offense, the actor was:

(1) a judge or justice of a federal court;

(2) an active judicial officer, as defined by Section 411.201, Government Code; or

(3) a district attorney, assistant district attorney, criminal district attorney, assistant criminal district attorney, county attorney, or assistant county attorney.

(i) Subsections (b)(4), (b)(5), (b)(6), and (c) do not apply if the actor was not given effective notice under Section 30.06.

(j) Subsections (a) and (b)(1) do not apply to a historical reenactment performed in compliance with the rules of the Texas Alcoholic Beverage Commission.

(k) It is a defense to prosecution under Subsection (b)(1) that the actor was not given effective notice under Section 411.204, Government Code.

Texas Penal Code § 46.04

UNLAWFUL POSSESSION OF FIREARM.

(a) A person who has been convicted of a felony commits an offense if he possesses a firearm:

    (1) after conviction and before the fifth anniversary of the person's release from confinement following conviction of the felony or the person's release from supervision under community supervision, parole, or mandatory supervision, whichever date is later; or

    (2) after the period described by Subdivision (1), at any location other than the premises at which the person lives.

(b) A person who has been convicted of an offense under Section 22.01, punishable as a Class A misdemeanor and involving a member of the person's family or household, commits an offense if the person possesses a firearm before the fifth anniversary of the later of:

    (1) the date of the person's release from confinement following conviction of the misdemeanor; or

    (2) the date of the person's release from community supervision following conviction of the misdemeanor.

(c) A person, other than a peace officer, as defined by Section 1.07, actively engaged in employment as a sworn, full-time paid employee of a state agency or political subdivision, who is subject to an order issued under Section 6.504 or Chapter 85, Family Code, under Article 17.292 or Chapter 7A, Code of Criminal Procedure, or by another jurisdiction as provided by Chapter 88, Family Code, commits an offense if the person possesses a firearm after receiving notice of the order and before expiration of the order.

(d) In this section, "family," "household," and "member of a household" have the meanings assigned by Chapter 71, Family Code.

(e) An offense under Subsection (a) is a felony of the third degree. An offense under Subsection (b) or (c) is a Class A misdemeanor.

(f) For the purposes of this section, an offense under the laws of this state, another state, or the United States is, except as provided by Subsection (g), a felony if, at the time it is committed, the offense:

(1) is designated by a law of this state as a felony;

(2) contains all the elements of an offense designated by a law of this state as a felony; or

(3) is punishable by confinement for one year or more in a penitentiary.

(g) An offense is not considered a felony for purposes of Subsection (f) if, at the time the person possesses a firearm, the offense:

(1) is not designated by a law of this state as a felony; and

(2) does not contain all the elements of any offense designated by a law of this state as a felony.

Texas Penal Code § 46.05
PROHIBITED WEAPONS.

(a) A person commits an offense if the person intentionally or knowingly possesses, manufactures, transports, repairs, or sells:

(1) an explosive weapon;

(2) a machine gun;

(3) a short-barrel firearm;

(4) a firearm silencer;

(5) knuckles;

(6) armor-piercing ammunition;

(7) a chemical dispensing device;

(8) a zip gun; or

(9) a tire deflation device.

(b) It is a defense to prosecution under this section that the actor's conduct was incidental to the performance of official duty by the armed forces or national guard, a governmental law enforcement agency, or a correctional facility.

(c) It is a defense to prosecution under this section that the actor's possession was pursuant to registration pursuant to the National Firearms Act, as amended.

(d) It is an affirmative defense to prosecution under this section that the actor's conduct:

    (1) was incidental to dealing with a short-barrel firearm or tire deflation device solely as an antique or curio;

    (2) was incidental to dealing with armor-piercing ammunition solely for the purpose of making the ammunition available to an organization, agency, or institution listed in Subsection (b); or

    (3) was incidental to dealing with a tire deflation device solely for the purpose of making the device available to an organization, agency, or institution listed in Subsection (b).

(e) An offense under Subsection (a)(1), (2), (3), (4), (6), (7), or (8) is a felony of the third degree. An offense under Subsection (a)(9) is a state jail felony. An offense under Subsection (a)(5) is a Class A misdemeanor.

(f) It is a defense to prosecution under this section for the possession of a chemical dispensing device that the actor is a security officer and has received training on the use of the chemical dispensing device by a training program that is:

    (1) provided by the Texas Commission on Law Enforcement; or

    (2) approved for the purposes described by this subsection by the Texas Private Security Board of the Department of Public Safety.

(g) In Subsection (f), "security officer" means a commissioned security officer as defined by Section 1702.002, Occupations Code, or a noncommissioned security officer registered under Section 1702.221, Occupations Code.

Texas Penal Code § 46.06

UNLAWFUL TRANSFER OF CERTAIN WEAPONS.

(a) A person commits an offense if the person:

    (1) sells, rents, leases, loans, or gives a handgun to any person knowing that the person to whom the handgun is to be delivered intends to use it unlawfully or in the commission of an unlawful act;

    (2) intentionally or knowingly sells, rents, leases, or gives or offers to sell, rent, lease, or give to any child younger than 18 years any firearm, club, or illegal knife;

    (3) intentionally, knowingly, or recklessly sells a firearm or ammunition for a firearm to any person who is intoxicated;

    (4) knowingly sells a firearm or ammunition for a firearm to any person who has been convicted of a felony before the fifth anniversary of the later of the following dates:

        (A) the person's release from confinement following conviction of the felony; or

        (B) the person's release from supervision under community supervision, parole, or mandatory supervision following conviction of the felony;

    (5) sells, rents, leases, loans, or gives a handgun to any person knowing that an active protective order is directed to the person to whom the handgun is to be delivered; or

    (6) knowingly purchases, rents, leases, or receives as a loan or gift from another a handgun while an active protective order is directed to the actor.

(b) In this section:

    (1) "Intoxicated" means substantial impairment of mental or physical capacity resulting from introduction of any substance into the body.

    (2) "Active protective order" means a protective order issued under Title 4, Family Code, that is in effect. The term does not include a temporary protective order issued before the court holds a hearing on the matter.

(c) It is an affirmative defense to prosecution under Subsection (a)(2) that the transfer was to a minor whose parent or the person having legal custody of the minor had given written permission for the sale or, if the transfer was other than a sale, the parent or person having legal custody had given effective consent.

(d) An offense under this section is a Class A misdemeanor, except that an offense under Subsection (a)(2) is a state jail felony if the weapon that is the subject of the offense is a handgun.

Texas Penal Code § 46.11

PENALTY IF OFFENSE COMMITTED WITHIN WEAPON-FREE SCHOOL ZONE.

(a) Except as provided by Subsection (b), the punishment prescribed for an offense under this chapter is increased to the punishment prescribed for the next highest category of offense if it is shown beyond a reasonable doubt on the trial of the offense that the actor committed the offense in a place that the actor knew was:

    (1) within 300 feet of the premises of a school; or

    (2) on premises where:

        (A) an official school function is taking place; or

        (B) an event sponsored or sanctioned by the University Interscholastic League is taking place.

(b) This section does not apply to an offense under Section 46.03(a)(1).

(c) In this section:

    (1) "Premises" has the meaning assigned by Section 481.134, Health and Safety Code.

    (2) "School" means a private or public elementary or secondary school.

Texas Penal Code § 46.13

MAKING A FIREARM ACCESSIBLE TO A CHILD.

(a) In this section:

    (1) "Child" means a person younger than 17 years of age.

    (2) "Readily dischargeable firearm" means a firearm that is loaded with ammunition, whether or not a round is in the chamber.

    (3) "Secure" means to take steps that a reasonable person would take to prevent the access to a readily dischargeable firearm by a child, including but not limited to placing a firearm in a locked container or temporarily rendering the firearm inoperable by a trigger lock or other means.

(b) A person commits an offense if a child gains access to a readily dischargeable firearm and the person with criminal negligence:

(1) failed to secure the firearm; or

(2) left the firearm in a place to which the person knew or should have known the child would gain access.

(c) It is an affirmative defense to prosecution under this section that the child's access to the firearm:

(1) was supervised by a person older than 18 years of age and was for hunting, sporting, or other lawful purposes;

(2) consisted of lawful defense by the child of people or property;

(3) was gained by entering property in violation of this code; or

(4) occurred during a time when the actor was engaged in an agricultural enterprise.

(d) Except as provided by Subsection (e), an offense under this section is a Class C misdemeanor.

(e) An offense under this section is a Class A misdemeanor if the child discharges the firearm and causes death or serious bodily injury to himself or another person.

(f) A peace officer or other person may not arrest the actor before the seventh day after the date on which the offense is committed if:

(1) the actor is a member of the family, as defined by Section 71.003, Family Code, of the child who discharged the firearm; and

(2) the child in discharging the firearm caused the death of or serious injury to the child.

(g) A dealer of firearms shall post in a conspicuous position on the premises where the dealer conducts business a sign that contains the following warning in block letters not less than one inch in height:

"IT IS UNLAWFUL TO STORE, TRANSPORT, OR ABANDON AN UNSECURED FIREARM IN A PLACE WHERE CHILDREN ARE LIKELY TO BE AND CAN OBTAIN ACCESS TO THE FIREARM."

APPENDIX B: SELECTED FEDERAL FORMS

ATF Form 4473 *Page 1*

OMB No. 1140-0020

U.S. Department of Justice
Bureau of Alcohol, Tobacco, Firearms and Explosives

**Firearms Transaction Record Part I -
Over-the-Counter**

WARNING: You may not receive a firearm if prohibited by Federal or State law. The information you provide will be used to determine whether you are prohibited under law from receiving a firearm. Certain violations of the Gun Control Act, 18 U.S.C. §§ 921 et. seq., are punishable by up to 10 years imprisonment and/or up to a $250,000 fine.

Transferor's Transaction Serial Number (If any)

Prepare in original only. All entries must be handwritten in ink. Read the Notices, Instructions, and Definitions on this form. "PLEASE PRINT."

Section A - Must Be Completed Personally By Transferee (Buyer)

1. Transferee's Full Name

Last Name	First Name	Middle Name (If no middle name, state "NMN")

2. Current Residence Address (U.S. Postal abbreviations are acceptable. Cannot be a post office box.)

Number and Street Address	City	County	State	IP Code

3. Place of Birth
U.S. City and State -OR- Foreign Country

4. Height
Ft. ____
In. ____

5. Weight (Lbs.)

6. Gender
☐ Male
☐ Female

7. Birth Date
Month Day Year

8. Social Security Number (Optional, but will help prevent misidentification)

9. Unique Personal Identification Number (UPIN) if applicable (See Instructions for Question 9.)

10.a. Ethnicity
☐ Hispanic or Latino
☐ Not Hispanic or Latino

10.b. Race (Check one or more boxes.)
☐ American Indian or Alaska Native
☐ Asian
☐ Black or African American
☐ Native Hawaiian or Other Pacific Islander
☐ White

11. Answer questions 11.a. (see exceptions) through 11.l. and 12 (if applicable) by checking or marking "yes" or "no" in the boxes to the right of the questions.

		Yes	No
a.	Are you the actual transferee/buyer of the firearm(s) listed on this form Warning: You are not the actual buyer if you are acquiring the firearm(s) on behalf of another person. If you are not the actual buyer, the dealer cannot transfer the firearm(s) to you. (See Instructions for Question 11.a.) Exception: If you are picking up a repaired firearm(s) for another person, you are not required to answer 11.a. and may proceed to question 11.b.	☐	☐
b.	Are you under indictment or information in any court for a felony, or any other crime, for which the judge could imprison you for more than one year (See Instructions for Question 11.b.)	☐	☐
c.	Have you ever been convicted in any court of a felony, or any other crime, for which the judge could have imprisoned you for more than one year, even if you received a shorter sentence including probation (See Instructions for Question 11.c.)	☐	☐
d.	Are you a fugitive from justice	☐	☐
e.	Are you an unlawful user of, or addicted to, marijuana or any depressant, stimulant, narcotic drug, or any other controlled substance	☐	☐
f.	Have you ever been adjudicated mentally defective (which includes a determination by a court, board, commission, or other lawful authority that you are a danger to yourself or to others or are incompetent to manage your own affairs) OR have you ever been committed to a mental institution (See Instructions for Question 11.f.)	☐	☐
g.	Have you been discharged from the Armed Forces under dishonorable conditions	☐	☐
h.	Are you subject to a court order restraining you from harassing, stalking, or threatening your child or an intimate partner or child of such partner (See Instructions for Question 11.h.)	☐	☐
i.	Have you ever been convicted in any court of a misdemeanor crime of domestic violence (See Instructions for Question 11.i.)	☐	☐
j.	Have you ever renounced your United States citizenship	☐	☐
k.	Are you an alien illegally in the United States	☐	☐
l.	Are you an alien admitted to the United States under a nonimmigrant visa (See Instructions for Question 11.l.) If you answered "no" to this question, do NOT respond to question 12 and proceed to question 13.	☐	☐
12.	If you are an alien admitted to the United States under a nonimmigrant visa, do you fall within any of the exceptions set forth in the instructions (If "yes," the licensee must complete question 20c.) (See Instructions for Question 12.) If question 11.l. is answered with a "no" response, then do NOT respond to question 12 and proceed to question 13.	☐	☐

13. What is your State of residence (if any) (See Instructions for Question 13.)

14. What is your country of citizenship (List/check more than one, if applicable. If you are a citizen of the United States, proceed to question 16.)
☐ United States of America
☐ Other (Specify) _____

15. If you are not a citizen of the United States, what is your U.S.-issued alien number or admission number

Note: Previous Editions Are Obsolete

Page 1 of 6

Transferee (Buyer) Continue to Next Page
STAPLE IF PAGES BECOME SEPARATED

ATF Form 4473 (5300.9) Part I
Revised April 2012

ATF Form 4473   *Page 2*

I certify that my answers to Section A are true, correct, and complete. I have read and understand the Notices, Instructions, and Definitions on ATF Form 4473. I understand that answering "yes" to question 11.a. if I am not the actual buyer is a crime punishable as a felony under Federal law, and may also violate State and/or local law. I understand that a person who answers "yes" to any of the questions 11.b. through 11.k. is prohibited from purchasing or receiving a firearm. I understand that a person who answers "yes" to question 11.l. is prohibited from purchasing or receiving a firearm, unless the person also answers "Yes" to question 12. I also understand that making any false oral or written statement, or exhibiting any false or misrepresented identification with respect to this transaction, is a crime punishable as a felony under Federal law, and may also violate State and/or local law. I further understand that the repetitive purchase of firearms for the purpose of resale for livelihood and profit without a Federal firearms license is a violation of law (See Instructions for Question 16).

16. Transferee's/Buyer's Signature	17. Certification Date

Section B - Must Be Completed By Transferor (Seller)

18. Type of firearm(s) to be transferred (check or mark all that apply):

☐ Handgun ☐ Long Gun (rifles or shotguns) ☐ Other Firearm (Frame, Receiver, etc. See Instructions for Question 18.)

19. If sale at a gun show or other qualifying event.

Name of Event _____

City, State _____

20a. Identification (e.g., Virginia Driver's license (VA DL) or other valid government-issued photo identification.) (See Instructions for Question 20.a.)

Issuing Authority and Type of Identification	Number on Identification	Expiration Date of Identification (if any)		
		Month	Day	Year

20b. Alternate Documentation (if driver's license or other identification document does not show current residence address) (See Instructions for Question 20.b.)

20c. Aliens Admitted to the United States Under a Nonimmigrant Visa Must Provide: Type of documentation showing an exception to the nonimmigrant visa prohibition. (See Instructions for Question 20.c.)

Questions 21, 22, or 23 Must Be Completed Prior To The Transfer Of The Firearm(s) (See Instructions for Questions 21, 22 and 23.)

21a. Date the transferee's identifying information in Section A was transmitted to NICS or the appropriate State agency: (Month/Day/Year)

Month	Day	Year

21b. The NICS or State transaction number (if provided) was:

21c. The response initially provided by NICS or the appropriate State agency was:

☐ Proceed
☐ Denied
☐ Cancelled

☐ Delayed
The firearm(s) may be transferred on _____ (Missing Disposition Information date provided by NICS) if State law permits (optional)

21d. If initial NICS or State response was "Delayed," the following response was received from NICS or the appropriate State agency:

☐ Proceed _____ (date)
☐ Denied _____ (date)
☐ Cancelled _____ (date)
☐ No resolution was provided within 3 business days.

21e. (Complete if applicable.) After the firearm was transferred, the following response was received from NICS or the appropriate State agency on: _____ (date).   ☐ Proceed   ☐ Denied   ☐ Cancelled

21f. The name and Brady identification number of the NICS examiner (Optional)

_____ (name)   _____ (number)

22. ☐ No NICS check was required because the transfer involved only National Firearms Act firearms(s). (See Instructions for Question 22.)

23. ☐ No NICS check was required because the buyer has a valid permit from the State where the transfer is to take place, which qualifies as an exemption to NICS (See Instructions for Question 23.)

Issuing State and Permit Type	Date of Issuance (if any)	Expiration Date (if any)	Permit Number (if any)

Section C - Must Be Completed Personally By Transferee (Buyer)

If the transfer of the firearm(s) takes place on a different day from the date that the transferee (buyer) signed Section A, the transferee must complete Section C immediately prior to the transfer of the firearm(s). (See Instructions for Question 24 and 25.)

I certify that my answers to the questions in Section A of this form are still true, correct and complete.

24. Transferee's/Buyer's Signature	25. Recertification Date

Transferor (Seller) Continue to Next Page
STAPLE IF PAGES BECOME SEPARATED

ATF Form 4473 (5300.9) Part I
Revised April 2012

ATF Form 4473 *Page 3*

Section D - Must Be Completed By Transferor (Seller)				
26. Manufacturer and/or Importer (If the manufacturer and importer are different, the FFL should include both.)	27. Model	28. Serial Number	29. Type (pistol, revolver, rifle, shotgun, receiver, frame, etc.) (See instructions for question 29)	30. Caliber or Gauge

30a. Total Number of Firearms (Please handwrite by printing e.g., one, two, three, etc. Do not use numerals.)

30b. Is any part of this transaction a Pawn Redemption ☐ Yes ☐ No

30c. For Use by FFL (See Instructions for Question 30c.)

Complete ATF Form 3310.4 For Multiple Purchases of Handguns Within 5 Consecutive Business Days

31. Trade/corporate name and address of transferor (seller) (Hand stamp may be used.)	32. Federal Firearms License Number (Must contain at least first three and last five digits of FFL. Number X-XX-XXXXX.) (Hand stamp may be used.)

The Person Transferring The Firearm(s) Must Complete Questions 33-36. For Denied/Cancelled Transactions, The Person Who Completed Section B Must Complete Questions 33-35.

I certify that my answers in Sections B and D are true, correct, and complete. I have read and understand the Notices, Instructions, and Definitions on ATF Form 4473. On the basis of: (1) the statements in Section A (and Section C if the transfer does not occur on the day Section A was completed); (2) my verification of the identification noted in question 20a (and my reverification at the time of transfer if the transfer does not occur on the day Section A was completed); and (3) the information in the current State Laws and Published Ordinances, it is my belief that it is not unlawful for me to sell, deliver, transport, or otherwise dispose of the firearm(s) listed on this form to the person identified in Section A.

33. Transferor's/Seller's Name (Please print)	34. Transferor's/Seller's Signature	35. Transferor's/Seller's Title	36. Date Transferred

NOTICES, INSTRUCTIONS AND DEFINITIONS

Purpose of the Form: The information and certification on this form are designed so that a person licensed under 18 U.S.C. § 923 may determine if he or she may lawfully sell or deliver a firearm to the person identified in Section A, and to alert the buyer of certain restrictions on the receipt and possession of firearms. This form should only be used for sales or transfers where the seller is licensed under 18 U.S.C. § 923. The seller of a firearm must determine the lawfulness of the transaction and maintain proper records of the transaction. Consequently, the seller must be familiar with the provisions of 18 U.S.C. §§ 921-931 and the regulations in 27 CFR Part 478. In determining the lawfulness of the sale or delivery of a long gun (rifle or shotgun) to a resident of another State, the seller is presumed to know the applicable State laws and published ordinances in both the seller's State and the buyer's State.

After the seller has completed the firearms transaction, he or she must make the completed, original ATF Form 4473 (which includes the Notices, General Instructions, and Definitions), and any supporting documents, part of his or her permanent records. Such Forms 4473 must be retained for at least 20 years. Filing may be chronological (by date), alphabetical (by name), or numerical (by transaction serial number), as long as all of the seller's completed Forms 4473 are filed in the same manner. FORMS 4473 FOR DENIED/CANCELLED TRANSFERS MUST BE RETAINED: If the transfer of a firearm is denied/cancelled by NICS, or if for any other reason the transfer is not complete after a NICS check is initiated, the licensee must retain the ATF Form 4473 in his or her records for at least 5 years. Forms 4473 with respect to which a sale, delivery, or transfer did not take place shall be separately retained in alphabetical (by name) or chronological (by date of transferee's certification) order.

If you or the buyer discover that an ATF Form 4473 is incomplete or improperly completed after the firearm has been transferred, and you or the buyer wish to make a record of your discovery, then photocopy the inaccurate form and make any necessary additions or revisions to the photocopy. You only should make changes to Sections B and D. The buyer should only make changes to Sections A and C. Whoever made the changes should initial and date the changes. The corrected photocopy should be attached to the original Form 4473 and retained as part of your permanent records.

Over-the-Counter Transaction: The sale or other disposition of a firearm by a seller to a buyer, at the seller's licensed premises. This includes the sale or other disposition of a rifle or shotgun to a nonresident buyer on such premises.

State Laws and Published Ordinances: The publication (ATF P 5300.5) of State firearms laws and local ordinances ATF distributes to licensees.

Exportation of Firearms: The State or Commerce Department may require you to obtain a license prior to export.

Section A

Question 1. Transferee's Full Name: The buyer must personally complete Section A of this form and certify (sign) that the answers are true, correct, and complete. However, if the buyer is unable to read and/or write, the answers (other than the signature) may be completed by another person, excluding the seller. Two persons (other than the seller) must then sign as witnesses to the buyer's answers and signature.

When the buyer of a firearm is a corporation, company, association, partnership, or other such business entity, an officer authorized to act on behalf of the

ATF Form 4473 (5300.9) Part I
Revised April 2012

ATF Form 4　　　　　　　　　　　　　　　　　　　　　　　*Page 1*

U.S. Department of Justice
Bureau of Alcohol, Tobacco, Firearms and Explosives

OMB No. 1140-0014 (01/31/2014)

**Application for Tax Paid Transfer and
Registration of Firearm**

ATF Control Number

2a. Transferee's Name and Address *(Including tradename, if any) (See instruction 2)*

Submit in Duplicate to:
National Firearms Act Branch
Bureau of Alcohol, Tobacco, Firearms
and Explosives, P.O. Box 530298
Atlanta, GA 30353-0298

1. Type of Transfer *(Check one)*

☐ $5　　☐ $200

Submit with your application a check or money order for the appropriate amount made payable to the Bureau of Alcohol, Tobacco, Firearms and Explosives. Upon approval of this application, this office will acquire, affix and cancel the required "National Firearms Act" stamp for you. *(See instructions 2h, 2i and 3.)*

2b. County

3a. Transferor's Name and Address *(Including trade name, if any) (Executors: see instruction 2k)*

3b. Transferor's Telephone Number and Area Code

3d. Number, Street, City, State and Zip Code of Residence *(or Firearms Business Premises)* if Different from Item 3a.

3c. If Applicable: Decedent's Name, Address, and Date of Death

The above-named and undersigned transferor hereby makes application as required by Section 5812 of the National Firearms Act to transfer and register the firearm described below to the transferee.

4. Description of Firearm *(Complete items a through h)*

a. Name and Address of Manufacturer and/or Importer of Firearm	b. Type of Firearm *(See instruction 1c)*	c. Caliber, Gauge or Size *(Specify)*	d. Model		
			Length *(Inches)*	e. Of Barrel:	f. Overall:
			g. Serial Number		

h. Additional Description or Data Appearing on Firearm *(Attach additional sheet if necessary)*

5. Transferee's Federal Firearms License *(If any)*
(Give complete 15-digit number) (See instruction 2b)

First 6 digits	2 digits	2 digits	5 digits

6. Transferee's Special (Occupational) Tax Status *(If any)*

a. Employer Identification Number	b. Class

7. Transferor's Federal Firearms License *(If any)*
(Give complete 15-digit number) (See instruction 2b)

First 6 digits	2 digits	2 digits	5 digits

8. Transferor's Special (Occupational) Tax Status *(If any)*

a. Employer Identification Number	b. Class

Under Penalties of Perjury, I Declare that I have examined this application, and to the best of my knowledge and belief it is true, correct and complete, and that the transfer of the described firearm to the transferee and receipt and possession of it by the transferee are not prohibited by the provisions of Chapter 44, Title 18, United States Code; Chapter 53, Title 26, United States Code; or Title VII of the Omnibus Crime Control and Safe Streets Act, as amended, or any provisions of State or local law.

9. Consent to Disclosure of Information to Transferee *(See instruction k)* . I Do or Do Not *(Circle one)* Authorize ATF to Provide Information Relating to this Application to the Above-Named Transferee .

10. Signature of Transferor *(or authorized official)*	11. Name and Title of Authorized Official *(Print or type)*	12. Date

The Space Below is for the use of the Bureau of Alcohol, Tobacco, Firearms and Explosives

By authority of the Director, This Application has been Examined, and the Transfer and Registration of the Firearm Described herein and the Interstate Movement of that Firearm, when Applicable, to the Transferee are:

Stamp Denomination

☐ Approved *(with the following conditions, if any)*

☐ Disapproved *(For the following reasons)*

Signature of Authorized ATF Official　　　　　　　　　　　　　　　　　　　　　Date

ATF Form 4 (5320.4)
Revised March 2006

ATF Form 4   *Page 2*

Transferee Information

The following questions must be answered by any transferee who is **not** a Federal firearms licensee or government agency. The transferee shall give full details on a separate sheet for all "YES" answers. *(See instruction 2d)*

13. Are You:	Yes	No	14. Have You:	Yes	No
a. Charged by information or under indictment in any court for a crime punishable by imprisonment for a term exceeding one year?	☐	☐	a. Been convicted in any court of a crime for which the judge could have imprisoned you for more than one year, even if the judge actually gave you a shorter sentence?	☐	☐
b. A fugitive from justice?	☐	☐	b. Been discharged from the armed forces under dishonorable conditions?	☐	☐
c. An alien who is illegally or unlawfully in the United States?	☐	☐	c. Been adjudicated mentally defective or been committed to a mental institution?	☐	☐
d. Under 21 years of age?	☐	☐	d. Renounced your United States citizenship?	☐	☐
e. An unlawful user of or addicted to, marijuana, or any depressant, stimulant, or narcotic drug, or any other controlled substance?	☐	☐	e. Been convicted in any court of a misdemeanor crime of domestic violence? This includes any misdemeanor conviction involving the use or attempted use of physical force committed by a current or former spouse, parent, or guardian of the victim, or by a person with a similar relationship with the victim.	☐	☐
f. Subject to a court order restraining you from harassing, stalking or threatening an intimate partner or child of such partner?	☐	☐			

15. Transferee's Certification *(See instruction 2e)*

I_____, have a reasonable necessity to
           (Name of Transferee)

possess the machinegun, short-barreled rifle, short-barreled shotgun, or destructive device described on this application
for the following reason(s)_____

and my possession of the device or weapon would be consistent with public safety (18 U.S.C. 922(b) (4) and 27 CFR 478.98).

UNDER PENALTIES OF PERJURY, I declare that I have examined this application and the documents submitted in support thereof, and to the best of my knowledge and belief it is true, correct and complete.

_____   _____
       (Signature of Transferee)   *(Date)*

16. Photograph

Affix
Recent Photograph Here
(Approximately 2" x 2")
(See instruction 2f.)

17. Law Enforcement Certification *(See instruction 2e)*

I certify that I am the chief law enforcement officer of the organization named below having jurisdiction in the area of residence of

_____. I have no information indicating that the transferee will use the firearm or device
       (Name of Transferee)

described on this application for other than lawful purposes. I have no information that the receipt or possession of the firearm or device described in item 4 would be place the transferee in violation of State or local law.

_____   _____
  (Signature and Title of Chief Law Enforcement Officer)   *(Date)*

_____
           (Organization and Street Address)

_____   _____
           (County)   *(Telephone Number)*

Important Information for Currently Registered Firearms

If this registration document evidences the current registration of the firearm described on it, please note the following information.

Estate Procedures: For procedures regarding the transfer of firearms in an estate resulting from the death of the registrant identified in item 2a, the executor should contact the NFA Branch, Bureau of Alcohol, Tobacco, Firearms and Explosives, 244 Needy Road, Martinsburg, WV 25405.

Change of Address: Unless currently licensed under the Gun Control Act, the registrant shall notify the NFA Branch, Bureau of Alcohol, Tobacco, Firearms and Explosives, 244 Needy Road, Martinsburg, WV 25405, in writing, of any change to the address in Item 2a.

Change of Description: The registrant shall notify the NFA Branch, Bureau of Alcohol, Tobacco, Firearms and Explosives, 244 Needy Road, Martinsburg, WV 25405, in writing, of any change to the description of the firearm in Item 4.

Interstate Movement: If the firearm identified in item 4 is a machinegun, short-barreled rifle, short-barreled shotgun, or destructive device, the registrant may be required by 18 U.S.C. § 922(a)(4) to obtain permission from ATF prior to any transportation in interstate or foreign commerce.

Restriction on Possession: Any restriction *(see approval block on face of form)* on the possession of the firearm identified in item 4 continues with the further transfer of the firearm.

Persons Prohibited from Possessing Firearms: If the registrant becomes prohibited by 18 U.S.C. § 922 from possessing a firearm, the registrant shall notify the NFA Branch, Bureau of Alcohol, Tobacco, Firearms and Explosives, 244 Needy Road, Martinsburg, WV 25405, in writing, immediately upon becoming prohibited for guidance on the disposal of the firearm.

Proof of Registration: This approved application is the registrant's proof of registration and it shall be made available to any ATF officer upon request.

ATF Form 4 (5320.4)
Revised March 2006

ATF Form 1
Page 1

OMB No. 1140-0011 (06/30/2016)

U.S. Department of Justice
Bureau of Alcohol, Tobacco, Firearms and Explosives

Application to Make and Register a Firearm

ATF Control Number

To: National Firearms Act Branch, Bureau of Alcohol, Tobacco, Firearms and Explosives, P.O. Box 530298, Atlanta, GA 30353-0298

(Submit in duplicate. See instructions attached.)

As required by Sections 5821(b), 5822, and 5841 of the National Firearms Act, Title 26 U.S.C., Chapter 53, the undersigned hereby submits application to make and register the firearm described below.

1. Type of Application (check one)

a. Tax Paid. Submit your tax payment of $200 with the application. The tax may be paid by credit or debit card, check, or money order. Please complete item 17. Upon approval of the application, we will affix and cancel the required National Firearms Act Stamp. (See instructions 2c and 3)

2. Application is made by:
☐ Individual ☐ Corporation or Other Legal Entity ☐ Government Entity

3a. Trade Name (If any)

3b. Applicant's Name and Mailing Address (Type or print below and between the dots) (See instruction 2d)

b. Tax Exempt because firearm is being made on behalf of the United States, or any department, independent establishment, or agency thereof.

c. Tax Exempt because firearm is being made by or on behalf of any State or possession of the United States, or any political subdivision thereof, or any official police organization of such a government entity engaged in criminal investigations.

3c. If P.O. Box is Shown Above, Street Address Must Be Given Here

3d. County

3e. Telephone Area Code and Number

4. Description of Firearm (complete items a through i) (See instruction 2j)

a. Name and Location of Original Manufacturer of Firearm (Receiver) (If prototype, furnish plans and specifications)

b. Type of Firearm to be made (See instruction 1c)

c. Caliber or Gauge (Specify one)

d. Model

Length (Inches) e. Of Barrel: f. Overall:

g. Serial Number

h. Additional Description (Include all numbers and other identifying data to include maker's name, city and state which will appear on the firearm) (use additional sheet if necessary)

i. State Why You Intend To Make Firearm (Use additional sheet if necessary)

j. Is this firearm being reactivated? ☐ Yes ☐ No (See Definition 1k)

5. Applicant's Federal Firearms License (If any)

6. Special (Occupational) Tax Status (If applicable) (See definition 1f)

(Give complete 15-digit Number)

a. Employer Identification Number b. Class

Important: All individual applicants (including Federally Licensed Collectors) must complete the reverse side of this form and submit, in duplicate, FBI Form FD-258, Fingerprint Card.

Under Penalties of Perjury, I Declare that I have examined this application, including accompanying documents, and to the best of my knowledge and belief it is true, accurate and complete and the making and possession of the firearm described above would not constitute a violation of Chapter 44, Title 18, U.S.C., Chapter 53, Title 26, U.S.C., or any provisions of State or local law.

7. Signature of Applicant

8. Name and Title of Authorized Official

9. Date

The space below is for the use of the Bureau of Alcohol, Tobacco, Firearms and Explosives

By authority of the Director, Bureau of Alcohol, Tobacco, Firearms and Explosives, this application has been examined and the applicant's making and registration of the firearm described above is:

☐ Approved (With the following conditions, if any) ☐ Disapproved (For the following reasons)

Authorized ATF Official

Date

ATF Form 1 (5320.1)
Revised June 2014

ATF Form 1   *Page 2*

---

10. Law Enforcement Certification (See instruction 2g)

I certify that I am the chief law enforcement officer of the organization named below having jurisdiction in the area of residence of

_____
(Name of maker)

I have no information that the maker will use the firearm or device described on this application for other than lawful purposes. I have no information that Possession of the firearm described in Item 4 on the front of this form would place the maker in Violation of State or Local Law.

_____ (Signature of Chief Law Enforcement Officer)   _____ (Printed name)   _____ (Title and agency name)

_____ (Street address, city, State and zip code)

_____ (Telephone Number)   _____ (Date)

By (if delegated authority to sign for the chief law enforcement official):

_____ (Signature)   _____ (Printed name)   _____ (Title and agency name)

_____ (Street address, city, State and zip code)

_____ (Telephone Number)   _____ (Date)

Maker's Certification

A maker who is an individual must complete this Section.

11. Answer questions 11.a. through 11.j. Answer questions 13 through 16 if applicable. For any YES answer (other than for 11.i.), the applicant shall provide details on a separate sheet. (See instructions 7c and definitions)

	Yes	No	12. Photograph
a. Are you under indictment or information in any court for a felony, or any other crime, for which the judge could imprison you for more than one year?			
b. Have you ever been convicted in any court for a felony, or any other crime, for which the judge could imprison you for than one year, even if you received a shorter sentence including probation?			
c. Are you a fugitive from justice?			Affix
d. Are you an unlawful user of, or addicted to, marijuana or any depressant, stimulant, narcotic drug, or any other controlled substance?			Recent Photograph Here (Approximately 2" x 2") (See instruction 2e)
e. Have you ever been adjudicated mentally defective (which includes a determination by a court, board, commission, or other lawful authority that you are a danger to yourself or others or are incompetent to manage your own affairs) OR have you ever been committed to a mental institution?			
f. Have you been discharged from the Armed Forces under dishonorable conditions?			
g. Are you subject to a court order restraining you from harassing, stalking, or threatening your child or an intimate partner or child of such partner?			
h. Have you ever been convicted in any court of a misdemeanor crime of domestic violence?			
i. Are you a United States citizen?			
j. Have you ever renounced your United States citizenship?			

If you answered "NO" to question 11.i., please answer questions 13, 14, 15 and 16.

13. Answer questions 13.a. through 13.b., and 14 by checking or marking "Yes or "No" or "NA" in the boxes to the right of the questions.

	Yes	No
a. Are you an alien Illegally in the United States?		
b. Are you an alien admitted to the United States under a nonimmigrant visa? If the answer is "NO", do not respond to question 14 and proceed to questions 15 and 16.		

14. If you are an alien admitted to the United States under a nonimmigrant visa, do you fall within any of the exceptions set forth in the instructions (see definition 2.u.)? If the answer is "YES", a copy of the Documentation must be attached to the Application. ☐ Yes ☐ No ☐ N/A

15. What is your country of Citizenship if other than the United States? (Specify Country)

16. If you are not a Citizen of the United States, what is your U.S.-issued alien number or admission number?

CERTIFICATION: Under penalties imposed by 26 U.S.C. 5861, I certify that the statements contained in this Certification, and any attached documents in support thereof, are true and correct to the best of my knowledge and belief.

_____ Signature of Maker   _____ Date

ATF Form 1 (5320.1)
Revised June 2014

ATF Form 1   *Page 3*

17. Method of Payment Check one) See Instruction 2h)

☐ Check Enclosed) ☐ Cashier's Check or Money Order Enclosed) ☐ Visa ☐ Mastercard ☐ American Express ☐ Discover ☐ Diners Club

Credit/Debit Card Number No dashes)	Name as Printed on the Credit/Debit Card	Expiration Date Month year)

Credit/Debit Card Billing Address:

Address:

City: State: lp Code:

Please Complete to Ensure Payment Is Credited to the Correct Application:

I am Paying the making Tax for the Applicant: Total Amount:

I Authorl e ATF to Charge my Credit/Debit Card the Above Amount.

_____   _____

Signature of Cardholder   Date

Your credit/debit card will be charged the above stated amount upon receipt of your application. The charge will be reflected on your credit/debit card statement. In the event your application is NOT approved, the above amount will be credited to the credit/debit card noted above.

Important Information for Currently Registered Firearms

If this registration document evidences the current registration of the firearm described on it, please note the following information.

Estate Procedures: For procedures regarding the transfer of firearms in an estate resulting from the death of the registrant identified in item , the executor should contact the NFA Branch, Bureau of ATF, 244 Needy Road, Martinsburg, WV 25405.

Interstate Movement: If the firearm identified in item 4 is a machinegun, short barreled rifle, short barreled shotgun, or destructive device, the registrant may be required by 18 U.S.C. 22 a) 4) to obtain permission from ATF prior to any transportation in interstate or foreign commerce.

Change of Description or Address: The registrant shall notify the NFA Branch, Bureau of Alcohol, Tobacco, Firearms and Explosives, 244 Needy Road, Martinsburg, WV 25405, in writing, of any change to the description of the firearms in item 4, or any change to the address of the registrant.

Restrictions on Possession: Any restriction see approval block on face of form) on the possession of the firearm identified in item 4 continues with the further transfer of the firearm.

Persons Prohibited from Possessing Firearms: If the registrant becomes prohibited from possessing a firearm, please contact the NFA Branch for procedures on how to dispose of the firearm.

Proof of Registration: A person possessing a firearm registered as required by the NFA shall retain proof of registration which shall be made available to an ATF officer upon request.

Paperwork Reduction Act Notice

This form is in accordance with the Paperwork Reduction Act of 1 5. The information you provide is used to establish that a transferee's receipt and possession of the firearm would be in conformance with Federal, State, and local law. The data is used as proof of lawful registration of a firearm to the manufacturer. The furnishing of this information is mandatory 26 U.S.C. 5822).

The estimated average burden associated with this collection of information 1.6 hours per respondent or recordkeeper, depending on individual circumstances. Comments concerning the accuracy of this burden estimate and suggestions for reducing this burden should be addressed to Reports Management Officer, Information Technology Coordination Staff, Bureau of Alcohol, Tobacco, Firearms and Explosives, Washington, DC 20226.

An agency may not conduct or sponsor, and a person is not required to respond to, a collection of information unless it displays a currently valid OMB control number.

Privacy Act Information

1. **Authority.** Solicitation of this information is made pursuant to the National Firearms Act 26 U.S.C. 5821 and 5822). Disclosure of this information by the applicant is mandatory for any person other than a manufacturer qualified under the National Firearms Act) making a firearm as defined in the National Firearms Act.

2. **Purpose.** To verify payment of the tax imposed by 26 U.S.C. 5821 to determine that the making would not be in violation of law and to effect registration of the firearm.

. **Routine Uses.** The information will be used by ATF to make the determinations set forth in paragraph 2. In addition, to effect registration of the firearm, information as to the identification of the firearm, date of registration, and the identification and address of person entitled to possess the firearm will be entered into the National Firearms Registration and Transfer Record. No information obtained from a application, registration, or records required to be submitted by a natural person in order to comply with any provision of the National Firearms Act or regulations issued thereunder, shall, except in connection with prosecution or other action for furnishing false information, be used, directly or indirectly, as evidence against that person in any criminal proceeding with respect to a violation of law occurring prior to or concurrently with the filing of the application. The information from this application may only be disclosed to Federal authorities for purpose of prosecution for violation of the National Firearms Act.

4. **Effects of not Supplying Information Requested.** Failure to supply complete information will delay processing and may cause denial of the application.

ATF Form 1 5 20.1)
Revised June 2014

ABOUT THE ATTORNEY AUTHORS

KIRK EVANS
CO-AUTHOR

Kirk is the President of Texas Law Shield, LLP and has practiced law in Texas for over twenty years and has concentrated most of his work on litigation including constitutional issues and complex civil litigation. He has advised gun owners, instructors, ranges and law enforcement. He is an ardent supporter of each of our rights to keep and bear arms and is a proud gun owner.

Kirk is a graduate with honors from Texas A&M University and attended law school at the University of Houston where he graduated as editor of the Law Review. Kirk was recognized as a "Rising Star" in the legal profession by the Texas Monthly publication *Super Lawyers*.

Kirk is a frequent speaker on civil liability associated with gun ownership and has been a presenter at events across the United States, including the FBI Dallas CAAA Active Shooter Seminar, the national NRA Foundation Banquet and multiple civic and community organizations. In addition, Kirk has served as a media source for firearms law, including appearances on Fox News, KXAN in Austin, KSAT television in San Antonio, a national interview with Yahoo Sports, along with more than fifty radio interviews with stations across the country. Kirk has also authored a number of legal publications on firearms topics such as "Tribal Law and Your Firearms."

EDWIN WALKER
CO-AUTHOR

Edwin Walker is an independent firearms program attorney for the Texas Law Shield Firearms Legal Defense Program and a partner with Walker & Byington, PLLC. A native Texan, Edwin earned his bachelor's and law degree at the University of Houston and has been practicing law in Texas since 1993. Edwin's legal career has been focused primarily on criminal law and he is a proud member of the State Bar of Texas, Texas Criminal Defense Lawyer's Association and the Harris County Defense Lawyers Association. Edwin, currently living in La Porte, Texas, is at home speaking to crowds or on the radio, sharing his views on our Constitutional rights, or anything about music, politics, or Texas history.

MICHELE BYINGTON
CO-AUTHOR

Michele Byington is an independent firearms program attorney for Texas Law Shield's Firearms Legal Defense Program and a partner with the law firm of Walker & Byington, PLLC. Michele received her bachelor's degree from Texas A&M University and J.D. from South Texas College of Law. Michele proudly represents and advises gun owners all over the Great State of Texas. She has extensive knowledge of the processes of the BATFE and has assisted in hundreds of successful NFA Item transfers. Further, Michele lectures across the nation on firearms and self-defense issues. Michele lives in Houston where she never backs away from a challenge, never meets a stranger, and always finds time to laugh.